African Adventurer's Guide To

MOZAMBIQUE

African Adventurer's Guide To

MOZAMBIQUE

Willie & Sandra Olivier

SOUTHERN
BOOK PUBLISHERS

ISBN 1 86812 787 7
2 4 6 8 0 9 7 5 3 1

Published by
Southern Book Publishers
(A division of the Struik New Holland Group)
PO Box 5563, Rivonia 2128

Cover photograph by Anthony Bannister, ABPL
Cover design by Micha McKerr
Maps by CartoCom
Set in Optima 10/12
Designed and typeset by Micha McKerr
Reproduction by Creda Communications, Eliot Avenue, Eppindust II, Cape Town.
Printed and bound by Creda Communications, Eliot Avenue, Eppindust II, Cape Town.

CONTENTS

List of Maps

ACKNOWLEDGEMENTS

We are deeply indebted to a large number of people who kindly assisted us with information and accommodation during our research and various visits to Mozambique. Without their assistance our task would have been much harder and should anyone have been omitted inadvertently, we apologise sincerely.

Our gratitude is due especially to the following who assisted with accommodation: Eric and Mel Smith of Barra Reef; Margie MacDuff of Benguerra Lodge; Peter Thornicroft of Casa Msika; Paul Greyling of Guinjata Bay; Carlos Ferraz of the Pestana Hotel Group for accommodation at the Carlton Rovuma, Bazaruto Lodge and Inhaca Resort Hotel; David Ankers of the Polana Hotel and Pieter de Klerk and the staff of Zongoene Lodge

Numerous people also willingly shared their knowledge about tourism in Mozambique with us. We would like to thank David Ankers, Peter Bechtel of Helvetas, Peter de Klerk and Dick and Ria de Villiers of Paindane. Thanks also to Irwin Jakes of Campismo de Maxise, Roland Shubert of Paraiso de Chidenguele and Peter Thornicroft. Margie Toens of Paraiso Servicos was a mine of information about tourism in the Vilankulo area, while Arne Thorkildsen and Altie Steenkamp shared their knowledge on northern Mozambique with us.

Various people enthusiastically assisted us with information on diving, snorkelling and fishing. Our appreciation goes to Barra Lodge Dive Charters and Fishing Charters, Jakes and Veronica Bergh of Island Style Diving at Morrungulo, Jan Claassen for information on diving off Reserva Especial do Maputo. Louis Erasmus of Bazaruto Lodge was a mine of information on the Bazaruto Archipelago, while Eva Fleming introduced us to the wonders of Two Mile Reef. Paul Greyling and Colin Jefferies willingly shared their wealth of knowledge on diving and fishing at Guinjata Bay. Our thanks also to Pieter and Gigi Jacobs of CI Divers in Pemba; Jurgen Potgieter, who filled us in on the dive sites of Bazaruto; Duarte Rato, who gave invaluable information on various dive sites; and Les, Clint and Wayne of Praia do Sol, who supplied information on the dive sites off Bilene.

At Cahora Bassa Dam we were received hospitably by Gary Cripps, Marius Naude, Skip Bischoff (who also provided accommodation) and Phil Bezuidenhout of Ugezi Tiger Lodge.

Finally, our appreciation to the editorial staff at Southern: general manager Louise Grantham, commissioning editor Reneé Ferreira and copy-editor David Pearson, as well as Ingrid Booysen for the maps.

HOW TO USE THIS GUIDE

Having emerged from a devastating civil war in 1992, Mozambique's infrastructure and tourism facilities are still being rebuilt. As a result, exploring the country is not as easy as other southern African countries, making it an exciting destination for adventurous travellers and those prepared to set aside preconceived ideas and expectations of finding First World standards outside of tourist areas. However, new resorts, filling stations, banks and shops are opening up and the condition of the country's roads has improved dramatically. ***African Adventurer's Guide to Mozambique*** will help you to make the most of your visit by assisting you to plan your trip around your own particular interests and activities.

The structure of the book

As a general rule the Mozambican names of geographical features, streets and attractions have been used throughout the book, with English translations. Although the correct spelling of the country's name is Moçambique, we have used the more common spelling, Mozambique, mainly to facilitate listing in data bases. *All prices (e.g. border documentation, ferry charges, toll fees, departure taxes) are those applicable in October 1998 and are provided as a guide only.*

Chapters 1 to 5 provide a general introduction to the country and deal with the essentials of travelling to and in Mozambique. Chapter 2, *Why visit Mozambique?,* gives a general summary of the country's main tourist attractions. Detailed descriptions of all major attractions (game parks and reserves, monuments, towns and cities) in each region are provided at the start of Chapters 7 to 9, while other places of interest are dealt with in the relevant route description. Once you have a broad idea of what you want to do and see on your visit to Mozambique, the best times for visiting, and how to get around, you are ready to tackle the more detailed information in the second part of the book.

For practical reasons the country has been divided into three tourist regions – Southern, Central and Northern Mozambique, with Maputo described separately in Chapter 6. The regions, shown on the map on pp 60-61, were demarcated by the authors and are not official or administrative regions.

Chapter 10, *Where to stay in Mozambique,* provides a comprehensive list of accommodation establishments with postal addresses, telephone and fax numbers. Chapter 11 gives a list of Mozambican diplomatic missions abroad and diplomatic representatives accredited to Mozambique, as well as useful contact and emergency numbers and Portuguese words and phrases.

Planning your trip

Mozambique is renowned for its spectacular coastline, places of historical interest, culture, exciting birdwatching and magnificent landscapes. There are also thousands of kilometres of backroads ideally suited to those wishing to explore off-the-beaten track destinations. The information in Chapters 6 to 9 will help you plan a holiday to suit your specific interests and needs. Each chapter starts with a brief introduction to the attractions, history, landscape, vegetation, economic activities and people of the region, followed by a detailed description of its top attractions and in-depth descriptions of the main tourist routes. The main attractions are clearly cross-referenced to appropriate routes by means of a route symbol in the margin. In addition, symbols in the margin alongside the text draw attention to the different activities, attractions and accommodation options available. For ease of reference, a list of these can be found on the front cover flap.

The 11 routes describe all the places of interest along Mozambique's main tourist routes and major attractions referred to in the route descriptions are cross-referenced to the appropriate pages. Symbols in the margin and **bold entries** show at a glance which activities and features may be of interest to you. For practical reasons, such as the location of towns or cities used as starting points, some routes begin in a town or city that falls in a different region to the one being described. For example: Route 5 takes you through the central region, but starts at Inhassoro in southern Mozambique. Each route description is preceded by the direct distance, time, road conditions, the availability of fuel and linking routes. Distances and times are estimates and exclude detours and lengthy stops.

Names of selected accommodation establishments and restaurants are provided under the headings *Where to stay* and *Where to eat* in Maputo and Beira, as well as in the descriptions of top attractions and routes. These establishments have largely been selected on the basis of our own experiences and only the street address, telephone and fax numbers are provided. For postal addresses refer to Chapter 10.

Authors' notes

While every possible care has been taken to ensure that information is correct, it is inevitable that some of it will become outdated, as the country's infrastructure and tourism industry are changing and expanding rapidly. The authors will be pleased to receive any new information that can be incorporated into future editions. Please write to: Southern Book Publishers, PO Box 5563, Rivonia 2126 South Africa.

1

INTRODUCTION TO MOZAMBIQUE

Mozambique is a fascinating country, offering visitors a wide range of activities and experiences. Until the mid-1990s, however, it was known only to a handful of aid workers, staff of non-governmental organisations and South Africans who once regarded Mozambique as their holiday playground. When civil war broke out the stream of tourists dried up and the country became one of the world's forgotten corners. Following the end of the civil war in 1992 and democratic elections two years later, an increasing number of tourists are visiting this gem of a country.

Geography

Situated on the east coast of southern Africa, Mozambique covers an area of 799 380 km^2. It ranks 15th in Africa in terms of size, is slightly larger than Great Britain and France combined and slightly less than twice the size of the state of California in the USA. A long, narrow country, it is bordered to the north by Tanzania, in the south by Swaziland and South Africa's KwaZulu-Natal Province and by Zimbabwe in the west. In the northwest, Tete Province shares its international boundary with Zimbabwe, Zambia and Malawi, while the Indian Ocean's Mozambique Channel forms a natural boundary in the east.

With an average altitude of 360 m, it is relatively flat, with three distinct geographical regions. Covering about 44 per cent of the country, the *Planicie Moçambicana*, or coastal plains below 200 m, are dominant in the south of Mozambique. In the west the plains rise gradually to the Pequenos Libombos, a range of low mountains, while the coastal plains are punctuated by numerous lakes. North of the Rio Zambeze the coastal plains become narrower and are replaced by an upland region of *planaltos*, or high plateaus, ranging from 200 to 1 000 m above sea level. The most extensive upland region, the Planalto Moçambicano, covers most of Niassa Province and extends into western Nampula and northwestern

Zambezia provinces. Other upland regions are the Planalto de Chimoio in Manica Province, the Planalto de Lichinga in Niassa Province and the Planalto de Angonia and the Planalto de Márávia in northern Tete Province. *Montanhas* (mountains) occur at altitudes of above 1 000 m. Along the Zimbabwean border the Planalto de Chimoio rises steeply to the Chimanimani Mountains and Monte Binga, at 2 436 m the highest point in Mozambique. The country's second highest mountain, the 2 419 m-high Montes Namúli, lies in Zambezia Province, while Dómué in Tete Province rises to 2 095 m.

Mozambique's coastline stretches for 2 515 km from the mouth of the Rio Rovuma to Ponta do Ouro. It is characterised by numerous sweeping bays fringed with mangrove swamps, headlands and several islands off the coast. Best known among them are Ilha da Inhaca (see p 77), east of Maputo, and the Arquipélago do Bazaruto (see p 89). The historic Ilha de Moçambique (see p 153 and route 8) lies north of Quelimane, while the northernmost archipelago is a string of small coral islands, the Arquipélago das Quirimbas (see route 9).

The country is dissected by over 60 rivers; among them are the Rio Zambeze, which flows through Mozambique for 630 km and the Rio Limpopo. Other large rivers include the 650 km-long Rovuma which partly forms the northern boundary with Tanzania, and the Lugenda, Lúrio, Save, Búzi and Incomati rivers.

Despite the abundance of rivers, there are only three large dams – Cahora Bassa in Tete Province, Chicamba in Manica Province and Massingir in Gaza Province. The largest inland water body, Lago Niassa (see route 10) lies in the northwest of the country and forms a natural boundary with Malawi for some 300 km.

The vegetation of Mozambique is composed of some 17 vegetation types. Along the coast the vegetation ranges from mangrove swamps and magnificent high dune forests in the south to palm savannas just off the coast between the Rio Save and the Rio Búzi. Montane evergreen forests and montane grasslands occur at the upper elevations of high mountains, notably Monte Gorongosa, the eastern slopes of the Chimanimani range and Montes Namúli. In the arid Gaza Province the vegetation is dominated by mopane savanna which also occurs over large parts of Tete Province. Also occurring in Tete Province are magnificent tracts of baobab (*imbondeiro*) savannas. Grasslands occur on alluvial soils in the lower reaches of the major rivers in the south and central regions of the country; the most extensive area is the Marromeu floodplain grasslands in the Zambeze Delta. Well over 50 per cent of the country is, however, covered by miombo, a term used to describe broadleaved woodlands dominated by trees of the genus *Brachystegia*.

Large areas of coastal Gaza and Inhambane provinces have been planted under cashew nut trees, while coconut palms are characteristic in and around the city of Inhambane and much of Zambezia Province. A cause for concern is the large-scale deforestation taking place throughout the country. Large tracts of land are being cleared to obtain charcoal, which is the only source of income of many rural people. Following the repopulation of rural areas after the return of peace, large areas are also being cleared for subsistence agriculture.

Climate

Situated largely within the tropics, much of Mozambique enjoys a tropical or subtropical climate. Three distinct climatic zones can be distinguished. The coastal belt and the northern provinces of Zambezia, Nampula, Niassa and Cabo Delgado enjoy a humid tropical climate, while the interior of Maputo, Gaza, Inhambane and southern Tete provinces have a dry tropical climate. In the highlands of Manica, Lichinga and northern Tete Province, the climate is moderated by the altitude and temperatures are generally more pleasant throughout the year.

Most of the country's rainfall is recorded from December to March as violent thunderstorms. In the south the rainfall increases from an average of between 400 and 600 mm in Gaza Province to up to 1 000 mm along the coast. Rainfall in the central and northern provinces ranges between 1 000 mm and 1 400 mm, except in large areas of Tete Province where the average is between 400 mm and 800 mm. In the uplands and mountainous areas, rainfall averages over 1 400 mm a year.

The summer months from November to April are characterised by warm temperatures, accompanied by high humidity. Average annual temperatures over most of the country range from 22-26 °C, except in the upper Zambeze Valley and the area around Pemba, where the annual average exceeds 26 °C. In the highlands adjoining Zimbabwe, the uplands of Tete Province and the Planalto de Lichinga, average annual temperatures range from 18-22 °C.

The following table provides an indication of average monthly temperatures at a few localities in the country.

	Jan	Apr	Jul	Oct
Maputo	25	23	19	25
Beira	29	25	22	27
Nampula	26	24	22	27
Tete	30	29	26	31
Lichinga	21	18	16	22

History

Mozambique has a long and fascinating history which is intricately linked to the east coast of Africa, the Zimbabwean Plateau, the Portuguese voyages of discovery and the colonial powers' "Scramble for Africa" in the 1880s.

Early inhabitants

Prior to the arrival of Early Iron Age people in Mozambique between the third and fourth century, it was inhabited by San hunter-gatherers who lived in scattered groups throughout the country. The Early Iron Age people first populated the valleys along the coast and later the plateaux and highlands further west, displacing or assimilating the San in the process. They were skilled in mining gold, cultivated crops such as mapira and mexoeira (types of sorghum and millet) and practised animal husbandry. Between the 12th and the 14th centuries the Later Iron Age people migrated into Mozambique.

Muslim and Portuguese trade

By the 10th century Muslim traders had extended their commercial network from Kilwa, Mombassa and Malinde along the east African coast as far south as the "Land of Sofala". Extensive trade links existed with Great Zimbabwe and the Karanga kingdoms that arose after the decline of Great Zimbabwe at the end of the 15th century; the most prominent was with the legendary paramount chieftaincy of the Monomotapa. These kingdoms extended from the Zimbabwean plateau eastwards across present-day Manica and Sofala provinces, with the Rio Zambeze as the northern boundary. Fairs were held from time to time on the Zimbabwean escarpment and gold was traded for beads, pottery and cloth.

Portuguese exploration of Mozambique dates back to 1498 when Vasco da Gama landed in search of a sea passage to India. Henceforth the coast became an important stop where ships were replenished before they continued to India. Lured by reports of gold and silver being mined in the interior, a struggle for trade supremacy ensued between the Portuguese and Muslim traders. In 1505 the Portuguese ousted Muslims from Sofala and two years later a trade centre was also established at Ilha de Moçambique (see p 153). Much of the gold trade, however, remained in the hands of Muslims who moved to Angoche and had an intimate knowledge of the trade routes. It therefore became important for the Portuguese to gain direct control over the gold fields and in 1511 António Fernandes undertook an expedition to the realm of the Monomotapa. In 1531 a fair was established at Sena and two years later also at Tete, further upstream.

Owing to the decline in the production of gold on the Zimbabwean plateau in the 1500s, the focus of trade shifted to ivory. In the south of the country the ivory trade was in the hands of the Tsonga, while the Maravi of the Shire Highlands in Malawi and the Zambeze Valley controlled the ivory in the north of the country. Thousands of elephants were slaughtered and for two centuries ivory was the most important export from Africa: a phase in which Mozambique played an important role.

The 1760s saw the rise of the slave trade and the coastal settlements of Ibo, Ilha de Moçambique, Quelimane and Inhambane became important slaving ports. In 1828 alone some 30 000 slaves were exported from Mozambique to the French colonies of Mauritius, Réunion, the Comoros, Brazil, Cuba and north America. Despite the British and Portuguese anti-slavery treaty of 1842, the trade continued until the 1860s and it has been estimated that more than one million slaves were exported from Mozambique.

Colonisation and government of Mozambique

The first attempts by the Portuguese to colonise the interior were along the Zambeze Valley where the *Prazos da Coroa* (States of the Crown) system was implemented during the 17th and 18th centuries. Large tracts of land were granted to women on condition that they married a Portuguese – a move aimed at encouraging Portuguese men to settle in Mozambique. The term of the lease was three lifespans and *prazos* had to be passed on from mother to daughter. In return, the *prazeiros* (landholders) had to pay rent and render services, such as providing soldiers for the government and administering the area under their jurisdiction. Because they enjoyed considerable autonomy and had their own armies, the Portuguese Crown had little control over them.

Portugal's possessions in Mozambique were governed from Goa in India until 1752, when the first governor was appointed for the territory. Portuguese control was, however, limited to the district of Mozambique (the present Nampula Province), Tete and Sena along the Rio Zambeze and a few coastal settlements. In the south of the country, the Portuguese established their first permanent settlement in Baia de Lagoa only in 1782.

Following the break-up of the Portuguese South Atlantic Empire and Brazil's independence in 1822, Portugal turned its attention to Angola and Mozambique. Lacking the necessary capital to administer and develop the country, the Portuguese government granted land concessions to foreign companies, which controlled the administration and commerce of the concessions. The companies were required to bring development to the areas under their control, but at the same time the concessions enabled

Portugal to claim effective occupation of the areas. A concession between the Rio Save and Rio Zambeze was granted to the Companhia de Moçambique in 1891, while the land between the Rio Lúrio and the Rio Rovuma was allocated in 1894 to the Companhia do Niassa. Smaller concessions were awarded in Zambezia Province on former *prazos.*

Meanwhile, in the south of the country major political developments were taking place. The second decade of the 19th century witnessed the migration of Nguni people into Mozambique. One group migrated from Zimbabwe and ruled the area between the Rio Zambeze and the Rio Save for 10 years before the kingdom disintegrated. Another group, led by Soshangane, migrated into southern Mozambique in 1836 and established the Gaza kingdom, which extended from the Rio Incomati to just south of the Rio Zambeze.

Owing to its strategic location, the southern part of Mozambique was becoming increasingly important. In 1869 the Treaty of Friendship and Commerce between the Zuid-Afrikaansche Republiek (ZAR) and Portugal recognised Portugal's sovereignty over Delagoa Bay. Britain, however, disputed Portugal's claim over the area, but in 1875 the arbitrator, French President MacMahon, ruled in favour of Portugal. In 1876 the construction of a railway line to Lourenço Marques was proposed to provide an independent gateway to the sea for the Zuid-Afrikaansche Republiek and following the discovery of gold on the Witwatersrand in 1886 the strategic position of Delagoa Bay became even more important. Construction of the line, however, was only completed in 1894. The railway line and the port of Lourenço Marques provided a lucrative source of income for the Portuguese government, accounting for nearly a third of state income.

In January 1895 the Portuguese launched an attack against the Gaza monarchy, now led by Gungunhana, to reassert their authority over the area. After several battles, Gungunhana was captured on 28 December 1895 and sent into exile to the Azores.

The ZAR gold mines needed a vast workforce and towards the closing years of the 1800s large numbers of Mozambicans were recruited to work on those on the Witwatersrand. This resulted in an agreement on labour recruitment between the Portuguese government and the Zuid-Afrikaansche Republiek in 1897. Four years later a monopoly was granted to the Witwatersrand Native Labour Association to recruit labour in southern Mozambique and between 1904 and 1926 the number of migrant labourers fluctuated between 50 000 and 96 500.

Salazar and the Estado Novo

Following the ousting of the monarchy in Portugal in 1910, the new republican government, which ruled until 1926, introduced liberal reforms in Portugal's overseas colonies. Although the colonies were granted a great degree of self-government, they were still viewed as provinces of the mother country.

In May 1926, the Republican government in Portugal was overthrown by a military coup and heavy reliance was placed on António Salazar, an academic of Coimbra University, who devised the policies of the *Estado Novo,* or New State. Salazar, who became prime minister in 1932, enacted laws which restricted the autonomy of the Portuguese territories and ended the control of charter companies and the *prazos.* To reduce Portugal's dependence on imports, Mozambique was used to provide foodstuffs such as coffee, cocoa, sugar, rice and raw materials (especially cotton) to Portugal. At the same time Mozambique became an important market for exports from Portugal.

The system of *indigena* and *não-indigena,* inherited from the Republican government, was retained and in 1944 the *indigena* were required to register and carry identity cards. In the mid-1950s tens of thousands of peasant families were resettled in *aldeamentos* for administrative purposes and to boost crop-growing in the north of the country.

In 1951 the Portuguese Constitution was revised and Mozambique became an overseas province of Portugal. The change from colony to overseas province was aimed at emphasising the government's position that Portugal and its African territories were a single country.

The provision of health care to the *indigena* only improved after the Second Development Plan was implemented in 1958, while education was largely left to the church.

Although the boundaries of Mozambique were finally drawn in 1891 by Britain and Portugal, it took another 50 years before a unified government was created. At that time, the only areas under the direct administration of the colonial government were the district of Mozambique (now Nampula) and an area to the south of the Rio Zambeze around Tete. In addition, Britain also accepted Portugal's territorial claim over the area south of the Rio Save. The Companhia do Niassa's concession expired in 1929, while most of the *prazo* leases only expired in 1930. The concession of the Companhia de Moçambique, however, continued until 1941.

The liberation struggle

The nationalist movement that finally forced Portugal to hand over power to Mozambicans, Frelimo, was founded in Dar es Salaam in 1962 when three independence movements amalgamated. Two years later the *Luta Armada,* or armed struggle, was launched. The first phase of the armed struggle was fought in the northernmost reaches of Cabo Delgado and

Niassa provinces, bordering on Tanzania, from where operations were initially launched.

Following Operation Gordian Knot (see p 171) the liberation struggle shifted to Tete Province where Frelimo targeted the Cahora Bassa Dam. By 1972 the entire Tete Province (except for Cahora Bassa and the city of Tete) was under the control of Frelimo, as well as most of Cabo Delgado Province and the northern half of Niassa Province. From Tete Province Frelimo infiltrated further south, attacking Portuguese settlers and the Beira-Umtali (now Mutare) railway line.

Frelimo's infiltration of Tete provided a foothold for Zapu guerrillas fighting against the Rhodesian government of Ian Smith and disrupted the rail and road connection to Beira. The Smith government responded by deploying its troops to guard the Tete Corridor and the Beira Corridor and created the Renamo rebel movement in 1977 to counter Zapu and Frelimo.

The Carnation Revolution of April 1974, in which the Portuguese Prime Minister, Marcello Caetano, was ousted in a military coup led by the monocled General António de Spínola, brought about a swift change of events in Mozambique. Eager to dispose of its colonies as quickly as possible, the socialist government of Spínola began negotiations with Frelimo in June 1974 with a view to handing over power. Frelimo, however, refused to agree to a ceasefire until August 1974. Violence broke out and uncertainty about the future resulted in most of the 240 000 white settlers fleeing the country. Fleeing settlers withdrew their money from the banks, set buildings ablaze and sabotaged machinery and equipment.

Independence

After an agreement with the new Portuguese government a provisional government was formed by Frelimo and on 25 June 1975 Mozambique became independent. In 1977 Frelimo declared Mozambique a one-party state guided by the doctrine of Marxism-Leninism. Faced with a flight of capital and the abandonment of farms, companies and shops by fleeing settlers, unoccupied land and businesses were nationalised.

In the meanwhile, Renamo stepped up its military campaign in central Mozambique. Zimbabwe's independence in 1980 denied the rebels support they had previously enjoyed, but South Africa, fearful of a communist government in Mozambique, stepped in to fill the breach. The Beira and Tete corridors, once the target of Frelimo, now came frequently under attack by Renamo rebels, prompting the Zimbabwean government to deploy up to 12 000 troops to guard the Beira Corridor.

The signing of the Nkomati Accord between the Mozambican and South African governments on 16 March 1984 was meant to herald an end to the hostilities between the two countries. In terms of the accord, Mozambique agreed that its territory would not be used as a springboard for attacks on South Africa by ANC and PAC operatives, while South Africa undertook to cease all support to the Renamo movement. In August 1985, when Frelimo forces overran the Renamo headquarters in the Gorongosa area, documentary evidence was found that South Africa was still maintaining contact with the rebel movement. Not surprisingly, Mozambique abrogated the accord and, although it appears that the official South African government position was not to supply arms and logistical support to Renamo, hardline elements whithin the South African Defence Force continued covert support.

The ill-fated experiment in socialism and the near-total destruction of the country's infrastructure by Renamo forced the government to abandon socialism in favour of a transition to a free-market economy. In 1987 it agreed to a structural adjustment programme and two years later Frelimo transformed itself from a Marxist-Leninist to a social democratic party.

A new constitution, providing for multi-party democracy, human rights, freedom of the individual and property rights was adopted in 1990. By then it had become obvious that neither Frelimo, nor Renamo, could win a war that had killed, maimed and displaced millions of people.

With the mediation of Zimbabwe, Kenya, Italy and the Catholic Church, direct peace talks between the government and Renamo began in 1990 and an accord was signed on 4 October 1992 in Rome. The two-year transition to democratic rule was overseen by the United Nations Operations in Mozambique; this is regarded as the world body's most successful operation to date. Among its duties were the demobilisation of soldiers from both sides, the integration of former government and Renamo forces into a new national army and ensuring free and fair, democratic elections.

Mozambicans went to the polls for the first time ever in October 1994 and Frelimo President, Joaquim Chissano, received 53,3 per cent of the vote, while Renamo leader Afonso Dhlakama trailed with 33,3 per cent. The election for the Assembly was more closely fought, with Frelimo winning 44,3 per cent, or 129 seats, to Renamo's 33,7 per cent and 112 seats. Despite its defeat, Renamo accepted the outcome of the elections and the country has since enjoyed peace and tranquillity.

Population

The total population of Mozambique is estimated at 18,1 million (1997), giving the country an average population density of 20,8 people per square kilometre. About 30 per cent of the country's inhabitants live in urban areas, with the capital, Maputo, having an officially estimated population of just over one million. Unofficial estimates, however, put this figure considerably higher.

The population growth rate is estimated at 2,6 per cent (1997); 45 per cent of the population is under the age of 14. Life expectancy at birth is just under 45 years.

Mozambique is a multicultural country and among its diverse peoples are Africans, Arabs, Indians and Portuguese. The Makua, the largest population group, account for nearly 28 per cent of the country's population and live in the northern provinces of Nampula, Cabo Delgado and Niassa. Other cultural groups of the north include the Makonde of Cabo Delgado Province, the Yao of western Niassa, the Mwani and the Nyanya.

The central provinces of Manica and Sofala are inhabited mainly by Shona, Sena, Chuabo and Nyungwe people, while the Lomwe is the most numerous group in Zambezia.

The Tsonga (Shangaan) of the Gaza and Maputo provinces in southern Mozambique are the second largest cultural group and account for just over 12 per cent of the population. Also living in Maputo Province is the Ronga, while Inhambane Province is home to the Tswa, Chope and Tonga.

About 80 per cent of the country's population is engaged in subsistence farming. Other important employment sectors include industry, transport and communication, and fishing. Unemployment, estimated at 50 per cent in 1989, is set to decrease as more job opportunities become available.

Traditional religion is still widespread in Mozambique and although statistics are difficult to obtain, about 50 per cent of the population still practise traditional faiths that are often combined with other religions. About 16 per cent of people are Catholic and a similar percentage are Protestants, with some 22 per cent Muslims, a religion widespread in the north of the country.

Language

The country's cultural diversity is reflected in the over 60 languages and dialects spoken. Portuguese is the official language, despite the fact that it is the home language of just over 1 per cent of the population and is spoken by less than a quarter of the population. Until the mid-1990s very little English was spoken, but nowadays it is widely understood in resorts frequented by South African and Zimbabwean tourists and at upmarket hotels in Maputo and Beira. Outside of the cities, major towns and resorts, little English is spoken and it is advisable to learn a few commonly used phrases (see p 194), or to take a short course in Portuguese.

Economy

At the time of independence, Mozambique was the fourth most industrialised country in Africa, but an ill-considered experiment with socialism, followed by civil war and a devastating drought, virtually destroyed the country's economy. In 1992 it was ranked by the World Bank as the poorest country in the world, with a per capita GNP of US $60 and an average inflation rate of 38 per cent from 1980 to 1992. The Metical was hopelessly overvalued and decreased in value from 200 Mt to the US dollar in 1987 to over 5 600 Mt in little more than seven years.

The country's economic upswing over the last decade can be attributed to two major events – the launching of the Economic Recovery Programme in January 1987 and the ending of the civil war in 1992. The ERP signalled a radical departure from Marxism and provided for privatisation of over 1 000 state-owned firms, reduced state expenditure and liberalisation of the exchange rate, among others.

Following the democratic elections of 1994, foreign aid worth billions of US dollars has flowed into the country, while international investors have shown a keen interest in Mozambique. By mid-1999 approved and proposed investment projects amounted to over ten billion dollars, making Mozambique the country that attracted the most foreign investment in sub-Saharan Africa. Among the top investment projects are the US $1,3 billion Mozal aluminium smelter near Maputo and a US $2,5 billion gas, iron and steel project.

With about 36 million hectares of arable land, Mozambique has considerable potential for **agriculture**, but only about 7 million hectares are cultivated by the formal farming sector. Important export crops include cashew nuts, sugar, copra, citrus, tea and tropical fruit. Subsistence farming is practised on the remaining 80 per cent of the land; the most important crops are maize, mandioco, cashew nuts, citrus, tropical fruits, cotton, coffee, tea and cocoa. As a result of the introduction of state farms, which were unproductive, and the civil war, livestock production declined and even today few animals are to be seen.

The **fishing** industry is another sector that holds great potential for recovery. The nutrient-rich offshore waters of southern Mozambique are rich in prawns, shrimps, crab and rock lobster. Prawns occur from Beira northwards to Quelimane. The main pelagic fishing waters, where sardines, anchovy and mackerel are caught, are off the coast from just south of Beira to north of Quelimane, with tuna occurring in the deeper offshore waters along much of the coast.

Tourism is a rapidly expanding economic sector and has attracted considerable investments since the elections in 1994. Various zones have been earmarked for development; among them the coastline from Cabo Santa Maria to Ponta do Ouro, Inhaca, Beira and Pemba. Prime wildlife areas such as Parque Nacional da Gorongosa (see p 134), Reserva do Niassa (see p 161) and Reserva Especial do Maputo (see p 99 and route 2) have been, or are in the process of being, rehabilitated and will in time again become a major drawcard for tourists.

The country is rich in **minerals** and several international mining companies have been attracted to Mozambique following the announcement of incentives for foreign investors. The coal reserves at Moatize in Tete Province have been estimated conservatively at 2,2 billion tonnes. Among the other minerals are gold and bauxite in Manica Province, emeralds at Gilé in Zambezia Province and several heavy minerals along the coast.

Mozambique's **energy** sector is blessed with rich resources, including vast reserves of natural gas. The Pande gas field in Inhambane Province has an estimated 60 billion cubic metres of gas, while the Temane gas field, 60 km south of Pande, also has vast gas reserves. Oil exploration is being conducted in the Rovuma Basin in the north of the country and in the Zambeze basin. The Cahora Bassa hydro-electric scheme on the Rio Zambeze has a generating capacity of 2 000 MW. Although the 900 km line running through Mozambique to South Africa was repaired in 1997, a disagreement on tariffs between HCB and the South African electricity utility, Eskom, has stalled the flow of energy to South Africa.

Prior to independence, 40 per cent of exports from South Africa's industrial heartland passed through the port of Maputo, which is some 200 km closer than the harbour facilities at Durban. A year after the democratic elections in Mozambique and South Africa, the Maputo Corridor project was launched to revive international trade and attract foreign investment along the 563 km road between Gauteng and Maputo.

The R1,5 billion Maputo Development Corridor has provided a major stimulus for the country's economy. One of the corridor's major benefits is that it gives Gauteng harbour facilities that are some 200 km closer than those of Durban. The project involved the upgrading of the national road between Gauteng and Maputo, the upgrading of the rail link and the rehabilitation of the Port of Maputo.

Commerce and services account for about a third of the country's GDP, agriculture 26,5 per cent, fishing and industries 15 per cent, transport and communication 14 per cent and construction 10,6 per cent. The main export products are prawns, cashew nuts, cotton, sugar, copra, wood and minerals. With billions being invested in the country, however, the contribution of the various economic sectors to GDP is likely to change significantly over the next few years.

Government

Mozambique is a republic governed by a constitution adopted on 30 November 1990. The executive branch consists of a president, elected for a five-year term by popular vote, a prime minister appointed by the president and a cabinet. The 250 members of the unicameral legislative branch, the *Assembleia da República*, are also elected by popular vote for a five-year term. All citizens 18 years and older are eligible to vote. The third branch of government is the judicial branch. The Supreme Court comprises of judges appointed by the president and judges elected by the Assembly. The legal system is based on customary law and the Portuguese civil legal system.

On a regional level, the country is divided into 10 provinces (*provincias*), each with a provincial capital. Covering 129 055 km^2, Niassa Province is not only the largest but also the most sparsely populated province, while Maputo Province in the south is the smallest. The provinces are again divided into *distrito* (districts), while inhabitants of cities and towns are represented by elected city or town councils. Maputo and its satellite, Matola, have the largest population, followed by Beira (300 000), Nampula (200 000), Nacala, Chimoio, Quelimane and Tete.

Province	**Provincial Capital**	**Area km^2**
Maputo	Maputo	25 756
Maputo (City)	Maputo	602
Gaza	Xai-Xai	75 709
Inhambane	Inhambane	68 615
Sofala	Beira	68 015
Manica	Chimoio	61 661
Tete	Tete	100 724
Zambezia	Quelimane	105 008
Nampula	Nampula	81 606
Niassa	Lichinga	129 056
Cabo Delgado	Pemba	82 625

2

Why Visit Mozambique?

With its kilometres of pristine beaches, diverse landscapes and fascinating history, Mozambique offers something of interest for everyone. One of the top drawcards is its unspoilt 2 500 km-long coastline and its watersport activities – exploring magnificent coral reefs, snorkelling, world-class game fishing, or simply relaxing. Despite the civil war, there are still pockets of big game in the country's conservation areas that are now being rehabilitated. Birders can seek the elusive green-headed oriole on Monte Gorongosa, a megatick in any birder's book, or venture further afield to northern Mozambique, where several east African species reach the southern limit of their distribution.

Except where there are activities along the coast, much of Mozambique's tourist infrastructure is still undeveloped. This makes the country an ideal destination for adventure seekers and cyclists, trailists and rock climbers can blaze their own trails along little-known routes.

Angling

No matter what your interest in fishing is, Mozambique is an angler's paradise offering world-class marine fishing in the South Indian Ocean.

Marine angling

The coastline of Mozambique is legendary for its excellent catches. Deep-sea fishing is especially exciting with **black marlin** of up to 250 kg and **sailfish** of up to 22 kg among the most highly prized by anglers. Sought after **game fish** include king mackerel (or couta), wahoo, barracuda, bonito, dorado and the giant kingfish. October to March are generally the best months for black marlin, while June and July are good months for sailfish. Most game fish are present throughout the year.

Commonly caught **rock and surf angling** species include kingfish, queenfish, bonefish, springer, pompano and mata-hari. **Saltwater flyfishing** is rapidly gaining popularity and **Benguerra Island** (see p 91) offers excellent possibilities. The hot summer months, when the water is warm enough to attract game fish, are generally the best times to visit. Among the commonly caught species are pompano, kingfish, bonefish and king and queen mackerel.

Most lodges are geared for angling and boats with a skipper, tackle and bait can be hired for morning, afternoon or full-day fishing trips. Nowadays, many lodges support a catch-and-release policy and anything in excess of what can be consumed by lodge guests is released. Game fish and billfish are usually photographed, tagged and released, unless it is a record size specimen.

Freshwater angling

There are excellent opportunities for freshwater angling, especially tiger fishing.

Cahora Bassa (see route 7) is set to become the prime destination in southern Africa for **tiger fishing**. This is not surprising, considering the fact that the dam's rich fish resources were not exploited until around 1996.

The dam is home to some enormous tiger fish, with specimens of 6,5 kg not uncommon. Catches of 12 kg are possible, but the largest tiger fish caught to date reportedly weighed 14 kg. As no bush clearing was done when the dam was built, lines can become ensnared by submerged trees and boating your catch can be rather tricky. The best time for catching tiger fish at Cahora Bassa is generally from August to January, but December and January can be unbearably hot.

Although tiger fishing is the main attraction of Cahora Bassa, a variety of other fish species also occur. Among these are chessa, eastern bottlenose, brown squeaker, Manyame labeo and tilapia.

Barragem de Chicamba (**Chicamba Dam**) (see p 127 and route 7) offers excellent possibilities for bass angling and the Chicamba Classic is hosted annually in November by Casa Msika.

Angling regulations

To prevent the exploitation of the country's marine resources, fishing regulations are strictly enforced. Those violating the law are liable to a hefty fine and confiscation of their catch. Fish may not be sold for commercial purposes and anglers should note that there is a limit on the weight of fish allowed to be taken out of the country. The limit per *bona fide* angler is 6 kg, which may consist of 2 kg of each species, or 4 kg of one species and 2 kg of another. Information regarding the latest rules and regulations can be obtained from the Ministry of Industry, Commerce and Tourism, P O Box 641, Maputo, or tel (01) 42 50 11, fax 42 17 96.

Spearfishing

With an abundance of game fish and excellent visibility, opportunities for this sport are virtually limitless and an increasing number of spearfishing enthusiasts are attracted to the Mozambican coast.

There is a limit of two fish per person per day and a snorkel is the only permissible artificial breathing apparatus. A licence must be obtained from the Ministry of Industry, Commerce and Tourism, P O Box 641, Maputo, or tel (01) 42 50 11, fax 42 17 96.

Snorkelling

For snorkelling enthusiasts there are exciting opportunities all along the coast. Good snorkelling spots include **Ilha da Inhaca** (see p 77) and the nearby **Ilha dos Portugueses** (see p 80). At the **Pools of Eden** (see route 3), a shore entry about 8 km north of the Limpopo River, we have seen firefish and juvenile angel fish in knee-deep water, while the shore entry reef at **Paindane** (see route 3) will not disappoint even the most discerning snorkeller.

The **Arquipélago do Bazaruto** (see p 83 and route 4), with its diversity of fish and coral, has several good spots, including **Two Mile Reef** (see route 4) off Benguerra Island. This magnificent spot offers what must be the best snorkelling along the east coast of southern Africa and in a mere 45 minutes we saw a blue-spotted stingray, anemones, parrot fish, domino and clownfish in addition to a multitude of other colourful fish.

Further north, the unexplored reefs off the **Arquipélago das Quirimbas** (see p 151 and route 9) are totally unexplored and offer unlimited snorkelling opportunities.

Snorkelling equipment can be hired from most lodges and excursions are conducted. Owing to the large variance between high and low tides (up to 5 m at Bazaruto) snorkelling is limited to an hour before low tide, something keen snorkellers should bear in mind when planning their trip.

Scuba Diving

One of the country's top attractions is without doubt the excellent opportunities for scuba diving. Unlike the well-dived reefs of South Africa, those along the coast of Mozambique remained untouched for nearly two decades during the civil war. Add to the pristine condition of the reefs a bewildering variety of reef fish, hard and soft coral, some exciting wreck dives and good visibility and it is easy to understand why Mozambique is such an attractive scuba diving destination.

Ponta do Ouro and **Ponta Malongane** (see p 98 and route 2) in the far south, are extremely popular diving spots, while **Ilha da Inhaca** (see p 77), 24 km east of Maputo, offers a variety of dives. Travelling further up the coast, the reefs off **Bilene** (see route 3) hold several exciting possibilities. Other popular destinations are **Paindane** (see route 3), south of Inhambane, **Praia da Barra** (see route 3), near Inhambane and **Morrungulo** (see route 4), north of Inhambane. Among the country's best known diving destinations is the **Arquipélago do Bazaruto** (**Bazaruto Archipelago**) (see page 83 and route 4), which offers some of the most spectacular diving in Mozambique.

Still further north, the reefs off **Pemba** (see route 8) give divers an opportunity to do wall dives, while the potential of the **Arquipélago das Quirimbas** (**Quirimba Archipelago**) (see p 151 and route 9), a string of islands stretching from Pemba northwards to the Tanzanian border, remains largely unexploited.

Most upmarket resorts have dive shops with a full range of equipment for hire and offer courses ranging from Resort and Open Water 1 to Advanced. Several companies sell fully inclusive dive packages (see list of dive charters, camps and packages in Chapter 5) from Johannesburg.

Sailing

With its balmy weather, warm water and idyllic beaches, the Mozambican coast and the Arquipélago do Bazaruto are popular with sailing enthusiasts. Several resorts have yachts available for charter, while a number of companies offer live-aboard packages.

Island cruises are an ideal way to explore the aquamarine ocean off the **Arquipélago do Bazaruto** (see p 83). Days are spent diving, snorkelling, game fishing or simply soaking up the sun and the magnificent surroundings, while each night is spent anchored in a sheltered bay off the islands.

Those with a spirit of adventure can consider plying the ocean in a **dhow**, a maritime tradition inherited from early Muslim seafarers. These craft are often built without plans, their planks sealed with sacking and tar, while a triangular sail is hoisted to the head of a low mast. Romantic as it might seem though, be aware that these vessels rely on the wind and tidal conditions and it could take you days, instead of hours, to get to your destination. Also bear in mind that there are no toilet facilities on board and that you are fully exposed to the sun, making it essential to protect yourself against the elements.

If these warnings are not enough to dampen your spirit of adventure, you will enjoy a sense of freedom and an experience not easily forgotten. **Dhow trips** are especially popular from Vilankulo to the Arquipélago do

Bazaruto, from Maxise to Inhambane (see route 3) and Linga Linga (see route 4) and from Pemba (see route 8) and the coastal villages further north to Ibo and the Arquipélago das Quirimbas (see p 151).

To arrange a dhow trip, ask for the *senhor de barqa* and agree on the price, but point out that payment will only be made at the end of the journey, otherwise you might end up stranded on a remote island.

At the other end of the scale you can pay a brief visit to the Arquipélago do Bazaruto by taking a **luxury passenger cruise** operated by Starlight Cruises from Durban. The cruise liner *Symphony* anchors off the island and passengers are ferried to Bazaruto, where they can swim and sunbathe for a few hours before returning to the liner (South Africa tel (011) 807-5111, fax 807-5085).

Sea Kayaking

For a totally different perspective of Mozambique, consider a three-week sea kayaking trip from Pemba (see route 8) to the unspoilt coral islands of the Arquipélago das Quirimbas (see p 151). Along the way there will be numerous opportunities for snorkelling and diving. Distances covered daily range between 10 km and 40 km, requiring you to be fit. **Coastal Kayak Trails** has set departures for groups and offer fully inclusive trips from Johannesburg (South Africa tel (021) 439-1134).

If you do not have the time, or required level of fitness, pleasant day trips in sea kayaks can be undertaken from Vilankulo. **Contact Real Cape Adventures** (South Africa (021) 790-5611).

Other Water Sports

Hobiecat sailing, **windsurfing** and **paddle-skiing** are among other popular water sport activities offered by several resorts and lodges. At some lodges **parasailing** and **water-skiing** are offered, the latter usually early in the morning, depending on calm seas and the tide. It is advisable to check with the resort what activities are available when making reservations.

Opportunities for **surfing** are rather limited; the most rewarding spots are Ponta do Ouro, Tofo (beware of the strong backwash) and Tofinho beaches, south of Inhambane.

Birdwatching

With habitats and vegetation ranging from montane forests and grasslands in the western highlands bordering Zimbabwe to miombo woodlands, mangrove swamps, lakes and a 2 500 km-long coastline, Mozambique is home to more than 600 bird species. Of special interest are the 30-odd endemics and near endemics, as well as several east African species that reach the southern limit of their distribution in the north of the country.

The birdlife of **southern Mozambique** (see route 2) has been studied extensively and to date some 523 species have been recorded south of the Rio Save. Among the noteworthy species are sand forest birds such as Rudd's apalis, Neergaard's sunbird, Woodwards' batis, pinkthroated twinspot and lemon-breasted canary.

Species of interest in the montane forests and grasslands of the **highlands on the Mozambique and Zimbabwe border** include stripe-cheecked bulbul, Swynnerton's robin, Chirinda apalis, briar warbler, white-tailed flycatcher, bronze sunbird and red-faced crimsonwing.

Without doubt one of southern Africa's "megaticks" is the green-headed oriole, which occurs only in the montane forests of **Monte Gorongosa** (see p 134 and route 6). Another birding hot spot is the **Dondo Forest** and the **woodlands north of Dondo on the E.N. 213** (see route 5), which is a must for keen birders. Among the rare species recorded in the lowland forest and Miombo woodlands north of Dondo are eastern honeyguide, white-breasted alethe, Böhm's spinetail and black-headed apalis. Other interesting species you chance ticking include speckle-throated and little spotted woodpecker, red-winged warbler, Gunning's robin, violet-backed sunbird and olive-headed weaver.

The birdlife **north of the Rio Zambeze** has not been studied nearly as intensively as that of southern Mozambique, making this part of the country an exciting birding destination. In addition, well over 20 east African species reach the southernmost limit of their distribution here. Species recorded, or are likely to occur, include pale-billed hornbill, five species of bulbuls, red-capped forest weaver, long-billed apalis, white-tailed blue flycatcher, red double-collared sunbird and stripe-breasted canary.

Another exciting, but physically demanding, birding destination is Montes Namúli, north of Gurué. It is home to the rare Namúli apalis which was only discovered in 1932 and "rediscovered" by an expedition of biologists in 1998. Other rare and noteworthy species occurring here are the dapplethroat which has only been recorded from two localities in Tanzania, the Thyolo alethe, bar-tailed trogon and five species of greenbul.

From September to April, visitors to the coast and the islands of **Inhaca** (see p 77) and **Bazaruto** (see p 83 and route 4) should keep an eye out for the crab plover, as well as a variety of migrant waders which could include interesting vagrants. Lesser and greater flamingo can usually be seen foraging in the shallow waters of the intertidal beaches and sandflats off the islands.

An indispensable book for birders is *The Atlas of the Birds of Southern Mozambique* by Vincent Parker, who spent three years atlasing birds south of the Rio Save. The 300-page book contains distribution maps and information on 523 species. Also useful is *The Birds of Southern Mozambique* by Phillip Clancey.

Game Parks and Wildlife Viewing

The proposed **Bazaruto National Park** (see p 87 and route 4), will cover an area that has been a tourist destination since the late 1980s and is one of the most popular in Mozambique. Unlike the mainland parks and reserves with their big game, the islands offer visitors the opportunity to explore the fascinating marine life – brilliantly coloured reef fish, whale sharks, dolphins and the endangered dugong (see route 4).

The mainland national parks and game reserves were once a major attraction, but years of civil war and poaching have wiped out much of the once prolific big game populations. Several parks are in the process of being rehabilitated, or have been. However, it will take some time for game populations to recover and until such time visitors should rather focus on the wilderness experience provided by these areas.

Before re-opening the mainland parks to tourists, land-mines had to be cleared, game guards trained, roads rebuilt, staff accommodation constructed and tourism facilities established. The first park to be re-opened was the **Reserva Especial do Maputo** (see p 99 and route 2) which has been identified by the Peace Parks Foundation as a Trans Frontier Conservation Area (TFCA). The proposed 4 195 km^2 TFCA envisages linking the reserve with Ndumo and Tembe parks in South Africa and Swaziland's Hlane National Park and Mlawula and Ndzindza nature reserves. One of the major benefits of the park will be the restoration of the migration routes of elephants.

Considerable progress has also been made with the rehabilitation of the **Parque Nacional da Gorongosa** (see p 134 and route 6). Although the civil war and poaching reduced the once prolific wildlife populations to a mere fraction, the magnificent scenery and birdlife make this park a worthwhile destination. As a first step to re-opening the park, permission has been granted to specialist groups, such as birders, to visit it.

The **Reserva do Niassa** (see p 161 and route 11) in northern Niassa Province has the largest game populations of all the conservation areas in Mozambique and is in the process of being rehabilitated. Owing to the high costs of providing tourist facilities and its remote location, prices are likely to be high and aimed mainly at overseas visitors.

An exciting development is the proposed **Kruger/Banhine/Zinave/Gonarezhou TFCA** which will create the world's largest conservation area – a 95 712 km^2 wildlife sanctuary. This idea was first mooted in May 1990 when the president of World Wide Fund for Nature (WWF) South Africa, Dr Anton Rupert, discussed the idea with Mozambican President Joaquim Chissano. This project will see the amalgamation of the famed Kruger National Park in South Africa with Banhine and Zinave in Mozambique and Gonarezhou in southeastern Zimbabwe. One of the main benefits of the park will be that elephant and other game will be able to migrate freely, relieving the pressure on the Kruger National Park.

Other conservation areas still to be rehabilitated include **Reserva do Gilé** and **Reserva do Pomene** (see route 4), a tract of beautiful coastal forest north of Inhambane. There is also the **Reserva de Marromeu**, south of the Rio Zambeze. In the late 1970s Marromeu was a sanctuary to some 135 000 animals, including over 30 000 buffalo, 45 000 waterbuck, 1 700 hippo and 2 700 Burchell's zebra, as well as elephant, eland, sable, hartebeest and reedbuck. Although an air census conducted in 1994 showed a dramatic reduction in game numbers since 1979, the reserve has considerable potential as a tourist attraction.

In addition to the existing conservation areas, several new areas have been designated in Cabo Delgado Province (see route 9).

4x4 Driving

Once off the main tar and gravel roads, there are thousands of kilometres of tracks in varying condition to be explored. Although many of the gravel roads in rural areas have been rebuilt since 1994, there are still numerous routes that will appeal to those keen on exploring the country's off-the-beaten track destinations.

Interesting byways include the rugged 90 km track between **Metangula and Cóbuè** on Lago Niassa (see route 10), the desolate track between **Marrupa and Montepuez** (see route 11), and the track from **Marrupa to Reserva do Niassa** (see route 11). Also worthwhile exploring is the back-road that skirts several unspoilt lagoons north of **Bilene** (see route 3).

The **Reserva Especial do Maputo** (see p 99 and route 2) in the south of the country has a network of sandy tracks negotiable only by four-wheel drive vehicle. To minimise damage to the track caused by excessive wheel-spinning, or worse, getting bogged down, it is advisable to deflate the tyres of your vehicle when travelling in the reserve.

When travelling along off-the-beaten tracks, bear in mind that these roads usually carry very little traffic and that help could be a long way off;

often days away (see p 53). This makes a two-vehicle party advisable and you should carry spares and a good tool kit with you. Land-mines are still a fact of life in many remote areas and you should avoid tracks that are not in regular use. If in doubt, enquire from local inhabitants whether there are any *minen.*

To protect the ecologically sensitive coastline from damage by vehicles, beach driving, except at designated places, has been banned along the entire coast. These regulations are being strictly enforced and offenders are subject to heavy fines. In the **Reserva Especial do Maputo** (see p 99) it is possible to buy a beach driving permit which allows you to travel from Milibangalala to Ponta Dobela.

History and Culture

With its colourful history and mixture of African, Arab and Portuguese cultures, Mozambique has much to offer visitors interested in history and culture. Heading the list of historical attractions is the fascinating **Ilha de Moçambique** (see p 153 and route 8) with its narrow streets, crumbling buildings and reed and thatch dwellings. Its seafaring history and the conservation of its architectural heritage was considered so important that the island was declared a World Heritage Site in 1991.

Another fascinating historical attraction is **Ilha do Ibo** (see p 151), the best known island of the **Arquipélago das Quirimbas** (see p 151 and route 9). Once a thriving trade centre, its importance began waning in the early 1900s and it gradually faded into obscurity. Getting to Ibo by dhow is an adventure in itself and on the island you can wander among the remains of once stately buildings that have been reduced to crumbling ruins by time and the elements.

Bearing testimony to the long seafaring history of the coast and well worth exploring are the ***farols*** (lighthouses) that have warned mariners against treacherous reefs and capes for centuries. Especially worthwhile visiting are those on **Ilha do Bazaruto** (see p 89 and route 4) and the mouth of the **Rio Limpopo** (see route 3).

Cultural experiences in Mozambique range from intricate Makonde wood carvings (see p 23 and route 8) and the Nhau dancers of Tete Province to Inhambane's annual music festival and the white *muciro* masks of the Makua women.

Traditional dancing, singing and music still play an important role in the lives of Mozambican people. In Tete Province **Nhau dances** are still performed during initiation rituals. These complex dances, accompanied by the sound of drum beats, are performed with large wooden masks.

Wooden *mapico* masks are used in northern Cabo Delgado Province by the **Makonde** (see route 8) who still practise customs such as sharpening of the teeth and facial scarring, a painful ritual that involves the carving of patterns on the face.

Traditional music is another important aspect of Mozambican cultural life. The people of Niassa Province use a wind instrument, made from hollowed calabashes, to produce a sound not unlike that of a trumpet.

Further south, the Chope of Inhambane Province are renowned for playing their music on the *timbila*, a percussion instrument resembling a xylophone. The centre of this musical tradition, known as Timbila Ta Mupetane Ta Venáncio, is situated about 22 km north of the town of Quissico. The instruments are manufactured here and it takes about three weeks to build a half-metre long *timbila*. An orchestra can consist of up to 23 *timbila* of varying sizes and 45 musicians. An annual musical festival is held in Inhambane (see p 95).

In Nampula and Cabo Delgado provinces **Makua** women with their faces painted white are still commonly seen. A white powder is obtained by pounding the root of a tree and mixing it with water to form a paste which is applied to the face. The mask, known as *muciro*, is used as a skin lotion and as a sunscreen.

Shopping

Roadside stalls and markets are by far the best places to look out for pottery, basketry and cane furniture.

Makonde wood carvings are much in demand worldwide and can be bought from Makonde co-operatives in Maputo, Beira, Nampula, Pemba and Mueda. Take a close-up look at the Makonde sculptures. They usually tell a story and figures are portrayed in a characteristically supernatural way, revealing an almost eerie "oriental" influence on the African cultural tradition.

Other goods to buy are **Nhau wooden masks** and **drums** and **Makua mats**. Also popular are musical instruments such as the *timbila*, and the **calabash trumpet** that is common in Niassa Province.

In **Maputo** (see p 63) **curios** ranging from wood carvings to beautiful batiks are sold outside the Hotel Polana, the Hotel Cardoso and opposite Restaurante Piri-Piri. Paintings are also popular and typically reflect the style of Malangatana – numerous faces with empty eyes and sad faces.

Well worth a visit in Maputo is the *Mercado Artesanato*, or Saturday Market, at the Praça 25 de Junho. A wide variety of crafts ranging from wooden replicas of cellphones and cars and wire trinkets to beautiful batiks, wood carvings and paintings are offered for sale. The initial price is usually much higher than what the seller expects, so be prepared to bargain, or you run the risk of being overcharged.

Not to be missed are the colourful and bustling municipal markets (***Mercado Municipal***) found in all cities and towns. Reminiscent of Oriental bazaars with their narrow alleys, the tightly packed stalls sell everything imaginable and this is where the local people buy their fruit, vegetables, meat and other household requirements.

Trailing and Rock Climbing

Although totally undeveloped, there is considerable potential for hiking, backpacking and mountain climbing in Mozambique. For that real Robinson Crusoe feeling you can go beachcombing along the shores of the **Arquipélago do Bazaruto** (**Bazaruto Archipelago**) (see p 83), or stroll along kilometres of pristine beaches.

Areas of particular interest to backpackers include the **western highland areas of Chimanimani and Monte Binga** (at 2 436 m the highest point in the country) (see route 7) which form the international boundary with Zimbabwe. Also likely to be of interest to backpackers is **Monte Gorongosa** (see route 6) which is 1 863 m at its highest point.

Because there are no demarcated trails and as there might still be landmines on some of the remote tracks and paths it is advisable to hire the services of a local guide to accompany you.

The faces of Mozambique's spectacular *monte-ilhas,* or granite island mountains, present exciting challenges and opportunities to rock climbers. The faces of the domes punctuating the landscape of **Nampula** Province (see p 163) are reputedly among the highest in the world; some are 650 m to 700 m of sheer rock. Among these are **Malema**, a trio of sugarloaf mountains near Cuamba, and the **Ribáuè** *monte-ilha.* Other areas likely to be of interest are **Gorongosa** in Sofala Province, the **Panda** *inselberg* in Manica Province and the 2 419 m-high **Namúli**, the second highest peak in the country in northern Zambezia Province.

Prior to climbing any mountain, it is advisable to obtain the necessary permission from the *secretario* of the district in which the mountain is situated. Although this can be time-consuming, it is important to respect local traditions and customs.

Hunting and Hunting Safaris

Until the 1970s, Mozambique was one of Africa's top hunting destinations; but as a result of the civil war hunting was only reopened in 1994.

The hunting season stretches from 1 April to 30 October and there are several large hunting concession areas. Some of these are in the Marromeu complex and the buffer zones around Reserva do Niassa. Trophy fees range from US$ 3 700 for lion to US$ 2 300 for sable and US$ 1 330 for buffalo. The ban on hunting of elephants has been lifted.

For details contact **Zambeze Delta Safaris**, e-mail safaris@silcom.com, or **Safari Marketers**, South Africa tel and fax (011) 462-6960, e-mail smsafari@iafrica.com. Information on hunting concessionaires can be obtained from the Directorate of Forestry and Wildlife Conservation (Direção Nacional de Florestas e Fauna Bravia), tel (01) 46 00 36.

3

PLANNING YOUR TRIP

Planning Your Itinerary

Part of the enjoyment of any holiday is preparation, while the success depends to a large extent on sound planning. Unlike other southern African countries such as South Africa, Namibia and Zimbabwe that are easy on travellers, you will need to plan your visit to Mozambique carefully to ensure an enjoyable experience.

Except for an increasing number of resorts along the coast, Mozambique's tourism industry is still largely undeveloped and it is hence a great country for adventurous travellers. This will require you to have a flexible itinerary; for example a dhow trip that usually takes a few hours might take you days.

Most roads between major centres in the southern and central areas of the country have been rehabilitated and are, therefore, negotiable by sedan car (see p 49). When calculating travelling times, count on averaging about 80 km an hour on major tar roads. To reach many of the coastal tourist attractions, however, a four-wheel drive vehicle, or a vehicle with a high ground clearance, is required, if only for the last few kilometres. In the north of the country there are few tar roads, but fortunately many of the major gravel roads have already been rebuilt.

Obtaining fuel in cities and towns along major routes is no longer a problem in southern and central Mozambique. In off-the-beaten track areas it can be unavailable, although new filling stations are opening up throughout the country. You should, however, have little difficulty in buying diesel in most larger towns. When travelling in the north of the country it is advisable to take extra fuel along, rather than risking buying it on the black market. Not only is the price exorbitant, but in some cases petrol has been diluted with paraffin, diesel or water.

Suggested Itineraries

The following suggested itineraries can be combined into longer tours, or adapted to suit personal preferences. Distances are approximate only and allowance should be made for detours.

10-Day Southern Tour

Day	Destination	Distance
1	Gauteng – Ponta do Ouro (via Pongola)	630 km
2	Ponta do Ouro	10 km
3	Ponta do Ouro – Ponta Malongane	10 km
4	Ponta Malongane	10 km
5	Ponta Malongane – Milibangalala (Reserva Especial do Maputo)	100 km
6	Milibangalala	20 km
7	Milibangalala – Maputo	110 km
8	Maputo	25 km
9	Maputo – Praia do Xai-Xai	220 km
10	Praia do Xai-Xai	20 km

18-Day Lagoon Coast & Islands Tour

Day	Destination	Distance
1	Maputo – Bilene	190 km
2	Bilene	10 km
3	Bilene – Zongoene Lodge	120 km
4	Zongoene Lodge	–
5	Zongoene Lodge – Praia do Xai-Xai	60 km
6	Praia do Xai-Xai	10 km
7	Praia do Xai-Xai – Chidenguele	80 km
8	Chidenguele	–
9	Chidenguele – Inhambane/Barra/ Guinjata Paindane	230 km
10	Inhambane/Barra/Guinjata/Paindane	20 km
11	Inhambane/Barra/Guinjata/Paindane	20 km
12	Inhambane – Morrungulo	175 km
13	Morrungulo	40 km
14	Morrungulo – Vilankulo/Inhassoro	180/230 km
15	Vilankulo/Inhassoro – Benguerra/Bazaruto	Fly/boat
16	Benguerra/Bazaruto	–
17	Benguerra/Bazaruto	–
18	Benguerra/Bazaruto – Vilankulo/Inhassoro	Fly/boat

14-Day Northern Coastal Tour

Day	Destination	Distance
1	Mutare – Beira	310 km
2	Beira	20 km
3	Beira – Qulimane/Zalala (early start advisable)	500 km
4	Quelimane/Zalala	60 km
5	Quelimane – Ilha de Moçambique	
6	Ilha de Moçambique/Praia da Chocas	50 km
7	Ilha de Moçambique – Pemba	420 km
8	Pemba	30 km
9	Pemba – Quissanga/Ibo	dhow/115 km
10	Ibo	–
11	Ibo	–
12	Ibo – Quissanga – Pangane	dhow/150 km
13	Pangane	–
14	Pangane – Pemba	255 km

15-Day Northern Inland Tour

Day	Destination	Distance
1	Mt Selinda/Espungabera – Casa Msika	360 km
2	Casa Msika	10 km
3	Casa Msika – Cahora Bassa (early start advisable)	450 km
4	Cahora Bassa	100 km
5	Cahora Bassa	50 km
6	Cahora Bassa – Tete	150 km
7	Tete – Zomba (Malawi)	320 km
8	Zomba – Metangula (early start advisable)	465 km
9	Metangula	–
10	Metangula – Cóbuè	100 km
11	Cóbuè	–
12	Cóbuè – Lichinga	240 km
13	Lichinga – bush camping (depending on progress)	350 km
14	Bush camping (depending on progress) east of Maruppa	300 km
15	Bush Camp – Pemba	340 km

What to Pack

With its warm, subtropical and tropical climate, the most practical daytime wear in Mozambique is light cotton clothing (shirts, trousers or skirts) and a sun hat. Long-sleeved shirts and cotton trousers provide protection against the sun and are advisable for the evenings when mosquitoes are active. Although not a safeguard, they do help to protect against mosquito bites, as do socks. Keep rain gear handy in the summer when thunderstorms are a feature in the afternoons.

In winter the early mornings, evenings and nights can be cool, especially in the mountainous highlands between Mozambique and Zimbabwe, at Monte Gorongosa and the Makonde plateau. Remember to pack warm trousers, a jersey and a jacket. These items are also essential when visiting the coast, where it can occasionally be unpleasant.

Other items you should not neglect to pack include a first-aid kit (see p 33), mosquito prophylaxis (see p 36), mosquito net (if camping), mosquito spray, or roll-on repellent, lots of sunscreen cream, sunglasses, bathing costume and snorkelling gear. A cotton money belt is essential for keeping money and documents concealed on your body.

Also remember to pack comfortable walking shoes. Strops are useful if you're headed for Ilha da Inhaca or the Bazaruto archipelago, as they will protect your feet against the nasty cuts from razor clams when wading in the shallows off the western shores of the islands. A pair of flip-flops will come in handy when showering in communal ablutions.

Entry and Customs Regulations

A list of Mozambican diplomatic missions abroad and diplomatic representatives accredited to Mozambique, together with their addresses, telephone and fax numbers, is provided in Chapter 11.

Entry formalities

Visitors require a passport which must be valid for at least six months after the intended date of return from Mozambique. All visitors also require a visa, obtainable from the nearest Mozambican diplomatic mission (see p 189), or at the Direção Nacional Migração in Maputo. A number of travel companies in Johannesburg, South Africa, offer visa services for Mozambique, saving you the frustration of standing in long queues. Although a handling fee is charged, there is usually less of a delay and the additional cost is well worth it. Contact **VIP Visa Services** through Mozambique Connection, P O Box 2861, Rivonia 2128, tel South Africa (011) 803-4185, fax 803-3861 or the Mozambique National Tourist

Company, Noswall Hall, 10th Floor, 3 Stiemens Street, Cnr Bertha Street, Braamfontein 2001, tel (011) 339-7275, fax 339-7295.

Tourist visas are valid for 30 days for one entry, but can be extended for up to three months at any Provincial Immigration Department office while in Mozambique. A double entry visa is also valid for 30 days and is essential when travelling from Tete Province via Malawi to northern Mozambique. Take care not to overstay the period for which your visa is valid, as heavy penalties are payable for each day you remain in the country after your visa has expired.

Applications for visas must be accompanied by your passport, two passport photographs (not required if you have applied for a visa at the Consulate General in Johannesburg in the previous 12 months) and a completed visa application form. Visas are issued within six to eight working days (excluding Wednesdays and Mozambican public holidays). Urgent visas can be obtained within five working days, while very urgent visas are issued within two working days for an additional payment.

Border posts

Maputo's Mavelane airport, as well as the airports at Beira, Vilankulo and Inhambane, are recognised immigration points.

Overland travellers may enter and exit Mozambique at the following points:

Malawi	
Zóbuè/Mwanza	06:00-17:00
Namwera/Mandimba	06:00-17:00
Muloza/Milange	06:00-17:00
Dedza	06:00-17:00
South Africa	
Lebombo/Ressano Garcia	06:00-19:00
Kosi Bay/Ponta do Ouro	08:00-17:00
Swaziland	
Lomahasha/Namaacha	07:00-17:00
Zambia	
Cassacatiza	
Zimbabwe	
Forbes-Mutare/Machipanda	06:00-18:00
Mt Selinda/Espungabera	06:00-18:00
Nyamapanda/Cochemane	06:00-18:00
Mukumbura/Mecumbura	06:00-18:00
Kanyemba (boats only)	06:00-18:00

Customs

Visitors are exempt from paying import duty on personal effects, sporting and recreational equipment, other goods (including food) with a total value not exceeding US $100 and the following consumables: 5 *l* wine, 1 *l* spirits, 400 cigarettes, 100 cigarellos, 50 cigars, 250 ml toilet water, 50 ml perfume.

South African visitors have long been known to load their trailers with all the supplies necessary for the duration of their visit. While this was justifiable when supplies were unobtainable after Mozambique once again became accessible to tourists in 1994, this is no longer the case. In the south and central provinces shops are well stocked with a variety of food, but in the north the range of foodstuffs and goods is admittedly still limited. Because Mozambique's economy benefits very little from self-sufficient tourists, customs regulations are likely to be enforced much more strictly than in the past. The customs service is managed by a British company, Crown Agents, and efficiency and the collection of customs duties have improved significantly.

Although most foodstuffs are considerably more expensive than in South Africa, you should adopt an attitude of support for the country's economy, and especially of the informal sector. Take only the basics and head for the local market to buy whatever else you need. After all, this is where you will get the real feel of the country and its people.

Border post formalities

Border formalities are somewhat haphazard and vary from one border post to the next. Forms to be completed and fees payable differ considerably and the moods of officials no doubt play a role. Some of the smaller border posts might not have embarkation and disembarkation forms, but on departing from Mozambique an official could insist on such a form.

Formalities are more straightforward at Komatipoort (Lebombo)/Ressano Garcia than at smaller border posts. On arrival at the Komatipoort border post you will be required to take out third party insurance (*seguros*) before proceeding to immigration and customs. There is an IGI office at the border post and you will need to show the original registration papers of your vehicle. Policies cost R100 and are valid for 30 days. At some of the smaller border posts third party insurance is not always available. Should this be the case, you are advised to obtain insurance from the nearest Emose (Empresa Moçambicana De Seguros) office.

After completing immigration formalities you have to complete a re-importation of goods form (Form DA 65) for your vehicle, trailer and all identifiable items such as cameras, video cameras, radios etc. It is useful to keep a list with all the serial numbers at hand. Keep the form in a safe place as it must be surrendered to the Mozambican authorities on your departure.

At the Ressano Garcia border post on the Mozambican side you will be required to complete an embarkation/disembarkation form (*Registo De Embarque E Disembarque*) before presenting your passport. Both sections of the form must be completed and the lower section retained and handed to immigration officials when you leave the country. After your passport has been stamped (a fee of 28 800 meticais [Mt] is payable), proceed to customs where vehicle tax of 48 000 Mt is due.

You should be wary of people offering assistance to get you through immigration and customs quickly. These smooth, well-spoken operators might be mistaken for helpful officials, but demand exorbitant fees for their "services".

Formalities at Lebombo/Ressano Garcia are expected to be streamlined considerably once the Maputo Corridor becomes fully operational. At the time of writing (April 1999) various options were still under consideration and it is advisable to check with the authorities once the new border post is opened.

At some of the smaller border posts you might also have to complete a temporary import permit (*licença de importação temporária*).

Health

Visitors to Mozambique need to take a few common sense health precautions to ensure that they stay in good health. This is especially important when travelling in remote areas where medical facilities often lack the most basic medicines.

Medical insurance is absolutely essential as treatment in a private clinic is expensive and a substantial down payment is required before you will be admitted.

Private medical facilities in Maputo are of a good standard and are equipped to deal with most emergencies, including trauma cases. There are several clinics in Maputo, among them: Sommerschield Clinic, 52 Rua Pereira Lago, tel (01) 49 39 24; Cruz Azul, 414 Avenida Karl Marx, tel (01) 30 51 46; Clinica Especial, Avenida Eduardo Mondlane, tel (01) 42 46 33.

For up to date health travel advice you can visit the following websites: British Airways Travel Clinics at www.travelclinic.co.za; Centre for Disease Control and Prevention at www.cdc.gov/travel/eafrica.htm. South African travellers can also contact the **South African Institute for Medical Research**, or **Travelsafe Clinics** in Johannesburg, Pretoria and Cape Town.

First-aid kit

It is advisable to take a small but well-stocked medical kit along with you. The kit should contain: anti-malaria tablets, insect repellent, sunscreen cream and after-sun treatment cream, a broad spectrum antibiotic, local spray-on anaesthetic for stings or bites, anti-diarrhoea tablets, anti-histamine cream and tablets, pain killers, anti-inflammatory gel, antiseptic cream and solution, analgesic eardrops, eyedrops, eye ointment and oral rehydration powder. Other items to include are: sterile syringes, a thermometer, assortment of plasters, bandages (wide crêpe and narrow gauze), cotton wool, scissors, safety pins, sling, eye bath, tweezers.

Some of the medical problems that you could encounter during your travels are discussed below. By heeding the old saying "Prevention is better than cure" you can, however, reduce the risks considerably. For ease of reference this list is in alphabetic order.

HIV/AIDS

According to World Health Organization and UNAIDS statistics released in June 1998, an estimated 1,2 million people between the ages of 15 and 49 in Mozambique are HIV/AIDS positive. This gives the country an adult prevalence rate of 14,17 per cent, placing it seventh on the African continent in terms of HIV/AIDS infections.

Owing to widespread poverty, high unemployment and large numbers of war widows and orphaned children, sex for payment is seen by many destitute women and young girls as a means of earning an income, especially in the cities.

The only sure way to avoid HIV/AIDS, or other sexually transmitted diseases, is abstinence. Alternatively, condoms must be used as a preventative measure and you should ensure that you have a sufficient supply as they are not widely available.

Avoid blood transfusions, as blood may not be thoroughly screened. When travelling outside of Maputo and other major cities it is advisable to have single-use, disposable needles and syringes in your first-aid kit as they might not be available in remote rural areas.

Bilharzia

The World Health Organization has identified bilharzia as the most prevalent parasitic disease in the world after malaria. Humans are affected by two species of bilharzia: intestinal bilharzia and bladder, or urinary, bilharzia. The disease is caused by larvae penetrating the skin of its human host and migrating to the veins of the liver, or the mesentric vessels of the bowel. Here the larvae pair, to develop into mature worms that continue to produce eggs.

The best way to prevent bilharzia is to avoid contact with slow-flowing and stagnant water. A rash or itchy skin is usually the first symptom and after three to four weeks symptoms might include general fatigue, chills, fever, muscle aches and coughs. If left untreated, blood will appear in the urine. In rare cases the eggs can cause inflammation of the spinal cord and paralysis. Several drugs are available to treat bilharzia.

Cholera

Sporadic outbreaks of cholera occur in Mozambique and the risk is highest during the rainy season. Symptoms include severe watery diarrhoea and vomiting, resulting in massive loss of body fluids and salts that can be fatal. The injected vaccine is no longer recommended by the World Health Organization, but a newer oral vaccine has proved to be more effective, but not 100 per cent. Although immunisation is not required by visitors to Mozambique, it might be advisable to consider the oral vaccine if you are travelling outside of the major cities.

The risk of contracting the disease can be reduced if you follow a few basic rules. Drink only bottled water, or carbonated water and beverages made from boiling water (tea and coffee). When ordering bottled water, though, make sure that the seal is not broken as empty bottles are sometimes refilled with tap water and resold. Also do not brush your teeth with tap water and avoid ice which is made from it.

If you are doing an extended self-drive trip, ensure that you have enough water in containers for the duration of your visit. If in doubt about the quality of the water when refilling containers, boil such water before use. Bear in mind that water purification tablets are not effective against cholera.

When travelling outside of the main cities and beyond lodges, most of your purchases will be from markets where mainly fresh produce is sold. Peeled raw fruit should be avoided, while vegetables can be bleached. Other food, especially meat, fish and shellfish, should be thoroughly cooked. Always remember the adage, "If you cannot boil it, cook it, or peel it, forget it".

Adventurous eaters argue that it is safe to eat and drink whatever the local people consume. Should you have a tolerant stomach and opt for this philosophy, bear in mind that local people usually develop resistance or tolerance to some of the harmful bacteria in their food and this argument is therefore not entirely correct.

The most effective treatment is to drink lots of water, preferably with a rehydration solution, or you can make up your own solution by adding six teaspoons of sugar and half a teaspoon of salt to a litre of boiled or bottled water. Medical assistance should be sought.

Diarrhoea

Few travellers are fortunate enough to escape from diarrhoea, a disease caused by drinking, or eating, contaminated food. It is avoided by following the recommended hygiene practices for cholera and is best treated by drinking isotonic drinks, mixed to half strength, or an oral electrolyte mixture. Anti-diarrhoeal medication should be taken only if travelling cannot be avoided.

Heat-related conditions

Heat exhaustion is best prevented by remaining out of the sun during the heat of the day and by keeping the intake of fluids up. Wear a hat for protection against the sun.

Always bear in mind that high temperatures, especially in summer, can result in the rapid loss of body fluids, while high humidity prevents the evaporation of sweat, causing overheating of the body. Symptoms of heat exhaustion include sweating, a cold, clammy and pale skin, rapid and shallow breathing, a weak and rapid pulse, nausea and dizziness. Lie the person down in a cool place with feet elevated above the head, loosen tight clothing, remove excessive clothing and sponge the person down. Give the victim as much water, isotonic drinks or rehydration liquid as can be drunk.

Heatstroke is a more serious overheating condition that can result in unconsciousness and should be treated as a medical emergency.

Sunburn is the most likely discomfort you will suffer if you do not take the necessary precautions. Tempting as it might be to catch up on your suntan, avoid tanning between 10:00 and 15:00. Use a sunscreen cream with a sun protection factor suited to your skin type and activity, for example water sport. If you do not already have a suntan, limit your initial suntanning to 15 minutes, increasing the exposure by five minutes daily.

Sunscreen takes up to 30 minutes before reaching optimal effectiveness and it should therefore be applied well before you venture out into the sun. Sweating and drying will reduce its effectiveness and it must be re-applied frequently.

Be especially aware of the possibility of sunburn when swimming or snorkelling, and re-apply sunscreen after water-based activities. Also take care on overcast days when the effect of the sun is seemingly less severe. Other precautions you can take include wearing sunglasses, wearing a wide-brimmed hat and protecting your lips.

Hepatitis B

Hepatitis B, a viral infection of the liver, is one of the most serious forms of hepatitis and few people are aware that it is far more infectious than the AIDS virus. It is transmitted through the use of unsterilised needles, contact with infected blood, body fluids during sexual contact and the transfusion of unscreened blood or blood products. Symptoms include nausea, loss of appetite, vomiting, muscular aches, weakness, jaundiced skin and fever. A course of three vaccinations provides protection against infection for five years.

Jigger fleas

The jigger flea is a common inhabitant of sandy areas in tropical Africa. The fertilised female embeds herself into the skin of a human host, usually beneath the toenails or between the toes. As the eggs develop, the body, which is enclosed by inflamed flesh, swells to the size of a pea and the eggs are released through a small hole at the tip of the abdomen.

The risk of being bitten can be reduced by wearing closed footwear, and feet should be inspected regularly to remove the fleas before they develop. A severe pain underneath the toenail, or between the toes, and a hard, dark swelling are usually indicative of infection. The flea should be removed by enlarging the abdominal hole with a sterile needle and hooking it out. The wound should then be treated with an antiseptic ointment. In severe cases ulceration and gangrene can develop, resulting in the amputation of toes.

Malaria

Malaria is the cause of more deaths in Africa than any other parasitic disease and kills over one million people on the continent every year. In recent years the disease has spread into areas where it did not use to occur historically and parasites are becoming increasingly resistant to prophylaxis, giving rise to serious concern.

Because Mozambique falls within a year-round high risk malaria area it is advisable to consult a doctor and obtain medical advice. The risk of contracting malaria is especially high during the rainy season (November to April).

The most serious cases of malaria are caused by *Plasmodium falciparum* parasites that are injected into humans by an infected female *Anopheles* mosquito. The parasites enter the bloodstream, invading, infecting and destroying red blood cells.

Malaria is potentially fatal and a life-threatening situation can develop if it is not treated immediately. Symptoms can easily be mistaken for flu and include fever, hot and cold shivers, headache, body ache, nausea and diarrhoea. In cases of severe headaches, restlessness, unusual behaviour and convulsions, cerebral malaria should be suspected. Should any of these symptoms manifest themselves within seven to 14 days of entering a malaria area, or up to three months after leaving such an area, a doctor must be consulted immediately. It is important to tell the doctor that you had visited a malaria area.

It is often suggested that taking prophylaxis masks the symptoms, making diagnosis more difficult. The upside of taking prophylaxis, though, is that if malaria does develop, the severity of the disease can be reduced. As Dr Andrew Jamieson, the medical director of British Airways Travel Clinics in South Africa, puts it: "Avoiding anti-malaria tablets certainly does make it much easier for a doctor to clinch the diagnosis. He knows exactly what to enter on the death certificate".

In recent years the parasites have developed resistance to several anti-malaria drugs, especially Chloroquine and Fansidar. Travellers to Mozambique should, therefore, consult their doctor to obtain advice on the most appropriate prophylaxis.

After leaving a malaria area it is vitally important to continue taking the drugs for the prescribed period.

In addition to taking prophylaxis, other precautions include wearing socks, long-sleeved shirts and long trousers after sunset, applying a repellent (containing N, N-diethylmtolumide) to exposed skin and sleeping under a mosquito net impregnated with a pyrethroid insecticide. Rooms can be sprayed with insecticidal sprays, or you can burn mosquito coils.

Travellers venturing well off the beaten track where there are no medical facilities should consider taking along a malaria self-test kit and drugs to treat malaria. The test kit has been shown to be 92 per cent effective and should, therefore, be used as an emergency measure only and a doctor must be consulted at the earliest opportunity.

Marine-life stings and coral cuts

Along the coast there is a possibility of coming into contact with venomous marine animals. Among the most common hazards are **bluebottles** (easily identified by their blue airsac) and **jellyfish**, both of which release a powerful paralytic toxin when swimmers come into contact with the long tendrils. Symptoms include pain, red skin and slight swelling where the tentacles made contact, muscle cramps, nausea and in severe cases, breathing difficulties.

Minor symptoms can be treated by washing the affected area with surgical spirit, or ammonia and salt water (do not use fresh water). Alternatively, wrap your hand in a cloth and gently rub away attached tentacles. Immerse the affected area in very hot water, but take care not to cause scalding.

An encounter with a **stonefish**, an ugly shallow-water fish with short, poisonous spines, could be even more painful. Symptoms include severe pain, swelling and numbness of the affected area, followed by sweating, dizziness, nausea, general weakness and difficulty in breathing. In severe cases there is a possibility of paralysis and collapse within an hour. The affected area should be immersed in water that is as hot as the patient can bear (55 °C) until the pain subsides. Once the pain is relieved, take the affected area out of the water to prevent blistering. Re-immerse when pain returns. Also treat the person for shock and monitor breathing.

Treatment for **scorpionfish** and **firefish** wounds is the same as for stonefish poisoning.

Coral cuts can be painful and can take extremely long to heal. Cuts must be washed thoroughly with an antiseptic solution, taking care to remove any coral that might have become lodged in the skin. The wound should then be treated regularly with an antiseptic spray.

Meningitis

This highly contagious bacterial disease infects the membrane surrounding the brain or the spinal cord. It is transmitted when the carrier coughs, or sneezes, and can be fatal within a few hours. Symptoms include severe headache, fever, light sensitivity, purple rashes and a stiff neck that prevents the head from bending forward.

Before travelling in remote areas, ask your doctor for a prescription for a broad spectrum antibiotic for treatment in cases of emergency. However, medical help must be sought immediately.

Sleeping sickness

Also known as trypanosomiasis in humans and *nangana* in livestock, this parasitic disease is transmitted through the bite of an infected tsetse fly. This yellowish or brown blood-feeding fly is easily recognised by its scissor-like wings and a sharp pain will indicate a bite. Fortunately only a small percentage of flies are carriers of the disease, but if a bite becomes painful or inflamed, a doctor must be consulted immediately. Other symptoms include severe headache and swelling of the lymph glands.

There is no preventative medication, but the following measures will help to reduce the risk of contracting the disease: when travelling through tsetse fly infested areas, keep vehicle windows closed; wear long-sleeved shirts and trousers in dull colours; avoid floral or checked patterns and dark blue clothing and do not use aftershave or perfume.

Tick bites

Tick bites usually cause no more than a rash, or an itch, but when the *Rickettsia rickettsi* parasite enters the bloodstream, tick bite fever will develop within seven to 14 days. Ticks are best avoided by wearing long trousers, or clothing treated with a repellent. Inspect your body for ticks regularly.

If a tick is embedded in the skin it can be removed by burning it with a lighter, or covering it with a greasy substance. Clean the bite area with water and soap and apply an antiseptic ointment.

Symptoms of tick bite fever include swelling around the site of the bite, severe headache, body ache, intermittent spells of fever, nausea and swollen glands. Medical assistance should be sought without delay.

Safety and Security

Hijackings

Immediately after Mozambique became accessible to tourists in 1994 there were a number of hijacking incidents. In response, security forces were deployed along the Ressano Garcia to Maputo road and along the E.N. 1, south of Inchope, which resulted in a reduction in incidents. Isolated incidents still occur, but hijackings are usually non-violent, and the incidence is certainly much lower than in Johannesburg, or many other cities on the continent.

Police and traffic police road blocks are generally signposted. Traffic police can be recognised by their white shirts and black trousers, or skirts, while the police wear grey uniforms. They also display a force number.

As a general rule it is inadvisable to drive between towns after dark and preferable to avoid unnecessary stops. In addition, try not to drive at night in Maputo, Beira, Nampula and Nacala. If you do so, avoid poorly lit areas where there is little traffic, or driving late at night. Keep doors locked and be especially cautious at traffic lights and stop streets.

Should you be confronted by knife-wielding or gun-toting hijackers, don't resist – do exactly as you are told. It is better losing your vehicle and a few possessions than your life!

Theft and muggings

An increased police presence in cities and towns has resulted in a decrease in these types of crime. However, as in most other cities of the world pickpocketing, muggings and theft occur from time to time, but Maputo is certainly much safer than Johannesburg.

Avoid wearing expensive watches, jewellery and carrying costly handbags and cameras. A sure way of attracting the attention of muggers is to wear a moon bag; rather wear a cotton money belt concealed under your clothing. When walking about, cash and travellers' cheques are best left locked in your hotel room. Carry only as much cash on your person as you expect to need and avoid taking large amounts of cash out of your wallet or purse when buying something. As an additional safeguard, a small amount of cash should be kept in your pocket to pay for incidentals. Keep your credit card and the purchase slips of travellers' cheques separate from your cash.

Be especially cautious at markets, bus stops and crowded places where most muggings take place. Ensure that there are no valuables in the side pockets of day packs, or backpacks; they can be opened undetected in busy places. Should you be approached by strangers pretending to know you, or offering assistance, ignore them, but remain alert.

Self-drive visitors should avoid parking their vehicles in the vicinity of markets, bus stops or crowded places. Security guards are usually on duty at upmarket hotels and will be more than willing to look after your vehicle in exchange for a few cigarettes. Luggage and valuables are best kept in the boot of the vehicle, away from prying eyes.

If you are out at night, stick to busy streets and avoid poorly lit areas. Despite warnings not to venture onto the streets of Maputo at night, we walked about the main streets in the early evenings without feeling at all threatened. This does not, however, mean that muggings do not take place.

Mozambican law requires you to carry your passport on your person at all times; the best place is either in a shirt pocket with a button to prevent it from falling out, or a money belt. As perspiration will cause the ink in your passport and other documents to smudge it is advisable to first place documents in a plastic zip seal bag.

It is also worthwhile making certified photocopies of your passport, international driver's licence and all vehicle documentation and keeping them in a safe place, in case the originals are stolen, or lost.

In the event of a hijacking, theft, mugging, or documentation being lost, or retained by officials, the incident should be reported immediately to the nearest police station.

Land-mines

A tragic legacy of the bitter civil war are the thousands of land-mines, anti-personnel mines and other war material that have not yet been destroyed. Mines have been lifted on and alongside most major tar and gravel roads, but might still pose a risk on little-used tracks in remote areas. Mined areas that have not been cleared are usually demarcated with red warning tape and marked with skull-and-crossbones danger signs.

Should your touring take you on little-travelled backroads, always check with the local population about the possibility of *minen* and never drive on tracks that show no signs of being in regular use. Also take care not to drive, or walk, too far off the road.

Corruption and bribery

During the past few years, the government has been serious in its attempts to stamp out corruption. Officials have been retrained, or even redeployed, and during several visits to Mozambique we only experienced a single attempt at bribery.

Isolated incidents can still occur, though, in which case the best advice is to remain courteous but firm, if you are sure that you did not commit an offence. When issued with a bogus fine, insisting on a *recibo* (receipt) is usually enough to cause an official change of mind. Documents like your International Driving Permit and passport should only be handed to officials who are identifiable as police, traffic, or customs officials. Should documents be confiscated, the incident should be reported to the nearest police station.

Currency and Banks

The official currency of Mozambique is the metical (Mt) (plural meticais), divided into 100 centavos. Notes are available in denominations of Mt 100 000, 50 000, 10 000, 5 000, 1 000 and 500, with coins available in Mt 1 000 and 500. In October 1998 the bank exchange rates were 2 087 Mt to the South African rand (ZAR) and 11 795 Mt to the US dollar.

US dollars are widely accepted and easily exchanged, while the South African rand is readily accepted south of Beira. Payment at resorts and restaurants in southern and central Mozambique can sometimes be made in either meticais or rands. As there is often a considerable difference in the price, it will be worth your while to see which currency is the most advantageous to pay with. As from September 1999 the Malawian kwacha (MK) will be legal tender in Mozambique and the currency will probably be widely accepted in northern Mozambique. Except for the top hotels in Maputo, some upmarket lodges and resorts frequented by South Africans, credit cards are of little use.

When visiting Mozambique it is advisable to use travellers' cheques issued in US dollars rather than carrying large amounts of cash. Travellers' cheques are the safer option, despite the commission and clearing fees charged. Bank charges and fees vary considerably, depending on the bank and its location. In Maputo, some banks charge a minimum flat fee of 25 000 Mt to exchange US dollar notes, while banks in upmarket hotel complexes charge US $5 and upwards. In cities and towns further north, the minimum charge to exchange US dollar notes for local currency is 50 000 Mt. Commission and clearing fees for exchanging travellers' cheques range from 6 per cent to 7,5 per cent. Charges for exchanging currencies other than the US dollar and South African rand are much higher.

Ensure that you have sufficient cash or travellers' cheques for the duration of your visit. Transferring money to Mozambique is really only feasible to banks in Maputo and is an extremely slow process. However, this situation is likely to improve in future.

Avoid the temptation of exchanging money on the black market as you not only stand a chance of losing your money, but you could also have a brush with the law. Some shopkeepers will be willing to exchange money in cases of emergency.

The major commercial banks are Banco Comercial de Moçambique (BCM), Banco Standard Totta de Moçambique and Banco Internacional de Moçambique. The other banks, Banco Popular de Desenvolvimento (BPD), Banco de Fomento e Exterior and Banco Commercial de e Investimentos, are development and investment banks.

Banking hours

Banks are open Monday to Friday from 08:00-13:00 and 14:00-15:00 /16:00 (depending on the bank). Closed on Saturdays.

Public Holidays

Mozambique has nine public holidays:

New Year's Day	1 January
Heroes' Day	3 February
Good Friday and Easter Monday	April/May
Workers' Day	1 May
Independence Day	25 June
Victory Day	7 September
Armed Forces Day	25 September
Christmas Day	25 December

Business Hours

Shops	
Monday-Friday	08:30-12:30 and 15:00-18:30
Saturday	08:30-13:30
Offices	
Monday-Friday	08:00-12:30 and 14:00-17:30
Saturday	Closed

Time

Mozambique is in the same time zone as South Africa; two hours ahead of Greenwich Mean Time (GMT + 2) throughout the year.

Electricity

The power supply is 220/240 volts AC, but as fluctuations can occur it is advisable to ensure that appliances are surge-protected. Two-pin international plugs are generally used and a universal adapter plug is handy. In new buildings the trend is to install three pin round plugs similar to those used in South Africa.

Posts and Telecommunications

Based on our own experiences, the country's postal service is efficient. A postcard posted in Maputo took about 10 days to reach Cape Town, while cards posted in northern Mozambique reached Windhoek, Namibia in less than two weeks.

The main post office in Maputo is diagonally opposite Café Continental at Avenida 25 de Setembro. It is open from 07:45-12:00 and 14:00-17:00 (Monday-Friday) and on Saturday mornings. Express mail items can be handed in at the express mail service (EMS) office at 285 Avenida Zedequias Manganhela. International air courier services include those of DHL and Rennies, the licencee of FedEx.

Considering the destruction of the country's telecommunication system during the civil war, Telecommunicações De Moçambique has made remarkable progress to establish an efficient telecommunications system. International calls can be made with little difficulty from public call centres (*cabines públicas*) in all cities and major towns. There are several call centres in Maputo, the main one being in the 33 Andares building,

Avenida Zedequias Manganhela. Housed variously in buildings or air-conditioned containers, the call centres are well signposted and are usually open from 07:00-20:00 although times may vary. An operator will dial the required number and direct you to a call box equipped with a meter, enabling you to keep track of how long you are talking. The minimum call period is three minutes and thereafter charges are per minute. In October 1998 call charges to South Africa were: 25 800 Mt (US $2,21) for the first three minutes and 8 600 Mt (US $0,74) per minute thereafter. Charges to Europe were: 86 400 Mt (US $7,40) for the first three minutes and 28 800 Mt (US $2,47) per minute thereafter.

Metered local calls can be made from businesses, shops and restaurants indicated with *Telefone de Público* signposts, but charges are determined by the owner. In Maputo and other cities south of Beira, phone cards (telecartão) can be used to make local calls from public call boxes. Cards are sold at post offices and some shops in units of 50 000 Mt.

The international country code for Mozambique is 258 and the city code for Maputo is (01). Dialling codes for other cities are as follows: Beira (03), Chimoio (051), Inhambane (023), Lichinga (071), Manica (051) Nampula (06), Pemba (072), Quelimane (04), Tete (052), Xai-Xai (022). There are three telephone directories (*listas telefonicas de Moçambique*): South, covering Maputo, Gaza and Inhambane; Central and North, covering Cabo Delgado, Manica, Nampula, Niassa, Sofala, Tete and Zambezia, and a telefax-telex directory.

The South African cellular telephone companies, Vodacom and MTN, have agreements with the Mozambican company mCel.

Photography

As a matter of common courtesy and respect, never take photographs of people without asking their permission. In most cases they will agree and, except in the more touristy places, money is seldom asked for photographs to be taken.

Do not take photographs of government buildings such as police stations, the presidential palace, military installations, or uniformed officials without their consent. During the civil war severe restrictions were placed on photographers for security reasons and in remote areas officials might still suffer from this phobia. If you are confronted with an angry official demanding your camera and documents, you should simply stand your ground, no matter how intimidating the situation. Should the official insist that you pay a fine, ask politely for a *recibo* (receipt) and report the incident to the police.

Although colour print film and processing shops are widely available in Maputo and Beira, 35 mm transparency film is unobtainable and you will be well advised to ensure that you have sufficient stock for the duration of your visit.

Newspapers and Radio

Several newspapers are published in Portuguese in Maputo, the most widely read being the two dailies, *Noticias* and *Diário de Moçambique*. The latter is also distributed in Beira. *Mediafax* is an independent daily newspaper published by Mediacoop and distributed by fax to subscribers. The company also publishes a weekly, *Savana*, which is aimed at decision-makers.

No English newspapers or magazines are published in Maputo, but there is a good selection at Sensaçoes, at 657 Avenida Julius Nyerere and the kiosk in the Polana Hotel.

Mozambique's two national television stations, TVM and RTK, broadcast in Portuguese only, but most of the lodges and better class hotels have multi-channel satellite television. Radio Maputo, an English-language broadcast of Radio Moçambique, is on the air at 13:00 and 20:00, seven days a week on the FM/MW frequency. BBC broadcasts 24 hours a day on the 95.5 FM frequency.

4

How To Get There

Although the only inter-continental transport link is between Lisbon (Portugal) and Maputo, there are numerous convenient connecting flights between Johannesburg in South Africa and Maputo. Mozambique is also easily accessible by tar roads from South Africa, Swaziland, Zimbabwe and Malawi, and there are regular rail services between Mozambique, South Africa, Zimbabwe and Malawi.

Air

The national airline, ***Linhas Aéreas de Moçambique*** **(LAM)**, operates direct flights from Maputo to Lisbon on Fridays and from Lisbon to Maputo on Sundays. **TAP Air Portugal** has a scheduled flight from Lisbon to Maputo on Tuesdays and a Maputo to Lisbon flight on Wednesdays.

From Johannesburg **LAM** has daily flights, except on Saturdays, to Maputo, while **South African Airways** operates flights on Mondays, Thursdays, Fridays and Sundays between Johannesburg and Maputo. **SA Airlink** has return flights from Nelspruit to Vilankulo where immigration and custom formalities can be completed. Flights are scheduled for Tuesdays and Fridays with same-day connecting flights between Johannesburg and Nelspruit.

Maputo's Mavelane Airport is situated 4 km from the city centre and taxis operate between the airport and the city. Alternatively, if you are staying at one of Maputo's hotels you can make prior arrangements for a transfer. Beira International Airport is 18 km from the city and taxis are usually available. Vilankulo International Airport is about 4 km from the town and you will need to make arrangements to be met there. There has been talk of Inhambane's facility being upgraded to an international airport and if you are staying at one of the lodges it is advisable to make arrangements to be collected.

There is an international departure tax of US $20, payable in hard currency at the airport of departure.

Road

Mozambique has excellent tar road connections with South Africa, Swaziland, Zimbabwe and Malawi. The **Maputo Corridor** between Witbank and Maputo via Komatipoort/Ressano Garcia is in an advanced stage to completion, while the road from Lomahasha/Namaacha on the Swaziland border is generally in a good condition. The **Beira Corridor**, linking Mutare in Zimbabwe with Beira, has been rehabilitated and repairs are regularly carried out on sections that break up. The **Tete Corridor** between Nyamapanda/Cochemane and Tete is overall in a good condition, although there are a few bad sections and the occasional pothole, while the road from Tete to Zóbuè/Mwanza is in good condition.

There are also several gravel-surfaced roads linking Mozambique and its neighbouring countries. The route from northern KwaZulu-Natal via Ponta do Ouro to Maputo is suitable only for four-wheel drive vehicles or those with a high ground clearance.

The route via Mount Selinda/Espungabera is being upgraded and although a four-wheel drive vehicle is not required, sturdy transport with a high ground clearance is essential. The road between Mucumbura on the Zimbabwean border and Mágoè is negotiable by four-wheel drive vehicle only, but from Mágoè it has a good gravel surface.

The 58 km from Mangochi in Malawi to Namwera alternates between badly potholed and gravel stretches. From Mandimba, 5 km beyond Namwera, the gravel roads have been upgraded, but the Lichinga road can be very corrugated at times. An alternative from Malawi to northern Mozambique is the tar road from Limbe to Muloza/Milange. The road is tarred up to the Mozambican border, where you join a gravel road to Mocuba, from where you can either head for Nampula or Quelimane. Another approach route from Malawi is from Lilongwe to Dedza, from where it is 171 km to the E.N. 103 between Tete and Zóbué.

Although there is a road between Pafuri in South Africa's Kruger National Park and Mozambique there is no border post and this road cannot be used. There is also no road link from northern Mozambique across the Rio Rovuma into Tanzania, although it is possible to make the crossing by canoe. The Tanzanian immigration point at Mwambo is about 5 km north of the Rio Rovuma, while the Mozambican immigration office at Namiranga is about 2 km south of the river.

Bus

Panthera Azul operates a luxury bus service between Johannesburg and Maputo daily. Buses depart Johannesburg at 07:30, arriving in Maputo at

15:30. On Fridays there is a bus departing at 21:00, arriving in Maputo at 09:00 the following day. The company also offers services between Durban and Maputo on Thursdays and Sundays, departing at 07:30 and arriving in Maputo at 16:00: Johannesburg, tel (011) 337-7409, Durban, tel (031) 309-7798; Maputo tel (01) 49 42 38. **Intercape Mainliner**, Pretoria, tel (012) 654-4114 and **Translux**, Pretoria, tel (012) 315-3492, have daily services between Johannesburg and Maputo and in the reverse direction.

Tete is connected by a daily bus service operating from Harare to Blantyre and Blantyre to Harare, while Mutare to Beira and Beira to Mutare routes are served daily by buses.

Rail

The Komati, a mainline passenger train operated by **Spoornet**, has a daily service between Johannesburg and Komatipoort, departing Johannesburg at 18:10 and arriving at Komatipoort at 06:42 the following morning. At Komatipoort passengers board the **CFM** (**Caminhos de Ferro de Moçambique**) train to Maputo. Spoornet operates a direct mainline service from Durban to Maputo, departing Durban at 19:30 on Tuesdays and arriving in Maputo at 16:30 the following day. Spoornet, Johannesburg, tel (011) 773-2944; CFM, Maputo, tel (01) 43 08 94.

There are also passenger rail services between Mutare in Zimbabwe and Beira. The Malawi National Railways operates passenger train services from Liwonde to Nayuchi on the Malawi border on Mondays and Thursdays. From here it is a short (20 minutes) walk to Entrelagos where you can catch a connecting CFM train to Cuamba.

Sea

Cargo vessels call regularly at the ports of Maputo, Beira, Nacala, Quelimane, Pemba and Mocimboa da Praia, but there is no passenger service to Mozambique. Calls are made at Bazaruto and Ilha da Mozambique by the *Symphony*, a liner operated by **Starlight Cruises**.

Adventure travellers can sail by dhow from the village of Msimbati (there is an immigration office) in southern Tanzania to either Palma or Mocimboa da Praia. Once in Moçambique you must report to the immigration office at Palma to complete entry formalities.

5

Getting Around in Mozambique

Getting around in Mozambique is becoming increasingly easier than in the mid-1990s, irrespective of whether you are on a self-drive visit or reliant on public transport. Most of the major tar roads and gravel roads have been rehabilitated, filling stations are opening up everywhere and reliable bus services operate between the cities and major towns throughout the country.

By Road

Mozambique's road network was extensively damaged during the civil war, but many roads have been rehabilitated since 1994 and many more are scheduled for repair. Of the country's road network of 29 000 km, about 5 600 km are tarred. Main routes are indicated by the abbreviation E.N. (*Estrada Nacional*). Few roads have centre lines and distances are generally not indicated; the E.N. 1 from Maputo north and the Mandimba/Lichinga roads being notable exceptions. As roads are rehabilitated, signposting is likely to improve.

The country's main tar routes have all been rehabilitated, although stretches of road do break up from time to time. Major gravel roads have, likewise, been rehabilitated, or are in the process of repair. In remote rural areas, especially in the north of the country, many of the minor roads are still no more than tracks, requiring a four-wheel drive vehicle, or at least one with a high ground clearance. A brief report on the conditions of the country's main roads is now given. It would be useful when studying the route descriptions in the regional chapters to refer back to this section.

E.N. 4 Ressano Garcia to Maputo: The 39 km stretch of the tar road between Ressano Garcia and Moamba is being upgraded, while a new road is under construction from Moamba to Maputo (1999).

E.N. 201 Catembe to Ponta do Ouro: The road from Catembe to Salamanga has a good gravel surface and 17 km of good tar, but then deteriorates to a gravel track and finally a sandy track requiring four-wheel drive, although two-wheel drive vehicles with a high ground clearance are known to have travelled this route.

E.N. 1 Maputo to Inchope: The tar road from Maputo to the Rio Save is generally in a good condition, but heavy rains caused substantial damage to the road surface and bridges in the Inhassoro/Vilankulo area in the first quarter of 1999. North of the Rio Save the road alternates for 190 km between potholed tar, reasonably good tar and disintegrated stretches. Sections of the road were being rehabilitated in October 1998.

E.N. 216 Espungabera to Dombe and Barragem de Chicamba: The gravel road to Dombe has been rehabilitated and although it is in a reasonably good condition, it is best negotiated in a rugged vehicle, or a four-wheel drive vehicle. The road can become difficult to negotiate during the rainy season. From Dombe to Rotunda and along the eastern shores of Barragem de Chicamba the gravel road is in a fair condition, but could become rutted.

E.N. 6 Machipanda to Beira (Beira Corridor): The condition of the tar road is generally good, but as this road carries heavy traffic potholes do occur from time to time, while sections might break up.

E.N. 213 Beira to Caia (Rio Zambeze): This is one of the worst stretches of road in the country, requiring a four-wheel drive vehicle, or vehicle with a high ground clearance. You should allow at least seven hours to cover the 240 km stretch between Dondo and the Zambeze.

E.N. 213 Caia to Quelimane: North of the Rio Zambeze the road alternates between potholed tar and good tar sections which deteriorate as one approaches Nicaudala. The road from Nicaudala to Quelimane is in excellent condition, having been rehabilitated in 1998-99.

E.N. 7, 104 and 232 Quelimane to Nampula: The first 70 km to Nicaudala is a good tar surface followed by 28 km of gravel and 156 km of tar. The remaining 86 km to Alto Molócuè alternates between tar and gravel. About 107 km of the remaining 112 km to Rio Ligonha is gravel. Work on the rehabilitation of this road has started and several bridges have already been rebuilt. From Rio Ligonha to Nampula the tar road is in a fair condition.

E.N. 8 and 105 Nampula to Ilha de Moçambique: The tar surface between Nampula and Namialo has been patched, but the road is in a fair condition. Take care, however, of the odd pothole and frayed shoulders. From Namialo to the Ilha de Moçambique turnoff the surface is uneven and patched. The tar E.N. 105 to Ilha de Moçambique is narrow, but in good condition.

E.N. 106 Namialo to Pemba: This tar road is in good condition, except for uneven sections across bridges between Sunate and Pemba.

E.N. 243 Sunate to Mocimboa da Praia: The tar road from Sunate to Macomia is being rehabilitated and used to alternate between reasonably good and badly potholed stretches. North of Macomia the road is scheduled to be replaced by an all-weather gravel road.

E.N. 247 Mocimboa da Praia to Rio Rovuma: This sandy track is best negotiated in a four-wheel drive vehicle, or a vehicle with a high ground clearance.

E.N. 102 Chimoio to Tete: The condition of this tar road is good overall, except for the odd pothole, frayed road shoulders and some uneven patches at bridges.

E.N. 102 and E.N. 258 Tete to Songo: The tarred E.N. 258 has been rehabilitated and is in excellent condition.

E.N. 258 to Mágoè and Mucumbura: From the E.N. 258 turnoff to Mágoè the all-weather gravel road is in good condition, but the stretch of road between Mágoè and Mucumbura is negotiable by four-wheel drive vehicle only.

E.N. 103 Tete to Zóbuè (Tete Corridor): This tar road is in good condition.

E.N. 8 Mandimba to Nampula: The first 50 km of the gravel road from Mandimba to Cuamba was being rehabilitated in 1998, while the remaining 100 km to Cuamba is a good gravel road. From Cuamba to Nampula the road surface is being rehabilitated.

E.N. 249 Mandimba to Lichinga and Metangula: The gravel road from Mandimba to Lichinga has been rehabilitated and is in a good to fair condition, but can become rutted. Although narrow, the tar road from Lichinga to Maniamba is in good condition (sections were rehabilitated in 1998). The 29 km gravel road from Maniamba to Metangula is in good condition.

E.N. 242 Lichinga to Marrupa: The bridge over the Rio Luambala was washed away by floods in 1997 and had not been repaired by September 1998. Travelling was therefore only possible as far as Majune. Enquire before using this road. This is a rough track through a remote area and it is advisable to have a two-vehicle party.

E.N. 248 Cuamba to Marrupa: The road linking Cuamba and Marrupa has an excellent gravel surface, but beware of patches where the surface breaks up.

E.N. 242 Marrupa to Metoro: The road from Marrupa to Balama is nothing more than a bush track, negotiable in a vehicle with a high ground clearance, or a four-wheel drive. From Balama the road is gravel, in fair condition but corrugated. From Montepuez to Metoro a potholed tar road is followed. This is a remote route and is best negotiated in a two-vehicle party.

Motoring and traffic regulations

Driving is on the left-hand side of the road and the wearing of seat belts is compulsory. All vehicles are required to have a set of red warning triangles, while vehicles towing trailers or a caravan must display a triangle on the front of the towing vehicle. The other triangle must be displayed on the back of the trailer or caravan. The official Mozambique warning triangle is a yellow triangle painted on a blue background.

To avoid an unnecessary brush with the law, motorists are advised to adhere strictly to the speed limits. These are generally well indicated and vary from as little as 20 km/h in densely built up areas to 120 km/h on the open road. The lifting of a speed limit is indicated by a diagonal black line across the speed.

Although South African drivers' licences are recognised in Mozambique, officials might insist on an International Driving Permit. International Driving Permits are valid for one year and can be obtained from AA Auto Shops, or internationally recognised motoring organisations. International visitors are, likewise, advised to be in possession of an International Driving Permit. It is worthwhile making certified copies of your International Driving Permit.

Traffic checkpoints are found outside virtually every city or town, even in remote rural areas. The checkpoints are well-signposted and traffic officials are dressed in white shirts and black trousers or skirts. In most cases they will only ask to see your driver's licence, but might also ask for your vehicle's registration papers, *seguros* (third party insurance) and temporary import permit (see p 31). In some cases they might also check your lights, indicators and tyres. It is useful to keep all your vehicle documentation in a folder where documents can be easily accessed. If you are courteous, chances are that you might be waved through and we have never had any unpleasant experiences with traffic officials. Should you be "fined" for some trumped up charge, don't yield to pressure and if you do pay the "fine", insist on a *recibo* (receipt).

Fuel

Petrol (*gasolina*) and diesel (*gasoleo*) are widely available and new filling stations are opening throughout the country, many of them along the major tar roads and approach routes to cities and towns. However, petrol can be difficult to obtain in the far northern provinces of Niassa and the inland towns of Cabo Delgado, making it advisable to carry spare fuel between Cuamba and Montepuez.

Avoid asking for "petrol" which can be mistaken for paraffin, known in Portuguese as *petroleo*. Also avoid buying fuel at markets; not only will you pay exorbitant prices, but unscrupulous racketeers have been known to add paraffin and even water to fuel, with disastrous consequences for your vehicle's engine.

Motoring hints

Broken down vehicles left in the road and unroadworthy vehicles without lights are a constant menace on many of the country's roads, especially after dark, making it inadvisable to be on the road after sunset, unless absolutely essential. Red warning triangles are seldom used; the "Mozambican triangle" is a couple of branches placed in the road in front and behind the vehicle. Potholes under repair are usually indicated by placing a branch in the hole.

Ensure that your vehicle is mechanically sound, especially when venturing off the beaten track in the north of the country. When travelling in remote areas a second spare wheel and basic spares are essential. It is advisable to travel in a two-vehicle party in case of a breakdown.

Be especially cautious when travelling on gravel roads. Slow down to a reasonable speed and keep a constant watch for vehicles approaching from behind, allowing faster vehicles to overtake. Switch on headlights when travelling in the dust of a vehicle ahead of you, or when an oncoming vehicle approaches. Do not overtake unless you have a clear view.

Corrugations and disintegrated gravel surfaces could cause you to lose control over the vehicle, especially when travelling fast. Should this happen, do not apply brakes, or turn the steering wheel violently. Rather decelerate and bring the vehicle slowly back into the track.

Travelling along backroads during the summer months is best avoided, as the roads are likely to become impassable. In addition, many of the bridges in remote rural areas have not yet been repaired and you could be left stranded.

Tips for 4x4 driving

Tempting as it might be to set off on a trip when you have just acquired your first four-wheel drive vehicle, you should not venture into unfamiliar terrain and conditions until you are fully acquainted with it. The following are useful hints for inexperienced offroad drivers:

- Follow existing tracks – not only does this reduce the number of tracks, but often it is easier as the vehicle will simply follow the track in deep sand.
- Don't wait until your vehicle is bogged down in thick sand before trying to get it out. Stop on a hard surface, deflate tyres to about 1 kPa, lock front wheel hubs (if fitted) and engage four-wheel drive.

- Where beach driving is permitted you should time your trip to coincide with low tide, as the breakers roll right up to the dunes at high tide. This will either delay you, or even worse, you could lose your vehicle.
- After the rainy season grass growing in the centre of tracks can accumulate under protection plates and the driving shaft, creating a potential fire hazard. Stop for regular checks under the vehicle. Carry a fire extinguisher which is easily accessible in the event of an emergency.
- A fine mesh grille in front of the radiator is useful to prevent grass seeds from blocking the flow of air to the radiator, resulting in overheating. Keep a watch on your temperature gauge to ensure that the mesh does not block the air flow.

Environmental considerations

A four-wheel drive vehicle allows you to get to places which are inaccessible to other motorists, but also places a responsibility on you to take care of the environment (see p 21).

Stick to existing tracks as far as possible to avoid damage to the environment. Nowhere are the effects of new tracks more visible than along the route from northern KwaZulu-Natal to Ponta do Ouro. Here the ever-widening network of tracks has caused irreparable damage to the sensitive coastal environment.

Coastal areas are especially sensitive to disturbance and vehicles are permitted onto the beach only at designated places. Beach driving is not permitted above the high water mark and there is a maximum speed limit of 15 km/h. Outside of these areas *beach driving has been banned and is subject to heavy fines.*

Gone are the days of camping wherever you wish. Camping is only allowed at designated camp sites and it is prohibited to collect firewood. These regulations are being enforced increasingly strictly and transgressors are likely to be fined heavily.

Maps

The most detailed road map of Mozambique is the 1:2 000 000 map published by Ravenstein (map number 6821). The information regarding roads, especially tracks, is not always accurate and needs to be updated.

Less detailed, but still useful (especially when planning an overland route) is the Michelin map of Central and Southern Africa (map number 955). The map in the AA of South Africa publication, *Motoring in Mozambique,* is handy for motorists sticking to the main routes, but of limited use when venturing off the main roads.

Topographical maps are available in scales of 1:50 000, 1:250 000 and 1:500 000 from DINAGECA, 537 Avenida Josina Machel, Maputo. Topographical maps are generally outdated, some dating back to the Portuguese era, while only copies of maps of the more popular areas are sometimes available. Maps became prohibitively expensive in the latter half of 1998 when the price of 1:50 000 maps was increased to 250 000 Mt, and that of 1:250 000 maps increased to 200 000 Mt.

Vehicle hire

Car hire is becoming increasingly easy and several car hire companies are now represented in Maputo and Beira:

Maputo

Avis, 15 Avenida Mao Tsé Tung, tel (01) 44 49 73 and 49 45 50, fax 49 44 98; Mavalane International Airport, tel (01) 46 51 40 and 46 54 97, fax 46 54 93

Europcar, 1418 Avenida Julius Nyerere, tel (01) 49 73 38, fax 49 73 34

Hertz, 2006, Avenida 24 Julho, tel (01) 30 31 72, fax 49 49 82

Iberica Rent A Car, 1424 Avenida Guerra Popular, tel (01) 42 23 41 and 30 05 31; 1630 Avenida Maguiguana, tel (061) 42 71 98

Imperial Car Rental, 546 Avenida Julius Nyerere, tel (01) 49 35 43, fax 49 35 40

Beira

Avis, International Airport, tel (03) 30 12 63, fax 30 12 65

Hertz, tel (03) 32 23 15

Imperial Car Rental, 2163 Rua Correia Brito, tel (03) 30 26 50, fax 30 26 51

Interfranca, Avenida Eduardo Mondlane, tel (03) 32 24 80

Nampula

Imperial Car Rental, 26-A Rua Monomotapa, tel (06) 21 57 61, fax 21 57 60

Bus transport

The greatly improved road network, availability of fuel and improved economic conditions have all contributed to reliable regular bus services between cities and towns along the country's main roads.

There are numerous bus companies serving the cities and towns between Maputo and Beira. The **Oliviera** bus company is one of the best known and in Maputo its buses depart from Praça 16 de Junho in Avenida 24 de Junho. **Virginia** buses operate on several routes, including Maputo to Beira and Beira via Chimoio to Tete. The company has terminals in

Maputo (Avenida Karl Marx), Beira (197 Avenida Acordos Lusaka) and Tete (Avenida 25 de Junho). One of the major operators in the north of the country, **TransNorte**, operates between Lichinga, Cuamba, Nampula, Nacala and Pemba.

Buses are referred to as *machimbombos* and the bus terminus is known as the *Terminal de Machimbombos.*

Mozambique also has a thriving informal transport section and *chapas* are a popular mode of transport with the local population. A variety of vehicles ranging from mini-buses to light trucks, fitted with benches and a frame covered with canvas to provide protection against the elements, is used. In the north of the country *chapas* are often the only means of transport on routes not served by the mainliner buses. In Maputo *chapa cem* (mini-buses) are popular with commuters as they will stop to pick up or drop passengers anywhere. Although cheap, they are usually overcrowded with passengers hanging from the doors.

Taxis

In Maputo taxi ranks are at Mavalane Airport, outside the Hotel Polana and the Hotel Cardoso, the *Mercado Central* (central market), opposite Restaurante Piri-Piri and in Avenida Mao Tsé Tung. For radio taxis, contact Central Rádio Taxis, tel (01) 42 98 40, or Polana Taxis, tel (01) 49 32 55.

Hitchhiking

The concept of giving someone a free ride is unheard of in Mozambique and although you will have many offers if you are hitching around the country, expect to pay more or less the same price as that charged by *chapas.* In the southern and central provinces you should have little difficulty in hitching a lift, but in the remote northern regions you could have a long wait, especially between remote rural towns and settlements.

By Rail

Travelling by rail in Mozambique is generally slow and this mode of travel is seldom used by visitors. For information on the rail services from South Africa, Zimbabwe and Malawi to Mozambique see p 48.

By Air

Mozambique is a long, narrow country and distances from Maputo to the northern provinces of Zambezia, Nampula, Cabo Delgado, Niassa and Tete are vast. Pemba, for example, is 2 500 km by road from Maputo and it will take you several days to get there. Although more expensive, travelling by air is far quicker and more comfortable than travelling overland. A US $5 departure tax is payable in cash for all domestic flights.

Scheduled flights

The national airline, **LAM**, has regular scheduled domestic flights linking Maputo with Beira, Quelimane, Nampula, Pemba, Lichinga and Tete. **SabinAir** has return flights between Maputo, Magaruque, Benguerra, Bazaruto and Vilankulo on Mondays, Tuesdays and Fridays. The airline also operates flights from Maputo to Ilha da Inhaca on Fridays and Sundays.

Aircraft charter

A number of air charter companies operate from Maputo; among them **SabinAir** has a fleet of several aircraft. For details contact **Sabinair**, P O Box 465011, Maputo, tel (01) 46 51 08, fax 46 50 11; **Natair**, tel (01) 46 54 78, fax 49 18 72.

By Boat

The easiest way of getting to Catembe from Maputo is by ferry (the ferry terminal in Maputo is on Rua 10 de Novembro), while Ilha da Inhaca, the Arquipélago do Bazaruto and the Arquipélago das Quirimbas are accessible by boat. For boat transfers from Maputo to Inhaca, contact Rogerio Costa of **Turmar**, tel and fax (01) 49 87 35. Boat transfers from Inhassoro and Vilankulo to the Arquipélago do Bazaruto are expensive unless you are travelling in a group. For single travellers it will be cheaper to fly from Vilankulo to the island of your choice with SabinAir (see above). Transfer details are provided in the relevant descriptions of the attractions, or the route descriptions.

Tours and Safaris

The number of travel agencies and tour operators in Mozambique is expanding rapidly. Services include hotel and other accommodation reservations, transfers, excursions, car rental and conferences.

Travel agents and consultancies

Mextur, P O Box 1222, Maputo, tel (01) 42 84 27/8/9, fax 42 84 30

Mozambique National Tourist Company, tel (01) 42 17 94, fax 42 17 95, e-mail entur@virconn.com

Polana Tours, 1380 Avenida Julius Nyerere, Maputo, tel (01) 49 35 33/4, fax 49 35 38

Prosol, 809/11 Avenida Filipe Samuel Magaia, Maputo, tel (01) 42 53 22, fax 42 19 08

Sundown Travel, P O Box 423740, Maputo, tel (01) 42 58 42, fax 42 37 40

Turmol, 472 Avenida Karl Marx, Maputo, tel (01) 42 51 11/2, fax 42 44 70

Companies operating from South Africa

Mozambique Connection, tel (011) 803-4185, fax 803-3861, e-mail mozcon@pixie.co.za – self-drive safaris, 4x4 tours, fly-in packages, bookings for several hotels, lodges and resorts, visa service

Mozambique National Tourist Company, tel (011) 339-7275, fax 339-7295, e-mail entur@virconn.com – reservations for several hotels, lodges and resorts, visa service

Moçambique Tours, tel (031) 303-2190, fax 303-2396, e-mail mit@iafrica.com – specialises in fly and self-drive packages

Off Beat Safaris, tel and fax (015) 793-2422, e-mail offbeatsafaris@hotmail.com – scheduled overland and camping safaris and tailor-made tours

Sunway Safaris, tel (011) 888-6856, e-mail sunway@icon.co.za – camping and lodge tours

The Mozambique Travel Centre, tel (011) 608-0968, fax 608-0978 – bookings for accommodation, transport, visas, water sports

Dive charters, camps and packages

Following is a list of companies and resorts offering dive services. Other than for Hotel Seta, the telephone numbers are for South Africa.

African Watersports (Ponta do Ouro), tel and fax (013) 245-1691

Barra Lodge (Inhambane), tel (011) 314-3355, fax 314-3239, e-mail barra@pixie.co.za

Bazaruto Lodge (Bazaruto), tel (011) 447-3528, fax 788-6499

Benguerra Lodge (Benguerra), tel (011) 483-2734, fax 728-3767, e-mail benguela@icon.co.za

Blue International (Ponta do Ouro), tel (011) 465-9624, fax 465-8225

Blue Wilderness Dive Expeditions (Southern Mozambique), tel and fax (0323) 973-2348, e-mail bluewild@sco.eastcoast.co.za

CI Divers (Pemba), African Adventure Centre, tel (011) 660-3542

Dive Africa (Inhaca), tel (012) 333-7110, fax 333-7911

Dive The World (Mozambique), tel (011) 791-2634/5/6/7, fax 791-0337

Guinjata Bay (Inhambane), tel (cellphone code 083, RSA) 283-6918, fax (013) 741-3149

Hotel Seta (Inhassoro), tel and fax Harare, Zimbabwe (+263 4) 87-0930, e-mail welch@icon.co.zw

Indigo Bay Lodge (Bazaruto), tel (011) 268-0151, fax 268-0160

Intercontinental Explorers (Ponta Malongane), tel (012) 348-4262, fax 348-1252

Island Style Diving (Morrungulo), tel (011) 791-2634/5/6/7, fax 791-0337

Marlin Lodge (Benguerra), tel (012) 543-2134, fax 543-2135, e-mail marlinlodge@mweb.co.za

Motel do Mar (Ponta do Ouro), tel (012) 362-1355, fax 362-1321, e-mail ponta@icon.co.za

Oceanic Dive Charters (Ponta do Ouro, Inhaca), tel and fax (011) 886-0680

Planet Scuba (Ponta do Ouro), tel (082) 809-7971 or 443-9554, e-mail andyle@ga.co.za

Scuba Adventures (Ponta do Ouro), tel (011) 234-0917/8

Sea Blue Diving (Southern Mozambique, Ponta Milibangalala), tel (082) 462-4916, fax (013) 752-2536

Simply Scuba (Ponta Malongane), tel (031) 502-5261, fax 502-5263

Zongoene Lodge (Rio Limpopo), tel (012) 346-1286, fax 346-1269, e-mail zongoene@statis.co.za

Kayak tours

Coastal Kayak Trails, tel and fax (021) 439-1134, e-mail ctrail@fast.co.za – sea kayak expeditions are arranged for groups from Pemba to the Arquipélago das Quirimbas; distances range from 10 km up to 40 km per day and paddling experience and a reasonable degree of fitness essential

Real Cape Adventures, tel and fax (021) 790-5611, e-mail johan@mweb.co.za – day sea kayak trips are undertaken from Vilankulo, the gateway to the Arquipélago do Bazaruto; three night/four day and seven night/eight day fully inclusive packages are available ex Johannesburg

Yacht charter

Mozambique Yacht Charters, tel (083) 255-3285 or 450-4468 - fully inclusive live aboard packages

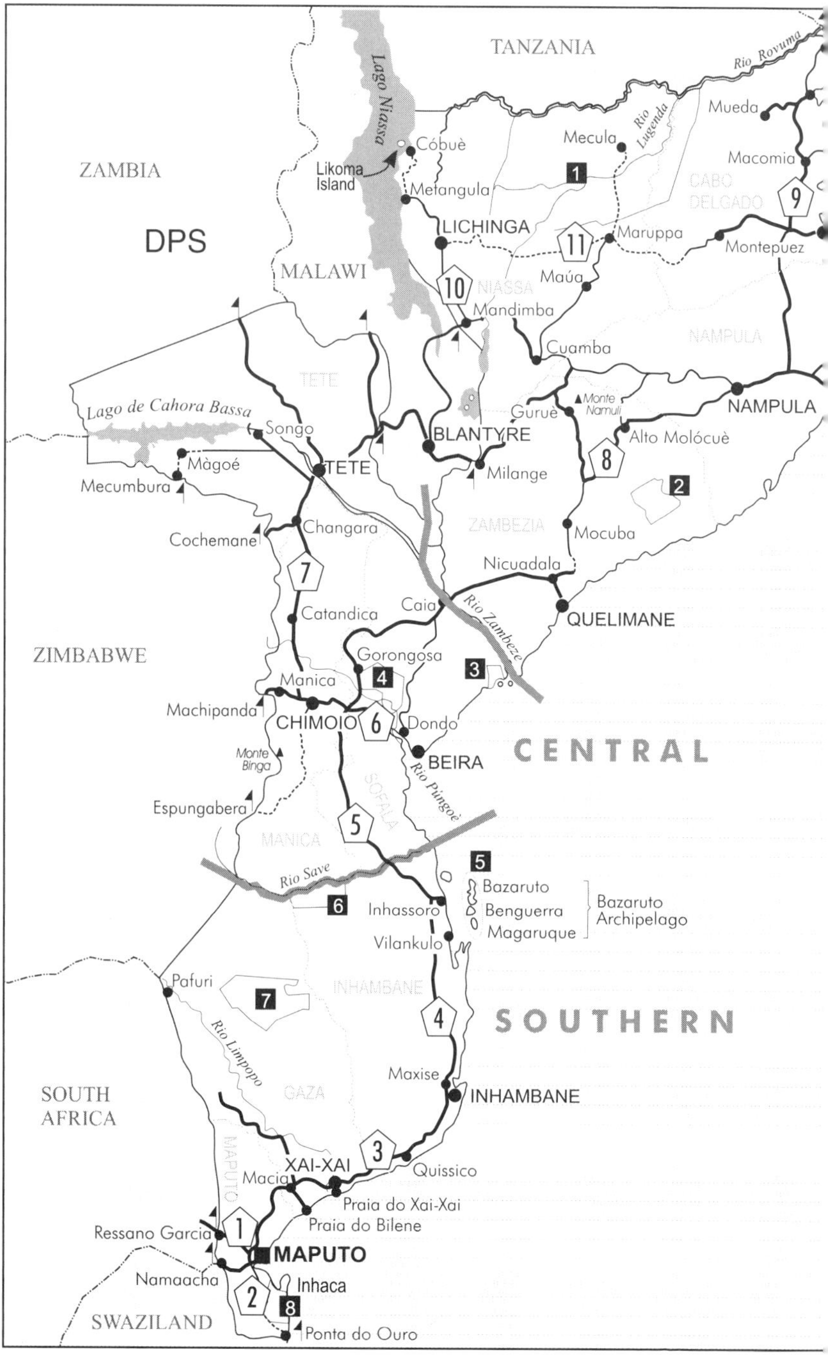
TANZANIA
Rio Rovuma
Lago Niassa
Rio Lugenda
Mueda
Mecula
Cóbuè
Macomia
ZAMBIA
Likoma Island
1
CABO DELGADO
Metangula
9
LICHINGA
Maruppa
DPS
11
Montepuez
MALAWI
10
NIASSA
Maúa
Mandimba
NAMPULA
Cuamba
TETE
Monte Namuli
Lago de Cahora Bassa
Gurué
NAMPULA
Songo
BLANTYRE
Alto Molócuè
Màgoé
TETE
8
Milange
Mecumbura
2
ZAMBEZIA
Changara
Mocuba
Cochemane
Nicuadala
7
Caia
Rio Zambeze
Catandica
QUELIMANE
ZIMBABWE
Gorongosa
3
4
Manica
Machipanda
CHIMOIO
6
Dondo
BEIRA
CENTRAL
Monte Binga
SOFALA
Rio Pingoè
Espungabera
5
MANICA
5
Rio Save
Bazaruto
6
Inhassoro
Benguerra
Bazaruto Archipelago
Magaruque
Vilankulo
Pafuri
7
INHAMBANE
4
SOUTHERN
Rio Limpopo
Maxise
SOUTH AFRICA
GAZA
INHAMBANE
MAPUTO
3
XAI-XAI
Quissico
Macia
Praia do Xai-Xai
Praia do Bilene
1
Ressano Garcia
MAPUTO
Namaacha
Inhaca
2
8
SWAZILAND
Ponta do Ouro

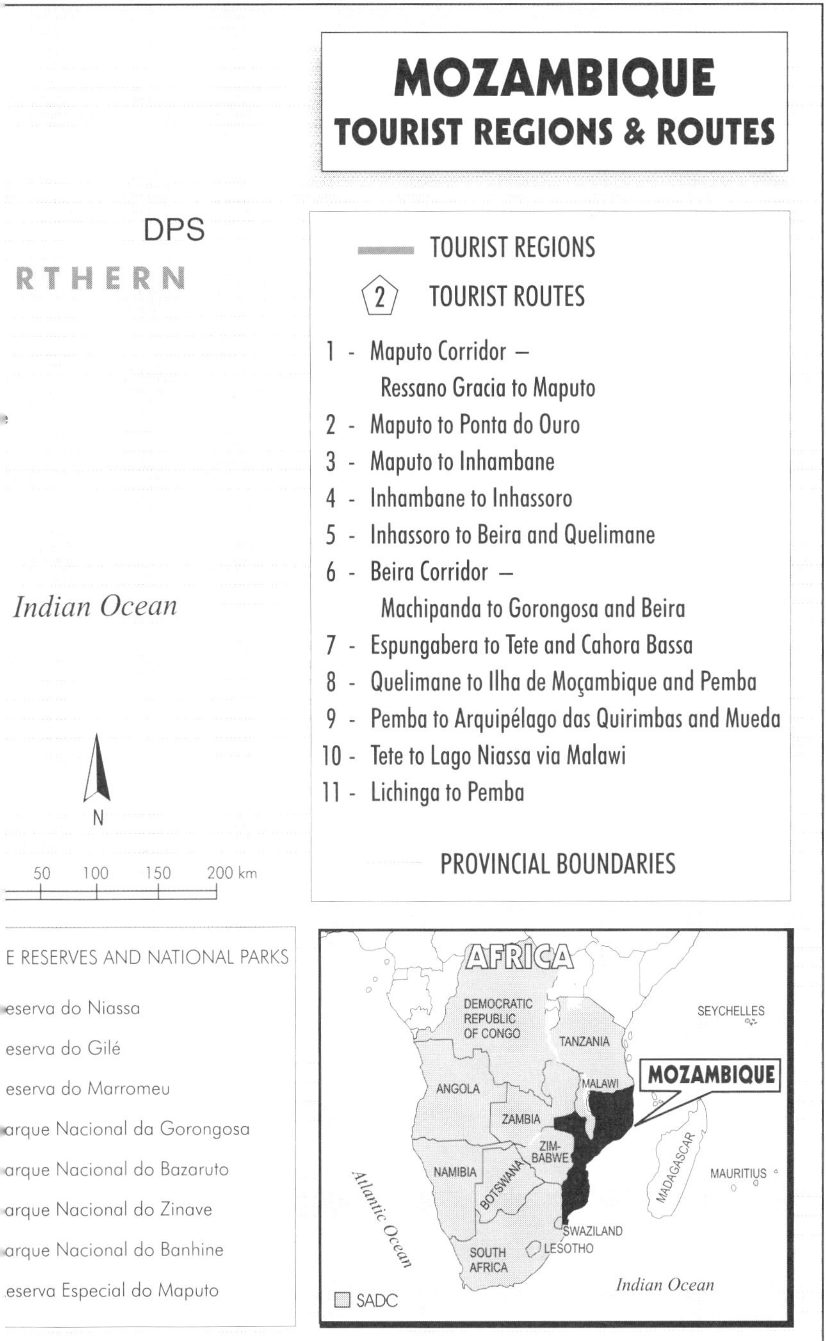
MOZAMBIQUE
TOURIST REGIONS & ROUTES
DPS
RTHERN
TOURIST REGIONS
2 TOURIST ROUTES
1 - Maputo Corridor – Ressano Gracia to Maputo
2 - Maputo to Ponta do Ouro
3 - Maputo to Inhambane
4 - Inhambane to Inhassoro
5 - Inhassoro to Beira and Quelimane
6 - Beira Corridor – Machipanda to Gorongosa and Beira
7 - Espungabera to Tete and Cahora Bassa
8 - Quelimane to Ilha de Moçambique and Pemba
9 - Pemba to Arquipélago das Quirimbas and Mueda
10 - Tete to Lago Niassa via Malawi
11 - Lichinga to Pemba
PROVINCIAL BOUNDARIES
Indian Ocean
N
50 100 150 200 km
E RESERVES AND NATIONAL PARKS
eserva do Niassa
eserva do Gilé
eserva do Marromeu
arque Nacional da Gorongosa
arque Nacional do Bazaruto
arque Nacional do Zinave
arque Nacional do Banhine
eserva Especial do Maputo
AFRICA
DEMOCRATIC REPUBLIC OF CONGO
TANZANIA
SEYCHELLES
MOZAMBIQUE
MALAWI
ANGOLA
ZAMBIA
ZIM-BABWE
NAMIBIA
BOTSWANA
MADAGASCAR
MAURITIUS
Atlantic Ocean
SWAZILAND
LESOTHO
SOUTH AFRICA
Indian Ocean
SADC

Distance Chart

Beira																			
803	Blantyre																		
860	505	Cassacatia																	
192	611	668	Chimoio																
567	606	663	375	Harare															
796	1343	1400	732	1107	Inhambane														
1587	1727	1784	1295	1123	1015	Johannesburg													
1275	1822	1879	1211	1772	545	470	Komatipoort/Ressana Garcia												
1226	403	908	1014	1009	1766	2132	2225	Lichinga											
1056	1015	515	864	489	1596	1612	2082	1423	Lusaka										
1192	1739	1796	1128	1503	462	553	83	2142	2165	Maputo									
304	679	780	112	263	844	1183	1323	1101	1273	1240	Mutare								
942	669	1273	1078	1374	1663	2607	2137	661	1689	2054	1264	Nampula							
1269	1816	1873	1205	1580	539	591	125	2219	2207	77	1317	2131	Namaacha						
1368	1095	1699	1504	1701	2108	3131	2661	1087	2115	2570	1690	426	2655	Pemba					
1310	1857	1914	1246	1621	580	625	185	2260	2267	118	1358	2172	185	2696	Ponto do Ouro				
465	452	961	601	976	1205	2154	1684	1212	1467	1601	713	551	1719	977	1719	Quelimane			
579	224	281	387	382	1119	2408	1598	627	796	1515	455	992	1592	1418	1633	680	Tete		
527	1074	1131	463	838	307	1256	786	1497	1465	703	575	1394	780	1839	821	936	850	Vilankulo	
988	1535	1592	924	1299	258	757	287	1939	1327	204	1036	1893	281	2374	322	1397	1311	499	Xai-Xai

Map Legend

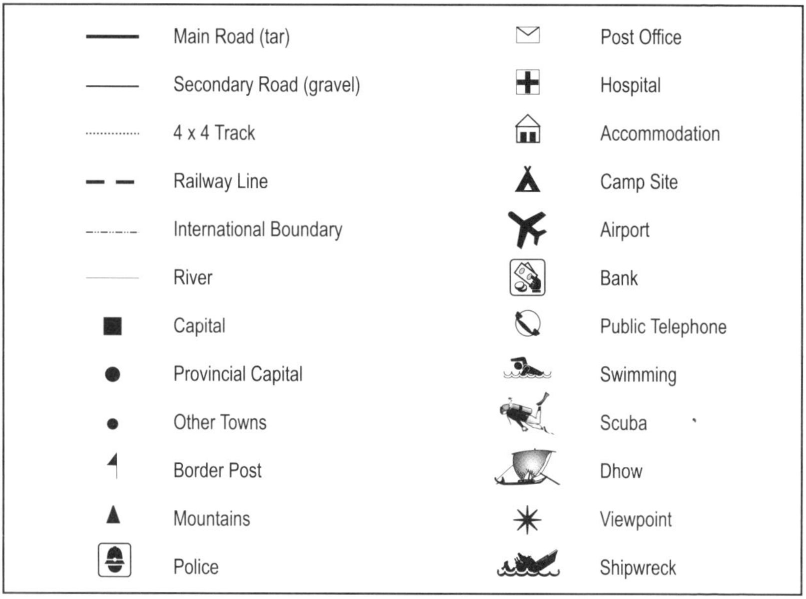

6

Maputo

Maputo, the capital of Mozambique, lies alongside the estuary of the Rio Esperito Santo and Baia de Maputo in the far south of the country. Designed along geometric lines, the city is characterised by wide avenidas lined with palm and flamboyant trees that are especially attractive in spring. International style high-rise buildings of the 1960s and 1970s dominate the skyline, creating a sharp contrast with derelict downtown buildings and the sprawling reed and mud residential areas on the city's outskirts.

With its rich blend of African, Portuguese and Oriental cultures Maputo is a cosmopolitan, vibrant city, bustling with overloaded chapas (mini-buses) and street vendors selling everything from plastic bags and cigarettes to paintings and batiks. Alongside Avenida Julius Nyerere are numerous pavement cafés, while delicious Portuguese pastries and cakes are sold by pastelarias. Most of the revolutionary slogans that once praised the virtues of Frelimo have been obliterated by time and coats of paint, but street names like Avenida Vladimir Lenine, Karl Marx and Mao Tsé Tung are silent reminders of the country's failed experiment with socialism.

History

Originally known as Mpfumo, after a local chief, the settlement was later named Albion by the British. Still later it was renamed in honour of the Portuguese trader Lourenço Marques, who explored the area in 1545. The bay became known as Baia a Lagoa, a reference to the many lakes further inland. Ivory was the main reason for the Portuguese interest in the area and within the first 17 years of Marques' expedition the Portuguese traded 561 tonnes of ivory in the area between the Rio Maputo and the Rio Incomati. Ilha da Inhaca and Xefina became important centres in the Portuguese ivory trade network.

For nearly three centuries, however, the Portuguese authorities established no permanent settlement in the bay as their attention centred further north around the trade settlements at

Ibo, Ilha de Moçambique, Quelimane, Sofala and Inhambane.

The growth of the port and the settlement was closely linked to political developments in the Indian Ocean and the interior of South Africa. During the 18th century Dutch and Austrian commercial interests established trading settlements at the bay, while British ships also conducted trade there. The Portuguese, however, only established their first permanent trading station at the bay in 1782, abandoning it temporarily 14 years later, after it was attacked by French pirates who arrived in three well-armed ships.

The Portuguese re-established a presence in 1800, but several political developments in the early 1800s rekindled Britain's territorial ambitions in southeastern Africa and in 1823 the British flag was raised on the southern banks of the Rio Maputo. Following the arrival of the Voortrekkers in the Transvaal in 1836, one of their priorities was to find a direct route (see p 70), free of British domination.

The discovery of diamonds at Kimberley in 1871 and gold on the Witwatersrand in 1886 greatly enhanced the strategic importance of Lourenço Marques. In 1869 Portuguese sovereignty over Delagoa Bay was recognised by the Treaty of Friendship and Commerce between the Zuid-Afrikaansche Republiek and Portugal. Britain, however, disputed Portugal's territorial claims, but in 1875 the French President, Marshal MacMahon, arbitrated in favour of Portugal.

To give the landlocked Zuid-Afrikaansche Republiek direct access to the sea and make it economically independent of the British colonies, the construction of a railway line was considered in 1876. Work only began in 1891 and the line was completed three years later. Despite the growing importance of Lourenço Marques and the port, the seat of government was only transferred from Ilha de Moçambique in 1898 – eight years after its status was elevated to that of a city.

In the years that followed, the railway line and port became an important gateway for the import and exports of goods to and from South Africa's industrial heartland, the Witwatersrand. Prior to independence in 1975, the port of Maputo handled about 40 per cent of all cargo from and to the Witwatersrand, while the railway provided a lucrative source of income for the Portuguese government.

At independence, the city's name was changed to Maputo, in honour of one of the Tsonga chiefs who once ruled the area south of Delagoa Bay. The collapse of the country's economy after independence and the civil war resulted in a massive influx of people to the city, which came to a virtual standstill.

Maputo's recovery since 1994 has been nothing short of remarkable. New buildings are rising over the city at a rapid rate, old ones have been spruced up and pavements are being repaired. Some downtown roads are still potholed and in back streets refuse continues to be discarded on the pavements, but overall it is a vast improvement from the early 1990s, when just about nothing worked and car wrecks cluttered the pavements of the once stately *avenidas*. It is just a matter of time before the city regains its former glory.

Situated on a high bluff overlooking the bay, the city's Polana suburb owes its name to one of the lesser Tsonga chiefs who once ruled over the area. Decidedly the upmarket part of the city, this is where most diplomatic missions are situated, and where diplomats, expatriates and the affluent live. Beautifully restored to its former British colonial glory in the early 1990s, the **Hotel Polana** is one of Maputo's most famous landmarks and one of Africa's great hotels. Designed by Sir Herbert Baker and built between 1918 and 1922, the hotel features a magnificent marble entrance hall with an ornate caged lift (see p 75).

Formerly known as Xilunguine, a name meaning "white men's place", the Baixa, or downtown, is the nucleus around which Maputo developed. The city's main commercial centre, it is a mixture of skyscrapers dating back to the 1960s and 1970s, high-rise flats, shops and offices. Here, too, can be found the post office, railway station and the port.

Maputo is a lot safer than it used to be in the mid-1990s and is certainly far safer than Johannesburg, or many other African cities. Bear in mind, though, that tourists are targets for pickpockets and confidence tricksters wherever you go, be it London's Underground or any other major city in the world; it is advisable to take a few common sense precautions when exploring Maputo (see p 39).

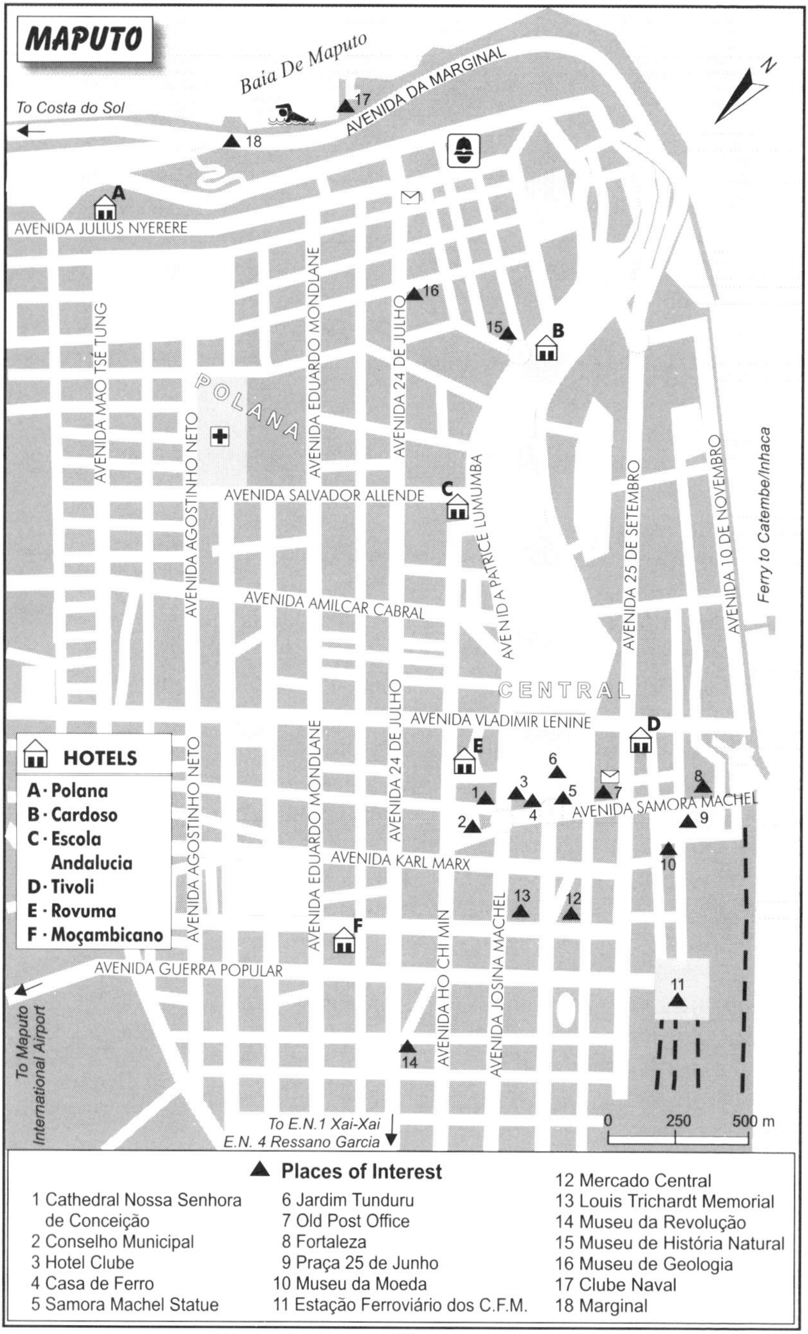
MAPUTO
Baia De Maputo
To Costa do Sol
AVENIDA DA MARGINAL
AVENIDA JULIUS NYERERE
AVENIDA MAO TSE TUNG
AVENIDA EDUARDO MONDLANE
AVENIDA 24 DE JULHO
POLANA
AVENIDA AGOSTINHO NETO
AVENIDA SALVADOR ALLENDE
AVENIDA PATRICE LUMUMBA
AVENIDA AMILCAR CABRAL
AVENIDA 25 DE SETEMBRO
AVENIDA 10 DE NOVEMBRO
Ferry to Catembe/Inhaca
CENTRAL
AVENIDA VLADIMIR LENINE
AVENIDA SAMORA MACHEL
AVENIDA KARL MARX
AVENIDA HO CHI MIN
AVENIDA JOSINA MACHEL
AVENIDA GUERRA POPULAR
To Maputo International Airport
To E.N.1 Xai-Xai
E.N. 4 Ressano Garcia
0 250 500 m
HOTELS
A · Polana
B · Cardoso
C · Escola Andalucia
D · Tivoli
E · Rovuma
F · Moçambicano
Places of Interest
1 Cathedral Nossa Senhora de Conceição
2 Conselho Municipal
3 Hotel Clube
4 Casa de Ferro
5 Samora Machel Statue
6 Jardim Tunduru
7 Old Post Office
8 Fortaleza
9 Praça 25 de Junho
10 Museu da Moeda
11 Estação Ferroviário dos C.F.M.
12 Mercado Central
13 Louis Trichardt Memorial
14 Museu da Revolução
15 Museu de História Natural
16 Museu de Geologia
17 Clube Naval
18 Marginal

What to do in Maputo

A walking tour

Numbers on the map on p 66 correspond with those in the text. An ideal place to start your **walking tour** of the Baixa is the Carlton Rovuma Hotel on the eastern side of the Praça Independência (Independence Square). Adjacent to the hotel is the **Catholic Cathedral** (1), built in 1944 and dedicated to Nossa Senhora de Conceição (The Lady of our Conception). Ironically the church, with its imposing spire and stained glass windows, was largely built with forced labour.

Overlooking downtown Maputo is the impressive **Conselho Municipal** (2), a bold three-storey building with central colonnades and arched windows, reflecting a neo-classical design. Completed in 1945, it houses the city council offices and the mayoral chambers. Of interest is the inlay in the pavement in front of the building which reads: "Aqui e Portugal" (This is Portugal).

From here, head down Avenida Samora Machel, past what was formerly known as the **Hotel Clube** (3). Situated in a peaceful garden setting, the red brick building now serves as the Centro Cultural Franco-Moçambicano (Franco-Mozambique Cultural Centre). Regular art exhibitions and other cultural activities are held here, and light refreshments can be enjoyed in a pleasant courtyard.

As you continue your walk, the pavement separating Avenida Samora Machel and the service road is unlikely to escape your attention. Laid out in light-coloured cobblestones, dark cobblestones were used for the borders and motifs. A short way on you will pass a curious looking building, the **Casa de Ferro** (4), or Iron House. The prefabricated building was designed by Alexandre Eiffel, three years after he completed building his most famous metal structure, the Eiffel Tower in Paris in 1889. The panels were shipped from abroad and assembled at the site, but the building turned out to be too hot and never served its original purpose as a residence of the Governor General. At the beginning of the 1900s it was used as a primary school and now houses the offices of the Museums Department.

Seemingly guarding the entrance to the botanical gardens, the **bronze statue of Samora Machel** (5) is mounted on a marble footpiece. The statue was unveiled in 1989 in honour of the country's first president, who played an important role in the liberation struggle. At the age of 33 he became Frelimo's commander and four years later succeeded the movement's first leader, Eduardo Mondlane, as president. After leading the country to independence, Machel ruled until 1986 when he was killed after the aircraft he was travelling in crashed into the mountains near Komatipoort. Evidence suggested that the aircraft was diverted off course by a radio beam; that act has been attributed to South African military saboteurs.

Behind the statue is the imposing neo-Manuelino style entrance gate to the **Jardim Tunduru** (6), or Botanical Gardens. Designed in 1885 by the well-known English horticulturist, Thomas Honney, it was originally known as the Vasco Da Gama Gardens in honour of the first European to set foot ashore in Mozambique. The garden has a variety of indigenous and exotic trees and plants imported from Portugal's overseas colonies and a cycad collection.

Continue to Avenida 25 de Setembro where two of the city's most famous cafés, the **Café Continental** and **Pastelaria Scala**, are situated. Turn left and as you make your way to the **post office** (*correio*) (7), take a closer look at the cobblestone pavement. Built in 1906, the building is in a good state of preservation and it is worthwhile stepping inside to look at the interior. Further along you reach the **national library** which dates back to 1904 and then a modern high-rise building on the corner of Avenida Vladimir Lenine and Avenida 25 de Setembro. The highest building in the Baixa, construction of the 33-storey building was stopped after independence and the uncompleted superstructure became known as the **Andares 33** (33-storey building). It was completed after peace returned to the country.

Turn right and then right again into Rua de Timor to reach the nucleus of the settlement around which the city developed. Of interest here is the **Fortaleza de Nossa Senhora da Conceição** (8), a red sandstone fort with four bastions, built between 1851 and 1867 to defend the Portuguese trading post. The historic building now serves as a military museum and the remains of the Gaza king, Gungunhana, are among the exhibits. One of the early rulers who resisted colonialism, he was captured after the defeat of the Gaza army by the Portuguese in late 1895 and sent into exile in the Azores. Also to be seen is a statue of António Enes, the Portuguese High Commissioner who ordered the attack on the king. Open from 07:00-17:00 on Saturdays and Sundays.

A short walk from the fort brings you to the **Praça 25 de Junho** (9), or 25th of June Square. A visit to the square is especially worthwhile on weekends when it is transformed into a colourful market, the **Mercado Artesanato**. A wide variety of crafts, ranging from batiks, paintings and wooden masks to carvings and realistic wooden replicas of cellphones and four-wheel drive vehicles, are sold and you will find the sellers more than willing to bargain over the price.

Diagonally across from the square is the well-known Yellow House, a plain flat-roofed building conspicuous only on account of its colour. One of the oldest buildings in the city, its simple structure belies the fact that it was once the seat of the first colonial government. It now houses the **Museu da Moeda** (10), or Money Museum, which traces the history of money in Mozambique back to the days of barter trade. Open on Tuesdays, Wednesdays, Thursdays and Saturdays from 09:00-12:00 and 14:00-16:30; Fridays from 09:00-12:00 and Sundays from 14:00-17:00.

Make your way now down Rua de Bagamoyo to the **Praça dos Trabalhadores** (Workers' Square), formerly known as Praça MacMahon in honour of the French President who ruled in favour of Portugal during the 1875 territorial dispute. Dominating the square is a large granite monument erected to honour Portuguese and Mozambican soldiers killed when German forces invaded the country during World War I. The work of the Portuguese sculptor Rui Gameiro, the statue depicts Athena, the Greek goddess of wisdom, practical wisdom and prudent warfare.

On the western side of the square is the **Estação Ferroviário dos Caminho de Ferro de Moçambique** (11), or railway station. The beautiful building, with its marble arches, wrought-iron work and interesting metal dome-shaped roof over its entrance, was built in 1910 and was once an important link between the ocean and the interior. The dome-shaped roof has variously been attributed to the engineer of the Eiffel Tower, Alexandre Eiffel, and an architect of the Eiffel School.

From the railway station, walk up Avenida Guerra Popular, turn right into Avenida 25 de Setembro and continue to the **Mercado Central** (12), or Central Market, dating back to 1901.

With its rows and rows of tightly packed stalls, the market is a hive of activity. Fresh prawns and fish, fruit, vegetables, spices and curios are sold. Not to be missed are the cashew nut counters where you can watch the nuts being roasted. As markets are often frequented by pickpockets and thieves, you will be well advised to be on the alert, although the authors never experienced any problems during several visits.

Exit through the northern entrance, turn left into Avenida Zedequias Manganhela and then right into Avenida Albert Luthuli which takes you past rows of small shops. At Avenida Josina Machel turn right and after a short while you will reach the **Louis Trichardt Trek Memorial** (13), set in a small sunken garden. Unveiled in 1968, the memorial was erected in honour of "Louis Trichardt and his people, the tamers of the bush" and commemorates the epic 1837/8 trek of the Voortrekker leader. In August 1837, Trichardt's party of 31 members set off from the Soutpansberg to Delagoa Bay in search of a route to the sea. After a journey of nearly eight months, the party reached Lourenço Marques where Trichardt and 22 others died of malaria. The trek is portrayed on murals and in beautiful mosaics on the floor of a pond.

If you are feeling tired and footsore, return to the Rovuma Hotel a short distance away. Alternatively, head for the **Museu da Revolução** (14) (Museum of the Revolution) in Avenida 24 de Julho, which depicts Frelimo's 10-year war against Portuguese colonialism with memorabilia from the struggle, posters, photographs and maps. The museum is open Mondays, Tuesdays, Thursdays and Fridays from 09:00-12:00 and 14:00-18:00; Saturdays 14:00-18:00 and Sundays 09:00-12:00 and 15:00-18:00.

Other places to see

The **Museu de História Natural** (15), or Natural History Museum, on the Praça da Travessia de Zambeze is housed in one of Maputo's most beautiful buildings. Featuring delicate turrets, arched windows and elaborate plasterwork which give it a Moorish appeal, it was restored in 1998. The most interesting exhibition is its unique collection of 14 elephant foetuses in various stages of development. The collection dates back to World War I when the Agriculture Ministry decided to open up the area south of Maputo for agriculture. In the process more than 2 000 elephants were slaughtered, but fortunately the supervisor of the hunt preserved the foetuses of pregnant cows in formalin.

Other displays focus on marine and bird life, while there is also a fascinating insect collection. Of interest in the garden are the exquisite murals painted by one of the country's foremost artists, Malangatana.

An interesting collection of minerals and precious stones occurring in Mozambique is on display in the **Museu de Geologia** (16) (Geology Museum) in Avenida 24 de Julho. The building with its Manuelino architecture was once the Maputo synagogue. Open Tuesdays to Fridays 15:00-18:00; Saturdays from 09:00-12:00 and 15:00-18:00.

One of Maputo's famous landmarks is the **Marginal** (18), the palm-lined avenue stretching along the beach to the Costa do Sol. From the ferry terminal in Avenida 10 de Novembro (the ferries to Catembe and Inhaca depart from here), drive eastwards along Avenida 10 de Novembro and bear to the right at the Praça Robert Mugabe, where you will join the Avenida da Marginal. After a short drive you will pass the **Clube Naval** (17) (Yacht Club) on your right. The imposing, whitewashed double-storey building and the yacht harbour date back to 1913. Further along you drive past **Praia da Polana** (Polana Beach). Cane furniture and handicrafts are sold at the traffic circle and as you continue along the causerina and palm-lined Marginal, the scenery is dominated by an uncompleted multi-storey building. Known as the Four Seasons, it was built as a hotel, but when foreign-owned property was nationalised, concrete was poured into all the ducts and service vents, rendering the building totally useless. Several attempts to complete the building have been unsuccessful.

About 2,5 km on you will see small fishing vessels on your right and the **bazar do peixe** (fish market) on your left. Fresh fish, prawns, rock lobsters, calamari and crabs can be bought here. One of the city's famous landmarks, the **Costa do Sol** (The Coast of the Sun), is reached a short way on and across the narrow channel **Xefina Grande** (see p 81) can be seen. As there is a considerable tidal difference, high tide is the best time for swimming.

Also worthwhile taking a look at is **Praça dos Herois**, or Heroes' Square, dedicated to the heroes of the liberation struggle. The monument is reached by taking Avenida Guerra Popular towards the airport until you reach a large traffic circle. The focal point of the circle is a white star-shaped monument (Frelimo's emblem) containing the remains of liberation struggle heroes, while pieces of wreckage of the aircraft in which President Machel was killed in 1986 are also displayed. On a nearby wall the history of Frelimo's liberation struggle is portrayed in colourful murals, painted by the renowned Mozambican artist Malangatana. Photographs may be taken of the wall, but it is strictly forbidden to photograph the monument.

Art, culture and entertainment

Art lovers should not miss the opportunity to visit the **Museu Nacional de Arte** (National Art Museum) at 1233 Avenida Ho Chi Min, where works of the country's leading artists, including the painters Malangatana and Naguib and the sculptor Alberto Chissano, are on permanent display. Exhibitions are also held from time to time. Open Tuesdays to Sundays 15:00-19:00. Regular art exhibitions are also held at the **Centro Cultural Franco-Moçambicano** (French-Mozambican Cultural Centre) in Avenida Samora Machel (see (3) on the walking tour and map of Maputo). Open Mondays to Fridays 08:00-12:00 and 14:00-17:00. Also worthwhile enquiring about is the **Centro de Estudos Brasileiros** where exhibitions of local and international artists can be seen. Located at 1728 Avenida 25 de Setembro, the centre is open Tuesdays to Fridays 09:00-13:00 and 15:00-19:00.

Maputo is known for its lively **nightlife**, but you will probably be well advised to venture out at night with someone who knows the city spots, or to move about in a group. One of the liveliest places is the **Feira Popular** alongside Avenida 25 de Setembro in the *baixa*. It has a fun fair and a large number of restaurants, each with its own specialities, and bars. Another popular spot is the long-established **Mini Golfe** along the Marginal. The complex features an open-air disco (weekdays excluding Monday), bar with live music (weekends), restaurant, putt-putt course, swimming pool and paddling pool.

One of the top **night clubs** is **Clube 7** at 2236 Avenida Vladimir Lenine. With its elegant and sophisticated ambience, this decidedly upmarket club is where the city's rich dance the night away. There is a hefty entrance fee for non-members. Open Thursdays-Saturdays. **Sheik** in Avenida Mao Tsé Tung is another popular venue over weekends.

Shopping

If you are looking for something to take back home, the **Mercado Artesanato** (see p 69) is probably the best place in Maputo to look for curios, but if you miss the Saturday market, visit the **Artedif**, a co-operative run by disabled people, on the Marginal. A variety of crafts, including leatherwork, ceramics and weavings, as well as curios, are sold here. Alternatively, take a look at the curios displayed on the pavement near the Hotel Polana, opposite the Piri Piri Restaurant, the Hotel Cardoso and Café Continental.

Travellers passing through Maputo can obtain all the necessary food and provisions from a variety of well-stocked supermarkets; one of the best options is **Shoprite**. It is reached by taking Avenida Guerra Popular towards the airport for about 600 m. The shopping centre also has a variety of other South African chain stores and restaurants.

A good selection of magazines and books is available at **Sensações**, 657 Avenida Julius Nyerere.

Where to eat in Maputo

Maputo offers a wide choice of restaurants, ranging from top-class establishments to cafés, coffee shops and *pastelarias*. Avenida Julius Nyerere is famous for its pavement cafés, while the Feira Popular also has a wide choice of eateries. Some of the better-known ones are listed here alphabetically.

A Grelha, 697 Avenida Julius Nyerere, tel (01) 49 40 95. Specialises in Italian and continental dishes.

Al'Andalus, 508 Avenida Patrice Lumumba, tel (01) 42 30 51. Situated in the Hotel Escola Andalucia, this restaurant with its marble wall panels offers a limited menu and reasonable service. There is also a pleasant garden bar near the hotel's swimming pool.

Bistro, 657 Avenida Julius Nyerere, tel (01) 49 76 44. One of the city's new breed of eateries, the Bistro features an interesting variety of tastefully presented continental dishes in an elegant setting.

Comandante, 707 Avenida Mártires de Mueda, tel (01) 49 10 71. Located in the four-star Hotel Cardoso, this elegant restaurant has an extensive menu and efficient service

Continental (Café), cnr Avenida 25 de Setembro and Avenida Samora Machel, tel (01) 30 20 05. This charming old-style café with pavement seating, a snack restaurant and bakery, is a landmark in the *baixa*.

Escorpião, Feira Popular, tel (01) 30 21 80. One of the Feira's best known restaurants. Specialises in Portuguese dishes at very reasonable prices.

Gil Vicente, Avenida Samora Machel, tel (01) 30 15 50. Small restaurant run by friendly Portuguese owner, next to the cinema. Variety of typical Portuguese dishes, offering good value for money.

La Bussola, 866 Avenida Julius Nyerere, tel (01) 49 64 56. Offers dining indoors or on the terrace and a lively bar. Specialises in Portuguese dishes.

Maputo (Café), 630 Avenida Julius Nyerere, tel (01) 49 32 07. A popular old-time café with outdoor and indoor seating. Snack meals.

Maritimo, Avenida da Marginal, tel (01) 49 63 45. Located at the Clube Naval, this terrace restaurant has a magnificent ocean view. Specialises in seafood and on Sundays a buffet is offered.

Mundo's, 657 Avenida Julius Nyerere, tel (01) 49 40 80. A popular meeting place of South African holiday-makers, this franchise restaurant has daily specials and a menu featuring pub food.

Polana, 1380 Avenida Julius Nyerere, tel (01) 49 10 03. The Hotel Polana's **Terraço** restaurant offers alfresco dining with a choice of international cuisine, or an excellent buffet. There is also a bar with a view overlooking Baia de Maputo.

Piri-Piri, 3842 Avenida Julius Nyerere, tel (01) 49 23 79. One of the city's best known restaurants with a reputation for its excellent peri-peri chicken and prawns. The basic interior is somewhat dated, but perhaps that's part of its attraction.

Restaurant 1908, cnr Avenida Eduardo Mondlane and Avenida Salvador Allende, tel (01) 42 48 34. A good choice if you fancy typical Mozambican fare, Italian dishes, or seafood. Prices are less expensive in the outdoor restaurant and there is also a take-away.

Ungumi, 1555 Avenida Julius Nyerere, tel (01) 49 09 51. Undoubtedly the best restaurant in Maputo, this upmarket restaurant is renowned for its international cuisine, extensive wine list and outstanding service. Expensive and aimed at the well-heeled.

Not to be missed is a visit to one of Maputo's numerous *pastelarias,* where a wide variety of mouthwatering Portuguese and continental cakes, pastries and breads can be bought. Among the well-known outlets are **Pastelaria Polana**, close to the hotel of that name, the **Pastelaria Scala** on the corner of Avenida 25 de Setembro and Avenida Samora Machel and **Pastelaria Nautilus** on the corner of Avenida Julius Nyerere and Avenida 24 de Junho.

Where to stay in Maputo

Visitors to Maputo have a choice of several accommodation establishments, ranging from top-class five- and four-star hotels to more modest pensões. Hotels are listed in alphabetic order according to their star rating, while pensões are listed alphabetically.

Hotels

Polana, 1380 Avenida Julius Nyerere, tel (01) 49 10 01, fax 49 14 80, e-mail mail@hpolana.uem.mz. One of Africa's classic hotels, the five-star Polana reflects the grace, sophistication and excellent service of a bygone era. The luxuriously furnished bedrooms in the main building and the Polana Mar (a newer annex) are air-conditioned, and have satellite television. The hotel has a restaurant, bar, coffee shop, a magnificent swimming pool and a tennis court. There are also two banks, a hairdresser, travel agent, curio shop, car rental agency and a news kiosk.

Escola Andalucia, Avenida Patrice Lumumba, tel (01) 42 30 51, fax 42 24 62. This pleasant four-star hotel with its 1950s style decor serves as a training school for the hotel industry. The air-conditioned rooms are small but adequate and have television. It also has two restaurants and a swimming pool with a nearby garden bar.

Cardoso, 707 Avenida Mártires de Mueda, tel (01) 49 10 71, fax 49 18 04. Prior to the 1994 elections, the building served as the headquarters of Renamo and was subsequently extensively renovated to become the city's first four-star hotel. Situated on a high bank overlooking the Rio Esperito Santo, the fourth-floor dining room, pool terrace and most of the rooms enjoy views over the bay.

Rovuma, 114 Rua de Sé, tel (01) 30 50 00, fax 30 53 05. Situated close to the Praça da Independência, this four-star hotel is conveniently situated in the *baixa*. It offers air-conditioned rooms with television, a restaurant with a buffet and à la carte menu, bar, swimming pool and gymnasium. The shopping centre has a terrace restaurant, book shop, bank, hairdresser and several other shops.

Moçambicano, 961 Avenida Filipe Samuel Magaia, tel (01) 42 92 52, fax 42 31 24. This three-star hotel has 49 air-conditioned rooms, a restaurant and pool bar. Good service.

Terminus, corner of Avenida Francisco Orlando Magumbwe and Avenida Sekou Touré, tel (01) 49 13 06, fax 49 12 84. This centrally located three-star hotel offers good air-conditioned rooms, with 17-channel satellite television, at reasonable prices. There is also a restaurant (specialising in fish, Portuguese and continental dishes), garden terrace, swimming pool and pool bar.

Hotel Tivoli, 1321 Avenida 25 de Setembro, tel (01) 42 43 53, fax 42 49 66. A conveniently located hotel in the *baixa*, the Tivoli has air-conditioned rooms with satellite television, a business centre, restaurant and bar.

Pensões

Hoyo-Hoyo Residencial, 837 Avenida Francisco Orlando Magumbwe, tel (01) 49 07 01, fax 49 07 24. Located in the heart of the Polana suburb, the Hoyo-Hoyo is a fairly recent addition to the city's accommodation establishments. Its neatly furnished rooms offer value for money accommodation.

Pensão Martins, 1098 Avenida 24 de Julho, tel (01) 42 49 30, fax 42 96 45. This neat guesthouse has reasonably priced rooms with or without *en suite* bathrooms. Other amenities include a restaurant, swimming pool and satellite television.

Residence Kaya Kwanga, 321 Rua D João de Castro, tel (01) 49 22 15, fax 49 27 04. Situated near the Mini Golfe complex along the Marginal, accommodation is in air-conditioned bungalows in a tranquil, private setting. Amenities at the club which forms part of the complex include a terrace restaurant, bar, swimming pool, tennis court and a children's playground.

Sommerschield House, Sommerschield suburb near Hotel Polana, South Africa tel (083) 726 0577. A new upmarket guesthouse offering air-conditioned rooms with *en suite* facilities, satellite television, swimming pool, bar and secure parking.

The Burger Inn, Bairro do Triunfo, tel (01) 45 52 11. This modest establishment close to the Costa do Sol offers clean, air-conditioned rooms and shared bathrooms at very reasonable prices. The ground floor restaurant has a fair selection of good local fare. South African credit cards are accepted.

Triunfo Guest House, Bairro do Triunfo South Africa tel (083) 726 0577. Situated close to the beachfront towards the Costa do Sol, this new guesthouse offers tastefully furnished, air-conditioned bedrooms with *en suite* facilities, television and swimming pool.

Ilha da Inhaca

Situated in the Baia de Maputo, 24 km east of the city, the tropical island of Inhaca (pronounced Inyaaka) lies amidst the turquoise waters of the Indian Ocean. Once a favourite retreat of wealthy Maputo residents and South African holiday-makers, the island is fast regaining its popularity following extensive renovations of the hotel, which has been taken over by the Pestana hotel group.

With a length of 12,5 km and a width of 7,5 km, the island owes its name to the Tsonga chief, Nhaca, whose chieftaincy extended from Maputo Bay southwards to St Lucia in South Africa's KwaZulu-Natal Province. Until about 30 000 years ago it formed part of the Machangulo Peninsula to the south, but rising sea levels slowly broke through and about 17 000 years ago its link with the mainland was finally severed.

During the 16th century, Portuguese ivory traders used Inhaca as a base from where they dispatched their boats to ply the rivers that flow into Maputo Bay. Relations with Nhaca were initially good, but after a quarrel with the chief in 1621 the Portuguese moved their trade to Xefina Island.

In the 1950s the island's population totalled about 2 000. The civil war, however, caused many people to flee the main-

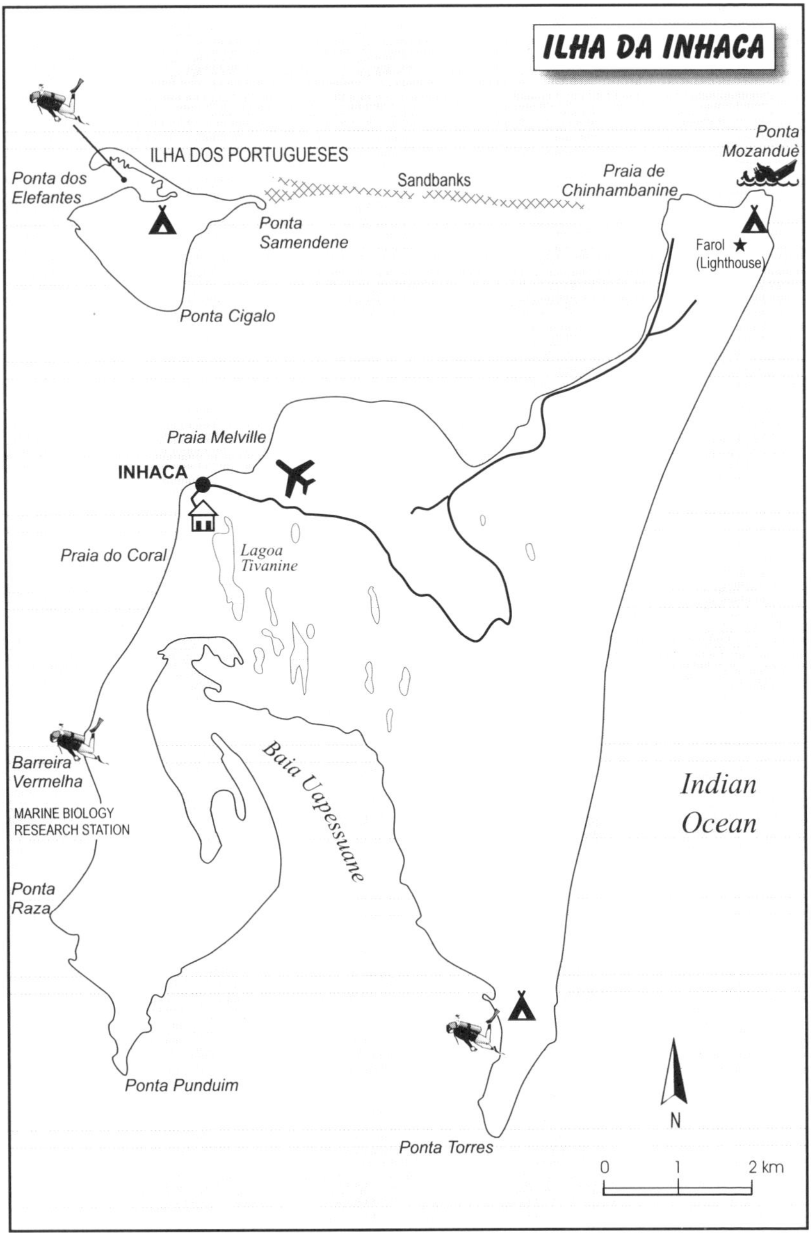
ILHA DA INHACA
ILHA DOS PORTUGUESES
Ponta dos Elefantes
Sandbanks
Praia de Chinhambanine
Ponta Mozanduè
Ponta Samendene
Farol ★ (Lighthouse)
Ponta Cigalo
Praia Melville
INHACA
Praia do Coral
Lagoa Tivanine
Barreira Vermelha
MARINE BIOLOGY RESEARCH STATION
Baia Uapessuane
Indian Ocean
Ponta Raza
Ponta Punduim
Ponta Torres
N
0
1
2 km

land, resulting in an increase to 3 500 people by 1980 and 5 200 by 1989. Following the democratic election of 1994, people slowly began returning to the mainland again, relieving the human pressure.

Inhaca offers good **diving** opportunities. At **Baixo Danae**, 10 km northeast of the lighthouse, divers can explore the wreck of the steamship, after which the reef was named, in the company of gamefish and brindle bass. Another **shipwreck**, lying in 5 m of water, can be explored just off the lighthouse, while **Cockburn**, northwest of Inhaca, is renowned for its brindle bass. Yet another option is the channel between **Cabo de Santa Maria** and **Ponta Torres**, where diving is only possible just before high tide on account of the strong currents.

Snorkellers can discover the fascinating underwater world of the reef just off **Barreira Vermelha** along the west coast and the wreck near the lighthouse. Another excellent snorkelling spot is along the eastern shores of **Baia Uapessuane** near Ponta Torres, but care should be taken against currents.

Diving, snorkelling and other water sport activities including **water-skiing**, **windsurfing**, **angling trips** and **parasailing** on the island are run by **Dive Africa**; in South Africa tel (012) 333-7110, fax 333-7911. Dive packages from Johannesburg can also be booked (see Dive charters, camps and packages in Chapter 5). Trips by tractor and four-wheel drive vehicle to the *farol* (lighthouse) are conducted by the hotel.

Of interest on the island is the **Estacão de Biologia Maritima**, or the Marine Biology Research Station, run by the Eduardo Mondlane University. The **museum** has an interesting collection of coral, tropical fish preserved in formalin (unfortunately their colours have faded over the years), the skeletal remains of a dugong, turtle carapaces and a variety of other exhibits relating to the island's ecology. Open Mondays to Saturdays from 08:00-11:30 and on Sundays and public holidays from 09:00-11:30. It is well worth a visit and is reached after a walk of about 45 minutes from the Inhaca Resort Hotel, which also offers trips by vehicle to the station.

Set among coconut trees, lawns and large trees, the **Inhaca Resort Hotel** comprises 40 brightly coloured units with twin beds and a bunk bed for two children, *en suite* bathrooms, telephone and satellite television. There is also a restaurant with an outside terrace, bar, games room and a salt water swimming pool, as well as conference facilities.

The well-established **Restaurante Lucas** in the village just behind the hotel specialises in seafood dishes and is popular with day visitors. The nearby market is a good place to buy coconuts, bread, fruit and vegetables.

The island has been declared a nature reserve and camping other than at designated sites is strictly prohibited. There are **two camp sites** for budget travellers; one at Coconut Bay near the lighthouse and the other near Ponta Torres close to the southern point of the island. Coconut Bay is a good hour's walk from Inhaca village, while the other site is even further.

Lying about 3 km northwest of the Inhaca Hotel is **Ilha dos Portugueses**, or Portuguese Island, which once served as a leper colony. It is most easily reached by arranging a boat transfer from the hotel, although it is theoretically possible to wade across at low tide.

Allow about two hours for a leisurely stroll around the island and if you are keen on salt water **flyfishing** or **snorkelling**, remember to take your gear along. On the northern side of the island a sandspit has formed a large lagoon offering excellent opportunities for these two activities. Although the reef in the lagoon has unfortunately been partly sanded in, snorkelling can still be rewarding.

For budget travellers there is a designated **camp site** among the dune forests along the northern shore of the island. Water and basic toilet facilities are available.

Inhaca can be reached by plane or by boat from Maputo. **Turmar**, tel and fax (01) 49 87 35, operates a speedboat service, departing at 09:00 from the jetty on Avenida 10 de Novembro and returning at 15:00 on the same day. The trip takes about an hour and it is advisable to wear shorts and sandals as it is usually necessary to wade through the shallows at Inhaca.

A cheaper, less luxurious and slower option for the more adventurous is to take the **ferry** which operates on Tuesdays, Thursdays, Saturdays and Sundays. It departs from the ferry terminal on Avenida 10 de Novembro at 07:30, arriving at Inhaca at around 10:30, depending on weather conditions. It returns to Maputo on the same day, leaving at 14:30.

Inhaca has a surfaced runway and is a mere 10 minutes by air from Maputo. **SabinAir**, P O Box 465011, Maputo, tel (01) 46 51 08, fax 46 50 11, operates **scheduled flights** to the island on Fridays and Sundays.

Xefina

At the mouth of the Rio Incomati a narrow sandspit extends southwards for several kilometres. On its landward side lies **Xefina Pequena** (Little Xefina), which is separated by a narrow gap from **Xefina do Meio** (In-between Xefina). The third island, **Xefina Grande** (Large Xefina) lies about 3 km offshore of the Costa do Sol.

Over the centuries, Xefina Grande has served as an ivory trading post, penal colony and a military installation. Of interest are the ruins of the old Portuguese fort and the rusty remains of the battery of heavy cannons that guarded the entrance to the harbour during World War II. Built on a sand dune which has since been eroded by the lapping waves, the guns have slid down the dune into the sea. **Nkomati Safaris** conducts day trips to Xefina Grande on board a 8,5 m twin-hulled catamaran. The price includes lunch.

7

SOUTHERN MOZAMBIQUE

With its kilometres of unspoilt beaches, pristine coral reefs and world-class bill and game fishing, the coast is southern Mozambique's main attraction. This is the most developed part of the country's coastline and there are numerous fine lodges and resorts, offering a wide range of accommodation options and activities. For wildlife enthusiasts the Reserva Especial do Maputo (see p 99 and route 2) offers exciting bird-watching opportunities and the possibility of seeing the reserve's famed elephants. Although still a far way off, the proposed Kruger/Banhine/Zinave/Gonarezhou Transfrontier Conservation Area (see p 21) is likely to be a major drawcard once it becomes a reality.

The provinces of Maputo, Gaza and Inhambane, south of the Rio Save, are dominated by the vast plains of the Planicie Moçambicana. Along the coast these plains are punctuated by a string of lakes and the floodplains of the Incomati and Save rivers, creating Mozambique's Lake District. The plains generally lie below 100 m except in the extreme west where they are replaced by highlands rising to an altitude of 500 m. Maputo Province borders in the west on South Africa and Swaziland, while Gaza shares its borders with South Africa and Zimbabwe. To the east the three provinces border on the Indian Ocean.

Vegetation varies from dune forests along the coast to miombo woodlands, while palm savannas occur on the river floodplains. Gaza Province is characterised by mopane and terminalia savanna, while the vegetation of the interior of Maputo Province is typically an acacia savanna.

Agriculture in Maputo Province centres mainly around citrus, with citrus and cashew nuts the main crops of Gaza Province. Inhambane Province is the second largest cashew growing area in Mozambique and prior to independence it was the country's main citrus producer. Extensive coconut plantations occur north and south of the city of Inhambane (see p 95 and route 3). The Indian Ocean here is a rich source of Mozambique's famed prawns and fish, providing a livelihood to thousands of people.

The population of Maputo Province is mainly represented by the Tsonga (Shangaan), which is also the most populous group in Gaza. Tswa and Chope are the dominant cultural groups in Inhambane Province.

It seems likely that the northern part of the coast was part of the "Land of Sofala" which is mentioned in 10th century reports of Muslim traders. Possible proof of this was provided in 1977 when a significant archaeological discovery was made at Chibuene, 5 km south of Vilankulo (see route 4). Although 250 km south of Sofala (see p 126), this site has so far proved to be the richest in imported goods and among the artefacts excavated are painted glassware, glass bottle fragments and glass beads dating back to before the first millennium.

Whilst seeking a sea route to India, the Portuguese navigator Vasco da Gama went ashore along the coast of southern Mozambique in 1498. The exact location is uncertain, but the reception from the local people was so friendly that he named the land Terra da Boa Gente, *or Land of the Friendly People. To this very day the traditional way of greeting by the people of Inhambane is open hands held in front of the chest; a sign that you come in peace and without weapons.*

Arquipélago do Bazaruto

Also referred to as the "Crown Jewels of the Western Indian Ocean" the Arquipélago do Bazaruto is a string of islands protruding from the mainland into the Mozambique Channel like five stepping stones. Surrounded by a translucent blue-green sea, the archipelago is a tropical paradise and a haven of tranquillity. On the landward side the extensive tidal flats, channels and sand banks are transformed into a mosaic of abstract patterns and shades of sapphire blue, indigo and aquamarine with the changing tides.

The archipelago formed part of Ponta São Sebastião as recently as 10 000 years ago, but tectonic movements and rising sea levels gradually severed its links with the mainland, as the sea broke through in low-lying areas. With that 14 mammal species also became isolated, among them bushbuck, red duiker, samango monkey and the four-toed elephant shrew. Some 45 reptiles and amphibians, including two new species and four new subspecies of fossorial reptiles, as well as freshwater crocodiles, likewise became stranded. Five turtle species have been recorded in the waters off the archipelago and at least two species, leatherback and loggerhead, breed on the shores of Bazaruto and Benguerra.

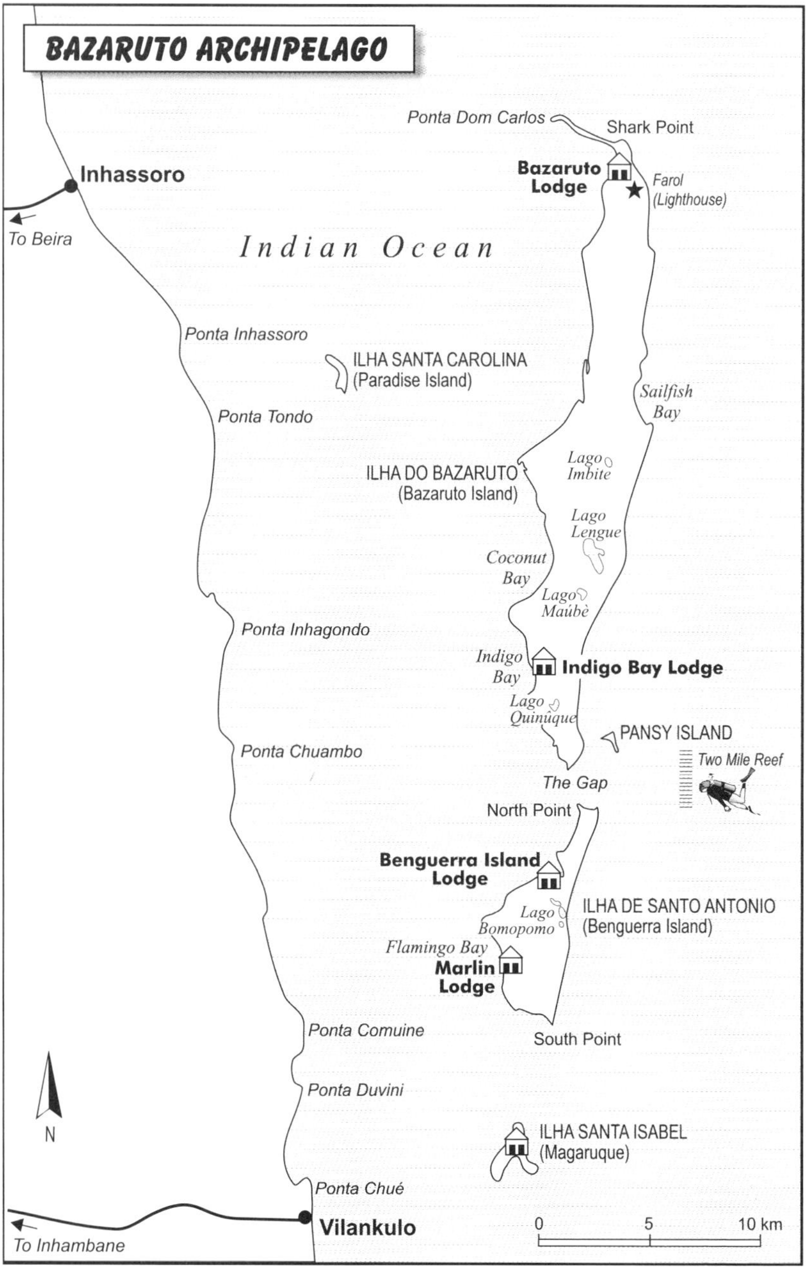
BAZARUTO ARCHIPELAGO
Ponta Dom Carlos
Shark Point
Bazaruto Lodge
Farol (Lighthouse)
Inhassoro
To Beira
Indian Ocean
Ponta Inhassoro
ILHA SANTA CAROLINA
(Paradise Island)
Sailfish Bay
Ponta Tondo
Lago Imbite
ILHA DO BAZARUTO
(Bazaruto Island)
Lago Lengue
Coconut Bay
Lago Maúbè
Ponta Inhagondo
Indigo Bay
Indigo Bay Lodge
Lago Quinúque
PANSY ISLAND
Two Mile Reef
Ponta Chuambo
The Gap
North Point
Benguerra Island Lodge
ILHA DE SANTO ANTONIO
(Benguerra Island)
Lago Bomopomo
Flamingo Bay
Marlin Lodge
Ponta Comuine
South Point
Ponta Duvini
N
ILHA SANTA ISABEL
(Magaruque)
Ponta Chué
Vilankulo
To Inhambane
0
5
10 km

The archipelago's bird list of some 150 species includes noteworthy birds such as the crab plover, a non-breeding visitor to the coast from September to April, olive bee-eater, black-headed apalis and blue-throated sunbird. Also to be seen are flocks of greater flamingo, while large numbers of migratory waders visit the fertile mudflats from September to April. Among the smaller creatures that are often overlooked, there are over 40 butterfly species that have been collected in the archipelago.

The warm tropical waters surrounding the archipelago support a stunning variety of fish, coral, marine mammals and plants. Some 2 000 fish species, representing over 80 per cent of the families of the Indo-Pacific region, occur here. **Gamefish** abound in the deep sea, while the pristine reefs off the islands attract a rich diversity of **tropical fish**, starfish and other marine creatures in hues of bright yellow, brilliant blue and powder blue. These reefs were formed when sand particles were cemented into beach rock by precipitated calcium carbonate, formed when fresh water percolating from the islands combined with sea water. Floating coral larvae subsequently colonised the submerged beach rock, creating coral gardens of exquisite beauty. Among these are plate, staghorn, honeycomb and brain coral, as well as a variety of soft coral.

Among the archipelago's most interesting creatures is the **whale shark** – the largest fish in the world. Despite its name, it is not a whale, nor does it resemble a shark. It owes its name to its enormous size and attains lengths of up to 17 m. One of three large filter-feeding sharks, its feeding habits are more akin to those of whales than to sharks. Whale sharks occur in tropical and warm temperature oceans, favouring temperatures of 21-25 °C. Research by the South African Shark Research Institute into the migratory patterns of whale sharks has provided some interesting information. An 8 m-long male, fitted with a satellite tag at Cape Vidal along the KwaZulu-Natal coast was tracked at Xai-Xai, a straight distance of about 370 km, eight days later. Whale sharks are sighted fairly often by divers and deep-sea anglers along the Mozambican coast, especially from December to February. For many divers the highlight of any diving trip is to swim with these gentle creatures. Other **shark species** include black-tip, grey reef, tiger and Zambezi sharks. October to March is generally best for shark diving.

Several species of marine mammals inhabit the open sea and the sheltered bays of the archipelago, among them the secretive **dugong**. They live in the warm coastal waters of the Indian Ocean, occurring from southern Mozambique to northern Australia. Their numbers are declining worldwide and the dugong is classified as vulnerable to extinction. The main reason for their decline is accidental entanglement in gill nets set out by fishermen, but they are also caught for their meat, fat and oil. The Bazaruto population, estimated at around 110, is thought to be the last viable population along the African east coast. There is also a small population at Ilha Mefunvo (see route 9). Their almost human-like faces, pectoral mammae and fish-like tails probably gave rise to Greek mythology's legendary mermaids, who lured ships onto the rocks by enchanting mariners with their singing.

Dugongs live in groups of five to six, although they are known to congregate in much larger groups. They inhabit shallow water no deeper than 30 m as they feed on sea-grass in sheltered bays. With a length of up to 3 m, they can weigh up to 400 kg.

Other marine mammals include common, bottlenose, humpback and spinner **dolphins**, which are often seen in the bays on the leeward shores of the islands and the open sea. There are also two resident **whale** species (minke and southern right whales), while humpback whales are frequently sighted from September to November when they migrate up the coast to Madagascar.

The islands are home to several thousand people. During the civil war many people took refuge on the islands, resulting in an increase of the total population to 3 800. Following the 1994 elections, however, some people have voluntarily returned to the mainland. The islanders subsist mainly on artisanal fishing and an estimated 1 500 tonnes of dried fish are exported annually to the mainland. They also exploit the sand oysters, locally known as *mapalo*, but no harvesting takes place from November to February when reproduction takes place.

Dhows are a common sight on the waters around the archipelago and provide another dimension to its tropical atmosphere. Capable of carrying loads of up to three tonnes, they are used as water taxis, for fishing and transporting cargo to and from the mainland. Often only their sails can be seen above the horizon, but when they come ashore large crowds of islanders gather to meet friends or relatives, to catch up on the latest news, or to help empty the nets.

Realising the archipelago's biological uniqueness, the World Wide Fund for Nature and the Southern African Nature Foundation funded a masterplan between 1989 and 1991 for the management of the archipelago. One of the key recommendations of the masterplan was that the entire archipelago be proclaimed a national park. Although Benguerra, Magaruque and Bangue have been designated a national park, Bazaruto only has the status of a Zone of Surveillance. However, indications are that the park is likely to be proclaimed in 1999.

The Endangered Wildlife Trust (EWT) has been active in the area since 1990, when it initiated a project to integrate rural development with conservation. EWT provides financial support to the *guardas da fauna* – guards who are appointed by community leaders of the area. They work closely with the community to protect the archipelago's natural resources and among their duties are the monitoring of reefs to prevent the use of nets over them, patrolling the beaches during the turtle nesting season and encouraging the sustained use of plants. The base camp of the *guardas* on Bazaruto Island is situated at Zingarema, a few kilometres south of Bazaruto Lodge on the site of an earlier crocodile farming operation.

An angler's paradise, the archipelago is ranked as the best **marlin angling** destination in the western Indian Ocean. The All Africa record for black marlin (590 kg) was landed in these waters in November 1998, while several other specimens have weighed in at over 450 kg. The average weight for marlin is 350 kg and the months from October to early March are generally the best months for this species. Sailfish weigh in at an average of 32 kg, while the record for these waters stands at 59,5 kg. May to September again are good months for sailfish which are especially abundant in July and August.

Gamefish occur in abundance in the deep waters off the continental drop-off, 20 km seawards of the archipelago, and the inshore waters between Bazaruto and Paradise islands. A few hours out at sea are usually rewarded with a good catch and among the commonly caught species are pompano, queen and king mackerel, dorado, giant kingfish, wahoo, barracuda and bonito. Gamefishing is generally rewarding all year round, except for wahoo and dorado which are scarce during the winter.

Surfcasting is no less rewarding throughout the year and bonefish of over 20 kg (reputedly the largest in the world) and giant kingfish are eagerly sought after. Other surfcasting species include queenfish, springer, bonito, barracuda, stumpnose, pompano, skates, rays and sharks.

With its clear water and generally calm conditions the archipelago is attracting an increasing number of **saltwater fly-fishing enthusiasts**. Catches include queenfish of up to 13 kg, ladyfish of over 5,5 kg, bonefish, pompano and several kingfish species, including giant kingfish of over 20 kg.

Although serious anglers are drawn to the archipelago, an increasing number of families and tourists are nowadays attracted by the wide range of activities, or simply to relax. The archipelago's balmy weather, clear water and ocean breezes make ideal conditions for a variety of other **water sports**, including scuba diving, snorkelling, swimming, sailing, windsurfing and paddle-skiing.

At depths from 10-40 m, the reefs, with their ever-changing topography, diversity of hard and soft coral, as well as brilliantly coloured tropical fish, are an underwater paradise waiting to be discovered. Here **divers** and **snorkellers** can explore lush coral gardens of infinite beauty and swim with schools of vividly coloured tropical fishes. Water temperatures range from 28 °C in summer to 22 °C in winter, making diving possible all year round; visibility is generally best from April to July. With a tidal difference of up to 5 m, resulting in reduced visibility and strong currents, diving excursions are limited to high and low tides.

Scheduled flights are operated to Bazaruto, Benguerra and Magaruque from Maputo by **SabinAir** on Mondays, Tuesdays and Fridays. Flights depart at 10:15, arriving at Bazaruto about two hours later. Scheduled return flights are also operated by **SA Airlink** from Nelspruit, in South Africa's Mpumalanga Province, to Vilankulo, where customs and immigration facilities are completed before continuing to the island. Flights are scheduled for Tuesdays and Thursdays.

Another option is to arrange a transfer by speed boat from Inhassoro (see route 4) to Bazaruto, a trip of 30-45 minutes depending on sea conditions; from Vilankulo (see route 4) to Benguerra (20 minutes), or Magaruque.

Yet another option is a **dhow trip** from Vilankulo or Inhassoro. Adventurous and romantic as it may seem, bear in mind that a trip from Inhassoro to Bazaruto can take anything from three hours (if the winds are favourable) to three days. In addition, there are no lifejackets on board and there is a possibility that the dhow could sink.

Ilha do Bazaruto (Bazaruto Island)

The archipelago takes its name from the largest and best known of the five islands, Bazaruto. With a length of 31 km and just over 6 km at its widest, Bazaruto is a mosaic of massive dunes on the seaward shore, savanna grassland dotted with clusters of ilala palms, freshwater lakes and white, deserted beaches.

Legend has it that the Ophir pearls of the kingdom of Queen of Sheba came from these shores and in the 16th century the island was the southernmost outpost of a string of settlements established along the Mozambican coast by Muslim traders. It has also romantically been linked with the love affair between the Portuguese trader Lourenço Marques and a beautiful Moor, Mariame.

Originally known as Hucicas, or Vacicas, the strategic island has seen many uses. At the beginning of the 1900s it became a penal colony (the Alcatraz of Mozambique) and the 18-m high *farol* (lighthouse) perched on a high dune near the northern end of the island is testimony to their labour. Built in 1913-14, the paraffin-operated lighthouse became defunct in 1982 for 14 years, until a solar panel was installed in 1996 to provide power for the light. During World War I a Portuguese entrepreneur, Joaquim Alves, allegedly set up a base near the northern point of the island to refuel German U-boats. Possible evidence of this is a narrow-gauge railway line which is occasionally exposed by the sea in front of Bazaruto Lodge.

Bazaruto has been a popular tourist destination since 1989, when a small fishing camp was built near its northern point. Although it has long since shed its fishermen's image the pace and the atmosphere is still very much relaxed and informal. Facilities at **Bazaruto Lodge** consist of a central area comprising the reception, lounge and dining room under thatch, as well as a swimming pool with a thatched area where drinks and snack meals can be enjoyed. Breakfast times are flexible, snack lunches can be ordered and the buffet dinner is a feast of seafood and a wide variety of salads.

The A-framed thatch-roof chalets are tucked away among indigenous vegetation, lawns and palm trees and, depending on the tide, you could go to sleep or wake up with the waves lapping against the shore. Each chalet has a double bed, *en suite* bathroom, open-air shower, ceiling fan and mosquito net.

One of Bazaruto's main attractions is the excellent angling, with the Big Three – black marlin, sailfish and kingfish – being the main targets. Marlin are plentiful in the deep waters just off North Point, while the waters from Sailfish Bay (along the island's eastern shores) northwards to North Point provide excellent opportunities for sailfish and black marlin.

Gamefishing is no less rewarding and a few hours out at sea is usually rewarded with a handsome catch. **Surfcasting** is also popular and catches are made of kingfish (including giant kingfish), queenfish, jobfish, springer, king mackerel and bonito. Fully equipped boats and tackle can be hired.

Diving and **snorkelling** excursions are guided by the resident diving instructor and there is a fully equipped dive shop. With 37 km of reefs, Bazaruto has several excellent diving sites, ranging from 12-25 m deep. **Potholes** owes its name to the large potholes (some with swim-throughs) eroded into the rock shelves of Lighthouse Reef off the northern end of the island. Situated about 1 km out at sea, the **Greek Temple**, with its 3 m-high rock pillars, tunnels and overhangs, is reminiscent of an ancient ruin. It has a maximum depth of 16 m and offers divers an opportunity to see green turtles, large brindle bass, beautiful coral and a variety of colourful reef fish.

Snorkelling excursions are conducted from Bazaruto Lodge an hour before low tide. **Coral Gardens** and **Lighthouse Reef** are both shore entries, while **Aquarium** is accessed by boat.

Activities on Bazaruto are, however, not limited to fishing, diving and snorkelling. Visitors can hire a four-wheel drive vehicle for a **trip to the island's freshwater lakes**, set sail in a dhow for a **sunset cruise**, book an **island hopping cruise**, or a **boat trip** to nearby Ilha Santa Carolina, or Paradise Island, where a picnic can be enjoyed. Subject to the tide, **water-skiing** is offered in front of the lodge. Not to be missed is a **walk up to the lighthouse** for a magnificent view over the island (remember to obtain the key from the lodge), or combing long expanses of unspoilt beach.

Swimming is not possible in front of the lodge at low tide when vast sandflats are exposed. This is, however, amply compensated for by the swimming pool at the lodge, while a bay behind Ponta Dom Carlos, a sandspit at the northern tip of the island (a walk of about 30 minutes from the lodge), offers good swimming and shade.

Further south, along Bazaruto's southwestern shores, is Coconut Bay, named after the large grove of coconuts planted on the island by Joaquim Alves in the early 1950s. A short way on is **Indigo Bay Lodge**. Built on the dunes among natural vegetation, the central area comprises reception, lounge and dining room with a magnificent view over the sea and white sandy beach. Accommodation is in two-bedded wood and thatch chalets with *en suite* showers, ceiling fans, mosquito nets and balconies overlooking the sea. To protect the sensitive dune vegetation the chalets are linked to the central building by wooden boardwalks.

The lodge has a swimming pool and activities offered include angling, diving, snorkelling, windsurfing, hobiecat sailing, catamaran island hopping cruises, sundowner cruises and four-wheel drive trips to places of interest on the island.

Benguerra (Ilha de Santo Antonio)

At the southern point of Bazaruto a narrow channel, The Gap, separates the archipelago's second largest island, Benguerra, from its northern neighbour. About a quarter the size of Bazaruto, Benguerra is an idyllic island retreat with kilometres of white sandy beaches, sand dunes, two freshwater lakes and patches of evergreen dune forests.

The island is named after a local chief, and its tourism dates back to 1990 when a Zimbabwean family, the Landreys, built a fishing camp among a patch of forest on the western side of the island. Since then, it has developed into one of southern Africa's top lodges.

Built on stilts, the thatched central complex comprises the reception, a small curio shop, spacious lounge with comfortable furnishings and a bar. From the dining room you can watch red squirrels scuttling about the trees and a variety of forest birds. For lunch a mouthwatering buffet is set out, while delicious table d'hôte dinners, featuring seafood such as freshly caught fish, prawns and crab curry, are served.

Nestling among lush coastal forests of milkwoods, close to a palm-lined white beach, are 13 thatched chalets raised on stilts. Three of the sides are enclosed by matted reed walls, while roll-down blinds at the front ensure both privacy and allow guests to enjoy views of the surrounding vegetation and beach. The tastefully furnished chalets have *en suite* shower and toilets and are equipped with mosquito nets. Despite the relaxed atmosphere, the lodge has an ambience of sophistication and offers guests personalised attention.

A full range of **diving** activities is offered and **Two Mile Reef**, about 3 km east of The Gap between Bazaruto and Benguerra Island, offers superb opportunities for diving on the seaward side with depths ranging from 12 m to 26 m. Other diving spots include **Five Mile Reef**, **Fossil Reef**, which owes its name to the fossilised trees extending from the sea bed, and **Pompano Reef**, renowned for its abundance of pompano.

Snorkelling on the landward side of **Two Mile Reef** reveals an underwater wonder-world inhabited by powder blue surgeon fish, moorish idols, dominos, threadfin butterflyfish, parrot fish, bluespotted ray and a host of other species. **Aquarium**, a pool within Two Mile Reef, features an amazing variety of fish and spectacular hard and soft coral and is without doubt one of the best snorkelling spots along the entire Mozambican coast. Another snorkelling option is **South Point Reef**, a rocky reef just off the island's southern tip, which has moray eels as one of its attractions. Scuba diving and snorkelling excursions are conducted by the lodge's diving instructor and there is also a well equipped dive shop.

Anglers can set off to the gamefish-rich waters of Sailfish Bay off the eastern shores of Ilha do Bazaruto, Ponta São Sebastião and the blue waters off Two Mile Reef in search of marlin, sailfish, king mackerel, queenfish, kingfish and bonito. Although Bazaruto has the edge over Benguerra when it comes to **surfcasting**, anglers can try their hand and luck at North and South points on incoming and outgoing tides.

Saltwater flyfishing at the narrow channels between Bazaruto and Benguerra (also known as Kingfish Alley) and Benguerra and Magaruque is unsurpassed, while boat flyfishing at Five Mile and Six Mile reefs is also possible. Kingfish heads the want list of many anglers, while king mackerel, queenfish and pompano are commonly landed. Boats with tackle and a skipper can be hired at the lodge.

Four-wheel drive island tours are offered to South Point and the freshwater lakes which are inhabited by crocodiles, while boat trips to South Point and Pansy Island are other possibilities. At **Pansy Island**, a small sandy island just off North Point, large numbers of pansy shells, members of the sea urchin family, can be seen just below the surface of the sand. When they die, the short spines drop off to reveal a pattern resembling a petal and once washed ashore they are bleached pure white. Two species occur on the sandy island, one of which is endemic to Mozambique.

You can gain an insight into the way of life of the islanders by arranging **a visit to a herbalist** who will show you around the village. On the tour you will learn more about the significance of the spiritual huts dotted around the island, see how palm wine is made (and perhaps taste it) and get to know more about the islands' staple crop, cassava.

A variety of **birds** are attracted to the coastal forest and time spent birding around the lodge will be well rewarded. With a length of just over 11 km and 4,6 km at its widest, the island can be **walked** around in one day. The 35 km walk takes about eight hours and should not be attempted if you are not fit. And what better way is there to end the day than with a glass of ice cold wine, watching the sun setting while a dhow glides effortlessly through the water.

Further south, at Flamingo Bay, lies **Marlin Lodge**, which opened in October 1996. Its focal point is the large wood-and-thatch main lodge building comprising reception, dining room, lounge, bar and TV room. There is also a swimming pool. The chalets in two wings are linked to the main building by elevated walkways.

The lodge offers angling and diving, as well as a variety of other water sports – water-skiing, hobie sailing, boardsailing, snake-tubing and parasailing. Also on offer are quad bike trips, four-wheel drive island trips, picnics and sundowner cruises.

Magaruque (Ilha Santa Isabel)

Magaruque, originally named Ilha Santa Isabel, is the third-largest island in the archipelago. Separated from Benguerra by a narrow channel, it is a mere 1,6 km long by about 1,4 km wide and a **walk** around the island takes just three hours. Along its eastern shores, a long narrow sandspit extends into the sea to form a protected bay which is one of the favoured feeding grounds of the island's flamingo population.

The first tourism development on the island was initiated by Senhor Joaquim Alves, who constructed self-catering bungalows in the 1960s. In 1985 a Zimbabwean businessman obtained a lease over the property and built the main building comprising the reception area, lounge, dining area and bar. Accommodation at the **Hotel Ilha Magaruque** comprises of basic but comfortable thatched chalets with *en suite* facilities. The lodge has been scheduled for a major revamp.

Angling is but one of Magaruque's many attractions. Honeymoon Bay at the island's northern point offers good **rock and surf angling** possibilities, while **bill and gamefish** abound in the offshore waters.

Although there are only a few **diving** spots in close proximity to Magaruque, diving is another option. Highlights of **Channel Reef**, a dive with a maximum depth of 12 m in front of the lodge, include stonefish and moray eels, while the 26 m **Deep Hole**, off the eastern shores of the island, attracts schools of barracuda and stumpnose. Further afield are the dive sites off Benguerra and Ponta São Sebastião.

Bangue

Bangue, the southernmost and smallest of the islands, is also the youngest, having been formed about 3 000 years ago. Covering a mere 0,3 km^2, the uninhabited island is nothing more than a sandy islet which is largely submerged during high tide. Boat trips to Bangue from neighbouring islands and Vilankulo for picnics and saltwater flyfishing are popular.

Ilha Santa Carolina (Paradise Island)

Known to many South Africans as Paradise Island during the 1960s and the early 1970s, Santa Carolina was a popular holiday destination with South African big-game fishermen and honeymoon couples until the civil war broke out.

In the mid-1850s a Portuguese settlement was established on the island, which later served as the headquarters of the Portuguese penal colony on Bazaruto Island. It is said to have been named by the convicts after a nurse, Carolina, who took care of them.

The now derelict hotel was built by Joaquim Alves, a Portuguese businessman who used to have extensive interests in the Vilankulo area and the Bazaruto Archipelago. Following his death in Portugal in 1974, his assets were taken over by the Bank of Mozambique and the island gradually sank into obscurity. Plans to renovate the hotel stalled when the developer failed to fulfil a World Bank loan agreement. Fears have been expressed that the steel structure of the hotel has become so corroded that it will be difficult to restore the building.

Covering less than 1 km^2, the tiny bean-shaped island is the most stable of the islands in the archipelago and dates back some 125 000 years. The southern half comprises of large mangrove communities and salt marshes, while dune forest occurs in the north.

Boat trips to the island are popular from the lodges on the nearby islands and often include a picnic lunch.

Inhambane 3

The charming coastal city of Inhambane (pronounced Inyumbane) is situated on the shores of a sheltered bay formed by two sandy headlands. It is the administrative capital of the province of the same name and an important harbour where Union Castle ships docked during the grand old days of passenger liners. It is also the springboard to some of the most popular resorts along the coast of Mozambique.

The earliest mariners to visit the bay were Muslim traders who established a trading centre in "the Land of Sofala" by the 10th century. They were followed centuries later by the Portuguese who established a presence at Inhambane in 1534. The name Inhambane is said to be a corruption of Niambani, who was chief over the area when the Portuguese first arrived.

In 1560 Inhambane was identified by the Jesuits as the site for their first mission along the east African coast. The mission was short-lived, though, but during the 17th century Inhambane gained importance as a base for trade in ivory from the interior and cloth from India. In 1727 Bernardo Castro Soares was dispatched to Inhambane to establish a trading settlement and to build a fort. In 1763 the status of a town was conferred on it.

During the second half of the 18th century, Inhambane also became an important port for the export of slaves. By the

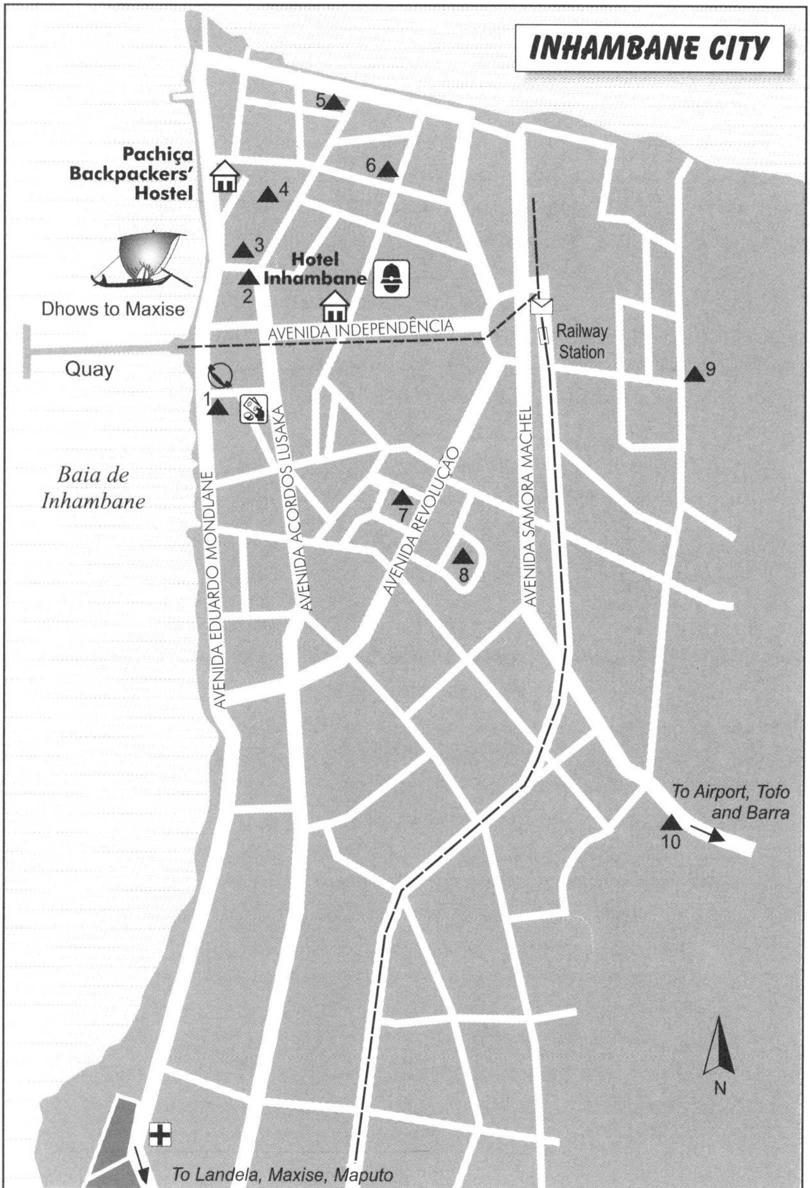

Places of Interest

1 Monument to Slavery and Forced Labour
2 Cathedral Nossa Senhora de Conceição
3 Catholic Church
4 Governor's Palace
5 Old Mosque
6 Museum
7 Mercado Central
8 Praça Herois
9 Carpenters' Co-operative
10 Market

1830s thousands of slaves were being shipped from its shores and by 1860 it was one of the principal ports along the Mozambican coast.

To develop the interior of Inhambane district, construction of the first section of the railway line between Inhambane and Inharrime to the south began in 1910. Although the railway line was originally planned to be linked to Xai-Xai as part of the "Grand Railway of the South", the grandiose plan failed to materialise and it remained a local line.

Among the relics of the Portuguese era are the **Cathedral of Nossa Senhora de Conceição** (Cathedral of Our Lady of the Conception), which dates back over two centuries. It was probably more by design than accident that the street it is situated in was renamed Avenida Karl Marx after independence. Also of interest is the **Monument to Slavery and Forced Labour**, a crumbling wall with a mural recalling the days when Inhambane featured prominently in the slave trade. Other city sights include the **museum**, the **mosque** dating back to around 1840 and the **dhow harbour**.

Inhambane is synonymous with dhows, a characteristic sight on the 24 km-long bay, which is a waterway to an estimated 200 of these vessels. During the annual **dhow race** which usually takes place to coincide with the International Day of Tourism, the crews of 30 to 40 dhows pit their skills in a race from Inhambane to Maxise.

A popular outing is to catch a **dhow** from Maxixse (see route 4) on the western shores of the bay to Inhambane and return after exploring the city on foot and enjoying a meal in one of the many restaurants. Not to be missed is a visit to the city's **Mercado Central**, or central market, with its wide variety of fresh fruit and vegetables, cashew nuts and fish.

Linga Linga

Linga Linga, north of Inhambane, is a little paradise that owes its pristine character largely to the fact that it is only accessible by boat. Jutting southwards for about 7,5 km, the peninsula is washed by the warm waters of the Indian Ocean along its eastern shores, while in the west it is bounded by Baia de Morrumbene. In the second decade of the 1900s a whaling station was established at Linga Linga, but it was forced to close down after a few years.

A mere 4 m from the low water mark, a channel up to 17 m deep in places creates excellent **angling** opportunities. Among the species to be caught are grunter, rock cod and yellowtail. The waters off Linga Linga are also home to an estimated 12 **dugongs**, while dolphins are also frequently seen. Another attraction of Linga Linga is the excellent **birding** that can be enjoyed here.

Day trips to Linga Linga can be organised through Erwin Jakes of Campismo de Maxise (see route 4), where safe parking is available at a small fee. At Barra Reef (see p 119) a 10 m yacht is available for charters to Linga Linga. There is an unofficial camp site, **Casa Lucia**, which caters for backpackers and those with an adventurous spirit. Basic facilities, comprising of a few tents and an open fireplace, are provided and you can either eat local fare, or take along your own provisions.

Ponta do Ouro

Ponta do Ouro, the Point of Gold, lies a few kilometres north of the border with South Africa. Here a sandy headland covered in magnificent coastal dune forest forms a sheltered bay which sweeps northwards for some 5 km. As Ponta do Ouro is easily accessible from South Africa's KwaZulu-Natal Province it is a popular destination with the South African angling and diving fraternity, especially during school holidays. Situated close to Maputo, it is also an ideal weekend retreat for wealthy Mozambicans.

There are four dive sites in close proximity to Ponta do Ouro, as well as nearly a dozen sites closer to Ponta Malongane which can also be explored. Well known among the nearby dive sites is **Checkers**, a flat 18 m-deep reef with a wide variety of reef fish, anemones and brightly coloured sponges. Several dive operations are based at the resort, offering courses from Open Water 1 to speciality. Equipment hire and airfills are available.

In addition to **diving** and **boat angling**, Ponta do Ouro is also popular with **surfing** enthusiasts, while **windsurfing**, **spearfishing**, **sunbathing** and safe **swimming** can be enjoyed along the kilometres of unspoilt beaches to the north of the resort. Not to be missed is a late afternoon walk up to the *farol* (lighthouse), from where you can enjoy a spectacular view of the coast.

Ponta Malongane

Ponta Malongane, another popular destination with South African holiday-makers, lies about 7 km north of Ponta do Ouro in the lee of a headland with dune forest sweeping down to a magnificent bay.

For **divers** there are 15 nearby reefs, ranging from 14-20 m in depth. Heading the list of popular sites is **Bass City**, five rocky outcrops projecting from the sandy sea bed. In addition to large potato bass (after which the site has been named), divers can expect to see devil firefish, lion fish, clown trigger fish and red-banded cleaner shrimps. The deepest dive, **Pinnacles**, drops down to 40 m and is ranked as one of the best shark diving spots in southern Africa. Among the species to be seen are hammerhead and Zambezi sharks and hence only experienced divers may undertake this dive. The waters off Ponta Malongane are often visited by whale sharks during the summer months and it is not uncommon for divers to swim with these fascinating creatures. There is a well-equipped dive camp with a thatch and wood lounge-dining area and tented accommodation. Other activities include **swimming** and **spearfishing**.

Reserva Especial do Maputo

Reserva Especial do Maputo, or Maputo Elephant Reserve, is a 50 000 ha mosaic of lakes, floodplains, mangrove swamps, woodlands and forested dunes sweeping down onto unspoilt beaches. Established in 1932, it extends from Baia de Maputo southwards to the southern tip of Lago Xinguta, but excludes the Machangulo peninsula. Its western boundary is partly formed by the Rio Maputo and the Rio Futi, while in the east the reserve is bounded by the Indian Ocean for 40 km.

The reserve was once a sanctuary to large herds of elephant, white rhino and a variety of other game species, but poaching during the civil war reduced animal numbers considerably. The entire white rhino population of 65 animals, introduced from the Umfolozi Game Reserve in South Africa's KwaZulu-Natal Province in 1967 was wiped out, while the elephant population decreased from an estimated 350 in 1971 to a mere 120 by the late 1980s.

The Rio Futi provides an ecological link with the Tembe area in northern KwaZulu-Natal and for centuries this fossil

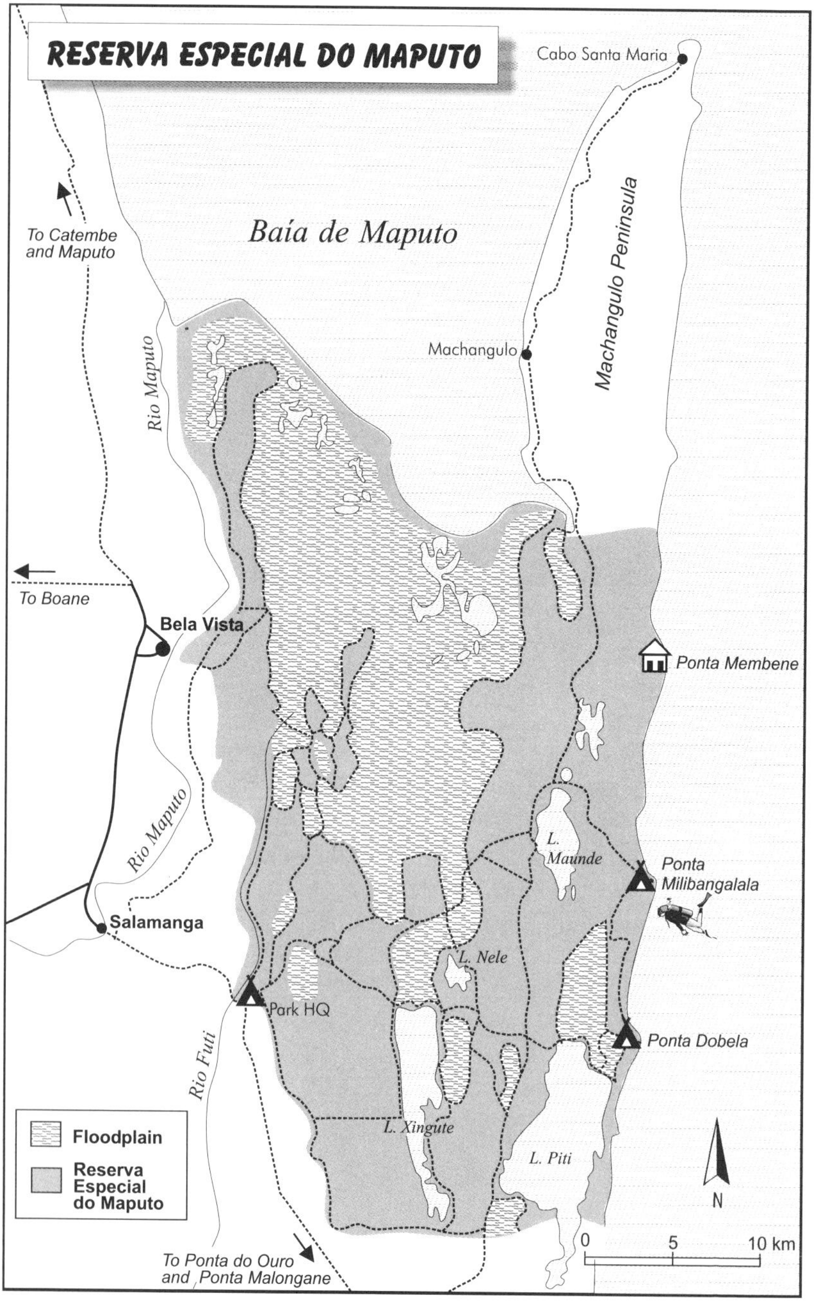
RESERVA ESPECIAL DO MAPUTO
Cabo Santa Maria
To Catembe and Maputo
Baía de Maputo
Machangulo Peninsula
Machangulo
Rio Maputo
To Boane
Bela Vista
Ponta Membene
Rio Maputo
L. Maunde
Ponta Milibangalala
Salamanga
L. Nele
Park HQ
Ponta Dobela
Rio Futi
Floodplain
Reserva Especial do Maputo
L. Xingute
L. Piti
N
0
5
10 km
To Ponta do Ouro and Ponta Malongane

river has been used as a migration route by elephants. During the winter months, the breeding herds congregate with their calves in the vicinity of the park headquarters before migrating southwards. Fearing that the elephants would be wiped out completely, KwaZulu-Natal conservation authorities fenced off the northern boundary of the Tembe Elephant Park in 1989.

Since 1994 the Endangered Wildlife Trust has provided considerable financial support to the National Directorate of Forestry and Wildlife to rehabilitate the reserve. The programme included educating the local population that the area is a reserve, halting poaching, training game guards and repairing tourism facilities.

Game numbers are increasing again and the park's elephant population currently numbers around 200, while the Tembe Elephant Park population is estimated at between 130 and 140 animals. Although their spoor and dung are frequently seen, the elephants are elusive and difficult to track down in the dense bush. Other animals you chance spotting include hippo, crocodile, nyala, red duiker, suni, vervet monkey and reedbuck.

The reserve offers excellent opportunities for **birdwatching** as several species reach the southern limit of their distribution in northern KwaZulu-Natal. Among these are Rudd's apalis, Woodwards' batis, Neergaard's sunbird and pink-throated twinspot. Commonly seen species include African fish eagle, crested guineafowl, olive bee-eater, woodland kingfisher and white helmetshrike, as well as grey, trumpeter and crowned hornbills.

One of the reserve's main attractions is the coast and the opportunities it presents for angling, diving, snorkelling and spearfishing. **Surfcasting** is rewarding and up to 14 species of fish have been caught within 10 days, among them bonefish, springer, stumpnose and mata-hari.

One of the advantages of **diving** here is that the reefs are still in a pristine condition, as Milibangalala is not yet as popular as Ponta Malongane and Ponta do Ouro further south. There are several good diving spots, ranging in depth from 8 m to 27 m at low tide. Among the attractions of diving along the coast here are whale sharks, manta and bluespotted rays, large potato bass, honeycomb eels, scorpion fish and turtles. One of the most popular dive sites is **Heaven's Gate**, with its schools of pelagic fish, yellow cup coral and prolific tropical fish.

Other options include **Ponta Dobela**, 7 km to the south, a pinnacle 17 km offshore, **Cabo Santa Maria** and several unexplored reefs. **Sea Blue Diving** has a tented diving camp at Ponta Milibangalala (South Africa tel (011) 803-4552, fax (807-1008).

At low tide **snorkellers** can explore two sites close to the camp site. A flat rock shelf provides easy shore entry to a 2 m deep gully sheltered to the south by a sandspit, and there is also a reef, about 100 m offshore, which should be attempted only by strong swimmers.

Swimming at high tide could be risky as there is a strong backwash. However, at low tide hours you can while away the hours by sitting in the shallow waters near the sandspit.

The park's tracks can only be explored in a **four-wheel drive vehicle** and it is advisable to deflate tyres before venturing onto the tracks which are very sandy across the dunes. A network of tracks criss-cross the bush to the north of the park headquarters, but the most used route is the track to the camp site at **Ponta Milibangalala**. Provided you are in possession of a beach driving permit, you can travel southwards along the beach for about 10 km to the camp site at **Ponta Dobela** at low tide. It is best to obtain the permit at park headquarters. Facilities at both camp sites are very basic, being limited to a bush toilet.

A more luxurious option is **Msala Bush Camp** near Ponta Membene. Situated alongside a small lagoon close to the beach, visitors are accommodated in dome tents sleeping two. Activities include game drives, tracking the park's elusive elephants on foot and birdwatching. A reef close to the camp offers excellent possibilities for snorkelling. The tariff is inclusive of meals, drinks and activities. Contact **Polana Tours**, tel (01) 49 35 33, fax 49 35 38.

The reserve, Tembe Elephant Park and the nearby Ndumu Game Reserve in KwaZulu-Natal have been identified by the Peace Parks Foundation and the World Bank as a transfrontier conservation area. Despite this, the Mozambican government awarded a controversial 226 000 ha tourism concession in southern Mozambique to an American entrepreneur, James Blanchard, in 1996.

Centred around the Reserva Especial do Maputo, the US$ 800 million project envisaged several upmarket hotels, floating casinos, a railway line, golf course and private nature reserve. However, since the announcement of the project there has been very little development and following Blanchard's death in March 1999 it remains to be seen whether these plans will materialise.

ROUTE 1

MAPUTO CORRIDOR – RESSANO GARCIA TO MAPUTO

DISTANCE: 94 km **TIME**: 1 hour **ROAD CONDITIONS**: Good tar **FUEL**: Maputo **LINKING ROUTES**: Routes 2 and 3

For most overland travellers, the border post at Ressano Garcia, 470 km from Johannesburg, is the gateway into Mozambique. The 94 km stretch of road is the final link of the Maputo Development Corridor, which has been described as the most advanced development corridor in Africa.

Prior to Mozambique's independence 40 per cent of the exports from South Africa's industrial heartland passed through the port of Maputo, which is some 200 km closer than the harbour facilities at Durban. During the civil war, however, the road was under constant attack by Renamo fighters and became potholed, overgrown by vegetation and littered with the wrecks of military vehicles.

One of the first roads to be rehabilitated after peace returned to the country, several armed robberies and hijackings initially took place. This prompted the Mozambican authorities to deploy troops along the road and for the past few years there have been no incidents. Years after the war, twisted wrecks of military vehicles alongside the road still served as reminders of this chapter in the country's history and during a nine month demining operation carried out in 1998, some 400 land-mines were cleared in a 60 m wide strip along the road.

A year after democratic elections in Mozambique and South Africa, the Maputo Development Corridor was launched to revive international trade and attract foreign investment along the road between Gauteng Province and Maputo. The revival of this outlet to the sea was, therefore, not only of considerable benefit to Gauteng, but has also provided a major stimulus for Mozambique's economy.

Work on the project, which involves the upgrading of the national road between Witbank and Moamba and the construction of a new road between Moamba and Maputo, started in 1997 and is scheduled for completion by the year 2001. There will be three toll plazas in South Africa and two in Mozambique. The upgrading of the rail link and the rehabilitation of the port of Maputo also form part of the project.

Several proposals, including drive-through passport control and advanced clearance, were under consideration to reduce delays at the border. At the time of writing no final decision had been taken, making it advisable to check with the South African Ministry of Home Affairs.

From the border post, the road winds down the eastern slopes of the Lebombo Mountains and then passes through acacia savanna and woodlands punctuated by marula trees as it descends gradually across the coastal plains. The section between the border and Moamba will be rehabilitated, but the new road from Moamba to Maputo will no longer make the detour south to Boane, near the junction of the road from Namaacha on the Swaziland border. As a result, the distance from Ressano Garcia to Maputo will be reduced by 36 km to about 94 km.

For many visitors to Mozambique, **Maputo** is the start of their visit to this fascinating country and the city is described in detail in Chapter 6.

ROUTE 2

MAPUTO TO PONTA DO OURO

DISTANCE: 230 km **TIME**: 1 day plus **ROAD CONDITIONS**: Gravel and sandy tracks requiring 4x4 **FUEL**: Maputo, Ponta do Ouro **LINKING ROUTES**: Route 1

The easiest and quickest way to reach **Catembe**, on the southern bank of the Rio Espirito Santo, from Maputo is by ferry, as by road it is a 120 km journey. The trip is an experience in itself, as throngs of people and overloaded trucks board the ferry, which operates from the terminal on Avenida 10 de Novembro. It leaves for Catembe at 05:00, 06:00, 07:00,

08:30 and then every two hours. Tickets (1 500 Mt per person and 45 000 Mt per vehicle) can be bought at the kiosk at the entrance gate to the pier.

Although the trip only lasts about 15 minutes you will enjoy good views of the Maputo skyline and the harbour a short way further upstream. About 100 m south of the Catembe ferry terminal you will join the E.N. 201. Turn left here and continue for 42 km along a gravel road which is in fair condition, before joining a tar road quite unexpectedly. The road joining in from the right is the route from Namaacha on the Swaziland border and the road from Maputo and Boane.

After about 3 km you will reach a turnoff to **Bela Vista**, situated on a bank overlooking the Rio Maputo; its name is translated as "beautiful view". Just over 1 km on there is another turnoff to Bela Vista. Both roads were badly potholed in September 1998 and as there is little of interest in the town, other than the view over the Rio Maputo, a detour serves little purpose.

The tar road continues for another 14 km until you reach the bridge over the Rio Maputo and the rather elaborate Temple Shree Ram. After the checkpoint at Salamanga, the road surface deteriorates and about 8,8 km beyond the checkpoint you will reach a bridge over the Rio Futi. About 200 m beyond the bridge turn left and travel for 2,6 km to a T-junction where you turn left again. On reaching the park headquarters of the Reserva Especial do Maputo (see p 99) 500 m further, turn right.

From the park headquarters, where entrance and camping fees are payable, follow the signposted track to Miradouro de Changas for 300 m and then keep left (signposted Ponta Dobella 42 km, Milibangalala 33 km). About 4,5 km further keep left, following the track signposted to Machangulo and Chlombane. The track traverses several forested dunes, alternated with grassy plains and extensive seasonally inundated reed-covered pans.

Among the trees to be seen are umdoni, or waterberry, monkey orange, terminalia, pod mahogany, toad tree and Cape honeysuckle. About 20,6 km beyond the park headquarters a major track joins in from the right; turn left and after about 2,4 km you will have a stunning view over Lago Munde. Keep right where a small track splits off to the left to Machangulo and a short way on you will be at the northern shores of the lake. Ignore another small track turning off to the left and after 1,2 km you will pass a small lake on your left. For the remaining 6,8 km to Ponta Milibangalala the track traverses undulating grass-covered dunes.

From Milibangalala, backtrack for 10,4 km; ignore the road to the park headquarters to the right and continue south. A short way beyond the junction the track heads up a steep dune with deep loose sand and 14 km on Lago Piti comes into view to the left. About 400 m further you will reach an old Portuguese trading store at a major junction; the track to the left ends at a small fishing settlement on the lake shore, while the faint track to the right heads to the park headquarters via Lago Xingute. Keep to the main track south and after 5,1 km you will reach the park's southern entrance gate. From here there are several tracks and despite the authors' meticulous notes, providing a detailed route description to Ponta Malongane is almost impossible. We also found the 1:250 000 topographical map of Bela Vista of little use; the best advice is to give free rein to your spirit of adventure and to follow the most used track, heading generally in a southerly direction.

By chance we unexpectedly ended up at the road signposted to **Ponta Mamoli**, a planned holiday resort which was abandoned after Mozambique became independent. The first 10,8 km to Ponta Mamoli is on a potholed tar road which gives way to a sandy track for 1,4 km. Ponta Mamoli is situated on a high dune overlooking the azure Indian Ocean to the east and Lago Mamoli to the west. The resort has been earmarked for a multi-million US dollar tourism development.

Backtrack to the circle where the tar starts and then head south for **Ponta Malongane** (see p 99). Tucked under a canopy of coastal dune forest, the **Ponta Malongane Resort** was built prior to the civil war. It then fell into disuse until it was renovated and opened in November 1995. Accommodation comprises two-bed and four-bed rondavels, and chalets sleeping four, five and six people. There are also 45 beautifully shaded camp sites (with electricity), served by communal ablutions with hot water and dome tents sleeping two people. Other amenities include a restaurant, bar and shop with basic foodstuffs and toiletries. There is a dive camp and dive shop for equipment rental. Resort courses are offered while dive charters are operated by **Intercontinental Explorers**, tel South Africa (012) 348-4262, fax 348-1252.

From Ponta Malongane follow the signposted sandy track to **Ponta do Ouro** (see p 98) for about 6 km until you join a tar road where you turn left for Motel do Mar and the Ponta do Ouro Holiday Resort.

Abandoned to the elements after independence, Ponta do Ouro was a ramshackle town until the mid-1990s. However, many of the derelict houses have been renovated and this once popular spot is regaining its place on the tourist map. Amenities include a small shop, market and filling station.

Visitors have a choice of a number of accommodation options. The **Motel do Mar**, which reopened in December 1995, offers fully serviced, self-catering four-bed beach cabanas, equipped with gas stove, fridge, crockery and cutlery. Other amenities include a restaurant specialising in Portuguese dishes, beach patio, bar and games room. Diving and deep-sea fishing charters operate from the motel.

The **Ponta do Ouro Holiday Resort** has two-bed huts with a gas cooker, basin, bedding and communal hot water ablutions and similarly equipped four-bed chalets, but with cold water shower. The four-bed luxury chalets are equipped with a gas cooker, kettle, cutlery, crockery, bedding and towels. There is also a camp site with hot water ablutions. For divers there is a dive camp, while equipment hire and dive packages are also available.

Retrace your tracks to the Ponta Malongane junction from where you continue straight along a sandy track. Bear left after 2 km and left again 2 km further on to reach the Ponta do Ouro/Kosi Bay border post after another 4,3 km.

At the border post, the road links up with the Lubombo Corridor, a 156 km highway linking the village of Hluhluwe with the Ponta do Ouro border post. Launched in May 1998, the corridor will be extended to Maputo at a later stage.

ROUTE 3

MAPUTO TO INHAMBANE

DISTANCE: 740 km **TIME**: 2 days plus **ROAD CONDITIONS**: Tar, except sandy tracks to the coastal resorts at Macaneta, Chidenguele, Závora, Baia dos Cocos, Guinjata Bay, Paindane,

Barra Reef and Barra Lodge **FUEL**: Maputo, Marracuene, Manhica, Bilene, Inhambane **LINKING ROUTES**: Routes 1 and 4

To get onto the E.N. 1 from the city centre, travel westwards along Avenida 24 de Julho to the circle at Praça 16 de Julho. Continue along Avenida da Oua for 1,4 km to a traffic light where you turn right into Avenida de Moçambique. After about 13,2 km you will pass the Marbor factory with an enormous metal and concrete statue, the work of renowned Mozambican artist Malangatana.

About 37 km north of Maputo you reach the village of **Marracuene**, which lies on a high bank overlooking the Incomati floodplains. The village is the gateway to **Macaneta** and the Incomati mouth, the closest resorts to Maputo. As a result, large numbers of people flock here during weekends and holidays, causing facilities to become rather crowded and quite lively.

As you enter Marracuene, look out for a tree-lined road on your right. Turn right and follow the rather potholed road for about 600 m until it curves to the left. The turnoff to **Marracuene Camping Park and Chalets (Parque de Campismo de Marracuene)** is signposted on the bend and from here it is about 4,3 km on a track (negotiable by sedan car) to the resort on the southern bank of the Rio Incomati. Amenities include five two-bedroomed, self-catering chalets with a bathroom, lounge, kitchen and outside fireplace. Camp sites with communal ablutions are also available. Other amenities include a restaurant on the riverside, and a boat and canoes can be hired by those keen on exploring the river.

At the Parque de Campismo de Marracuene signpost in the town the road veers to the left and after about 600 m you turn right onto a gravel road which descends to the Rio Incomati, reached less than 1 km on. A regular ferry service operates from 05:30-18:30. The return toll fee is 90 000 Mt.

Once across the river, continue along a track for about 5 km, where the road splits and deteriorates into a sandy track, negotiable only by four-wheel drive vehicle. The track to the left continues to **Jay's Lodge**, a popular stopover offering fully equipped and serviced self-catering chalets with *en suite* bathrooms, a restaurant and bar, as well as camp sites with hot water communal ablutions.

The **Incomati River Camp** is reached a short way on. Built on the banks of the Incomati River opposite Ilha Incanine, the camp offers accommodation in thatched bungalows sleeping two. There is a restaurant specialising in typical Mozambican fare, while river-based activities such as canoeing and cruises on the river can be undertaken.

To reach **Macaneta Lodge**, keep right at the split, continuing for another 5 km along a road accessible by sedan car. The resort lies in the shelter of the coastal dunes and accommodation includes two- and four-bed chalets, as well as camp sites with cold water ablutions. There is also a restaurant with thatched open-air eating areas and a bar.

From Marracuene the E.N. 1 winds inland to avoid the extensive floodplains of the Rio Incomati. About 48 km beyond Marracuene the road winds through the town of Manhica with its neat reed houses and 6 km after passing through Xiavane you cross the Rio Incomati into Inhambane Province. Further along the road winds through cashew nut plantations and 19 km after crossing the Rio Incomati you reach the turnoff to Bilene at Macia. Turn right here and follow the road, which has been rehabilitated and is in excellent condition, for 33 km to the circle at the entrance to the town.

Bilene lies on the shores of Lago Uembje, which stretches for 17 km parallel to the coast, from which it is separated by high forested dunes. In the 1840s the settlement was the capital of Soshangane, chief of the Gaza kingdom. Prior to independence the town was known as San Marthino; it owed its name to San Marthino do Porto in Portugal which is also situated alongside a lake.

The mouth of the lagoon is blocked by a sand bar, formed by the longshore drift of the Mozambique Current, for most of the year. However, after the summer rains the level of the lake rises to above that of the sea. Around April a channel is dug manually to let the lagoon flush and for a few months ski-boat anglers can head for the open sea through the mouth before it is washed closed again. When the mouth is closed a tractor is used to pull boats across the sand bar to the sea as the mouth is inaccessible overland, even with a four-wheel drive vehicle.

The lake offers safe swimming and is popular with water-skiing, boating and windsurfing enthusiasts. **Baixio da Lagoa**, southeast of Bilene, is an unspoilt 10 km-long reef with depths ranging from 7-18 m, while four unexplored pinnacles, 4 km offshore, offer dives from 9-18 m. The rocks off **Turtle Coves** offer good opportunities for snorkelling with an abundance of lion fish, eels and crabs. Dives can be arranged through the **Praia do Sol Resort**, which also offers deep-sea angling, water-skiing, sailing and windsurfing.

Once a popular holiday destination, Bilene became totally rundown during the war; its terrible effects are illustrated by the ruins of holiday flats and cottages at the water's edge in Parq Flores. Several accommodation establishments have, however, been renovated, while a number of new developments were underway in the second half of 1998. There are several restaurants, a filling station and a market in Bilene, but no bank or supermarket.

The town, however, offers a fair range of accommodation options ranging from self-catering chalets to fairly basic camp sites. The **Hotel Bilene** at the traffic circle as you enter the town has luxury suites in the main building and self-catering two-bedroom units with a kitchen equipped with tables and chairs, a two-plate stove and pots and a shower.

The turnoff to **Humula Complexo Turistico** is 200 m beyond the hotel. This new complex has two- and three-bedroom chalets with a lounge, television, kitchenette equipped with a stove (or gas plate) and fridge, bedding and a shower. There is also a swimming pool and open-air bar. It has the same drawback as the Hotel Bilene – it is some distance from the lake shore.

Continuing along the main road, you soon reach the beach road where you turn left to the **Palmeira Complexo** 300 m on. Visitors can either camp here under shady milkwood trees or stay in basic reed huts with shared ablutions. There is a restaurant and during the holiday season a variety of water sport activities is offered.

A few hundred metres on is **Parque Flores**, a complex which once featured a swimming pool, tennis courts, water features and flats along the lake shore. There is a large camp site shaded by pod mahogany and toad trees and basic two-bed rondavels with communal ablutions. The large rondavels have a lounge/kitchen equipped with a table, chairs, stove, kettle, cooking utensils and crockery.

Backtrack to the junction of the main road into the town and the beach road then continue straight. Soon you will see the **Central Férias do Bilene** on your right, a complex along the beach road owned by Mozambican Railways. It offers very basic accommodation and is an option of last resort. A short way on the tar road ends and a signpost indicates the turnoff to **Complexo Turistico Lagoa Azul**, which offers accommodation in basic two-bedroomed self-catering cottages.

At the end of the tar road a track continues for 1,5 km to the turnoff to the **Praia do Sol Resort**. It has thatch and stone one-, two- and three-bedroom fully-equipped self-catering chalets on stilts. Built on a hillside among coastal bush, each chalet has a wooden deck with a view over the lagoon. There is also a tented self-catering dive camp with a fully equipped kitchen and an open-air bar close to the lake shore. Perched on a hill a short way on is a new luxury holiday complex which was under construction in mid-1998. The planned complex will consist of 41 thatched chalets, a restaurant, bar, curio shop, supermarket and conference centre.

Retrace your tracks to Macia on the E.N. 2, turn right and about 16 km after passing through Chissano you will reach a factory on your left, where exquisite solid mahogany wood furniture is manufactured. A visit to the curio shop is worthwhile and you will find it hard to resist buying one of the delicately carved wooden fish, or other carvings.

About 5 km on you reach Chicombane village. Keep an eye out here for the signposted turnoff to the right to Zongoene Lodge, which is 34 km further along a gravel road. The road is negotiable by sedan car during the dry season, but after heavy rains is accessible only by four-wheel drive vehicle.

Situated just upstream of the mouth of the Rio Limpopo, **Zongoene Lodge** offers guests top-class accommodation. The main lodge, built from solid mahogany wood decorated with delicate carvings, comprises the lounge, dining room and bar leading onto a large wooden deck where meals can be enjoyed. The interior furnishings and decorations of the lounge and dining room are elegant, creating an atmosphere of sophistication and grace. The breakfast, buffet lunches and tastefully presented *table d'hôte* dinners are excellent and the service attentive.

Set among lawns and indigenous vegetation, the thatched A-frame pool chalets accommodate two people and have *en suite* facilities and a wooden deck, while two-bedroom family units (accommodating four) are also available. The swimming pool is much appreciated on a hot day.

The lodge offers visitors a host of activities. Several **quad bike trips**, each with an attraction of its own, are offered. Not to be missed is the **Lighthouse Trail**, a three hour trip through coconut groves and indigenous forest to the banks of the Rio Limpopo where ships used to moor. The trip then heads inland to the historic **Monte Belo *farol*** which dates back to 1914. Not to be missed is a climb to the top of the lighthouse, from where you can enjoy expansive views over the Limpopo Mouth estuary, which was at least 1 km wide in 1958.

The continental drop-off lies a mere 24 km offshore, providing opportunities for **gamefishing**. Commonly caught species include dorado, kingfish, queenfish, sailfish and wahoo. **Rock and surf angling** along the coast is popular too.

There are a number of local **dive sites**, while the 9-16 m **Bilene Reef**, a few kilometres to the south, is within easy reach of the lodge. The reef 2 km off Ponta Pabjini ranges from 13 m to 22 m in depth and potato bass, turtles, eels and rays are among the species to be seen here.

Snorkelling at low tide in the **Pools of Eden**, a series of rock pools enclosed by a long reef about 10 km north of the lodge, offers snorkellers the opportunity to see a wide variety of fish, including juvenile angel fish and firefish, in the shallow pools. It is one of the easiest shore entry snorkelling spots along the coast and is accessed by quad bike.

Several noteworthy **birds** are among the more than 340 species recorded in the area to date. Among these are white-backed night heron, black coucal, white-eared barbet, Rudd's apalis, Vanga flycatcher, Mozambique batis, Neergaard's sunbird and pink-throated twinspot. The rare crab plover has also been recorded.

Other activities include **sunset cruises** up the Limpopo River, **canoe trips** and **walks** among the mangrove community. There are plans to incorporate the lodge's 2 000 ha concession into a biosphere reserve stretching from Bilene to Xai-Xai. Among the game to be reintroduced into the reserve are roan, sable, tsessebe, Lichtenstein's hartebeest, nyala, the Sofala subspecies of Burchell's zebra, reedbuck, oribi and suni.

Continuing along the E.N. 1, you cross the Limpopo River (250 Mt toll fee) to reach the town of **Xai-Xai**, formerly known as João Belo, after the Portuguese Minister of Colonies in the mid-1920s. Xai-Xai, the capital of Gaza Province, is a sprawling city with a population of 50 000.

Situated on the northern bank of the Rio Limpopo, once navigable by coastal steamers as far as Xai-Xai, the town was developed during the early 1900s as a satellite port to Lourenço Marques to serve the interior of the lower Limpopo region. The development plans included a railway line and the first section of the Gaza Railway, a narrow-gauge (0,75 m) line from Xai-Xai to Languene, was opened in October 1909. The line with its branch lines was completed in 1915, but was never linked to the other lines of the Great South Railway as was originally envisaged. At around the same time the town became an important centre for migrant labourers recruited by the Witwatersrand Native Labour Organisation to work on the gold mines.

The 50 km narrow-gauge railway line between Xai-Xai and Manjacaze is still in operation, against all odds. The train, hauled by a vintage 1920s Pullman locomotive, leaves Xai-Xai on Friday mornings and returns on Sunday afternoon. It's no luxury steam safari though as frequent stops are made along the way to carry out repairs to the train and the railway line.

Xai-Xai has a BCM bank, filling stations, a variety of shops, *Mercado Central* (central market), restaurants and several accommodation options. However, because there are no tourist attractions in and around the town, most visitors only stop here to replenish supplies, or to buy fuel before heading for the popular nearby beach.

The city is served daily by Oliviera and Virginia buses operating between Maputo and Beira in both directions.

A signpost on the eastern outskirts of the town indicates the 15 km tar road to **Praia do Xai-Xai**, a small resort with a large tidal pool, formed by a protective reef, offering safe swimming. The resort is fast regaining its popularity, especially with South African holiday-makers who are attracted by the good **angling** and **diving** opportunities on the seaward side. Several reefs, with depths ranging from 5 m to 25 m, can be explored by scuba divers along 6 km of the coast.

Accommodation in Praia do Xai-Xai is available at the **Hotel Complexo Halley**, at the northern edge of the town close to the beach. Also situated here is the **Parque de Campismo** which offers camp sites (some with power points) and hot water ablutions, two- and four-bed bungalows served by communal ablutions and kitchens. There is also a restaurant and bar. Fishing and diving charters can be arranged through a company based at the camp site. The derelict **Hotel Xai-Xai** was being repaired in October 1998.

A worthwhile outing is a visit to the beach at **Wenela**, 1,4 km south of Xai-Xai. It is accessible on foot or by following a four-wheel drive track which branches off the tar road 300 m south of the Golfinho Azul restaurant. A reef just off the beach forms a large **tidal pool**, which drains empty at low tide but offers good swimming and rock angling opportunities. On the reef opposite Wenela House is a blow hole which spouts water into the air at high tide.

Back on the E.N. 1, the road traverses gently undulating countryside dotted with clumps of coconut palms and pleasant coastal bush. At Chidenguele a turnoff indicates the track to **Praia do Chidenguele**. Turn right into the village and opposite the trading store right again onto a sandy track. After about 1,7 km the track meanders along the southern edge of the 25 km-long Lagoa Nhanzume and 3 km later reaches the resort of **Paraiso de Chidenguele**.

The resort's tastefully furnished self-catering cottages are tucked away among indigenous coastal bush high up on the coastal dunes. Vehicles are left at a central parking area from where a footpath leads through the bush, with a profusion of cycads and interesting birdlife, to the accommodation units. When completed, the resort will consists of 16 chalets of varying sizes, sleeping two, four, six and eight people, and a restaurant.

The coast varies from sandy to rocky beach, providing opportunities for **rock and surf angling**. Close inshore a 25 m-wide gully, ranging in depth from 3-5 m, creates ideal conditions for **snorkelling**, while **diving** is possible at five easily accessible reefs.

North of Chidenguele the E.N. 1 winds further inland and then crosses into Inhambane Province. You then reach the town of Quissico, on a high hill overlooking the lagoon of the same name. Another 42 km on the road crosses Lago Poelela and then reaches the town of Inharrime.

Continuing further up the coast, the turnoff to Praia da Závora is reached 12 km beyond Inharrime. The resort is about 17 km further along a sandy track, negotiable in a four-wheel drive vehicle. **Praia da Závora** is renowned for its good **game-fishing**, and **snorkelling** enthusiasts can swim to the gully a short way offshore and explore the fascinating underwater world.

Accommodation options at **Závora Lodge** range from serviced, self-catering bungalows (sleeping four or six people) and houses (sleeping six or eight people) to camp sites with ablutions with cold water. There is also a restaurant and bar. Boats, paddle skis and rods are for hire, but there is no dive operation at the resort.

As you continue north along the E.N. 1, the coconut palms become increasingly dominant. At the roadside village of Lindela a signpost to the right indicates the road to Inhambane, the capital of Inhambane Province. Save for the odd pothole, the 33 km road is in good condition. Along the way the wrecks of numerous military vehicles involved in ambushes and landmine explosions serve as reminders of the country's civil war.

Just before entering Inhambane, a signpost opposite a fish factory indicates the turnoff to three of the resorts along the coast south of Inhambane. A four-wheel drive vehicle is essential to negotiate the tracks. Turn right here and after following a meandering track through cashew nut and coconut plantations for 14 km you reach a fork. The left-hand track continues for another 3 km to **Baia dos Cocos** (Coconut Bay), a small resort behind the dunes, a short way from the beach. Facilities here consist of camp sites (with little shade), served by ablutions with cold water. A few derelict rondavels decorated with faded murals of marine scenes suggest that the bay was once far more popular.

To reach Guinjata Bay, ignore the turnoff to Coconut Bay and continue straight. The road meanders through groves of coconut palms and after 6 km you look down onto the sea. About 1 km on you will reach the turnoff to **Guinjata Bay Resort**, which lies at the southern end of Jangamo Bay, a wide sweeping bay fringed by high vegetated dunes.

There are five **diving spots** with depths ranging from 10-24 m in close proximity to the resort and some divers have ranked the reefs on a par with the Maldives in terms of variety and abundance of fish. Best known is **Manta Reef**, a 10 m dive which has as its chief attractions manta rays with a wingspan of up to 6 m, moray eels up to 3 m long, enormous potato bass and turtles. Whale sharks are another attraction and at times up to 20 or more congregate in the bay.

With no less than 28 species of **gamefish**, the coast here is an angler's paradise. Marlin and sailfish occur in abundance and Guinjata holds the world record for kingfish; a 43,8 kg

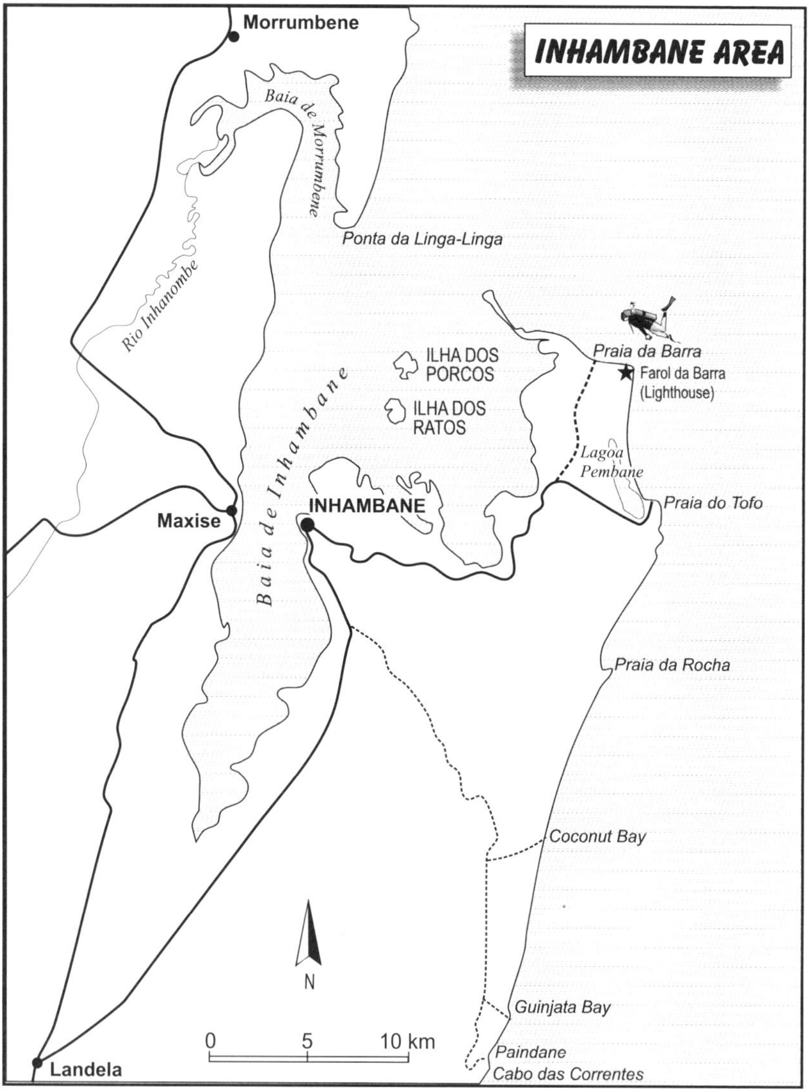
INHAMBANE AREA
Morrumbene
Baia de Morrumbene
Ponta da Linga-Linga
Rio Inhanombe
ILHA DOS PORCOS
ILHA DOS RATOS
Praia da Barra
Farol da Barra (Lighthouse)
Lagoa Pembane
Praia do Tofo
Baia de Inhambane
INHAMBANE
Maxise
Praia da Rocha
Coconut Bay
N
Guinjata Bay
0
5
10 km
Paindane
Cabo das Correntes
Landela

specimen was caught on a 15 kg line. Other commonly caught species include wahoo and dorado.

The beach offers safe **swimming** and **Paindane Reef** (see below), 3 km further south offers excellent opportunities for **snorkelling**. Other popular activities include **salt-water flyfishing** and **spearfishing**.

A wide range of accommodation is available; from basic self-catering four-bed rondavels with communal ablutions to luxury two- or three-bedroom reed chalets and fully equipped guest houses for eight, 12 or 20 people. Campers have a choice of open camp sites, or *baraca* shelters (reed huts with waist-high walls and cement floors) with tap water and power points. Other amenities include a restaurant, bar, laundry and freezer room. A full range of services and equipment, including boat hire, fishing charters and diving charters, is offered.

To reach **Paindane**, ignore the Guinjata Bay turnoff and continue straight along a sandy track that requires engaging four-wheel drive. The track meanders through coconut palms for 4 km and then ascends to the resort on the crest of the dunes at Cabo das Correntes (Cape of Currents).

At Paindane a 600 m-long reef embraces the coastline close inshore, providing easy access to what is widely acclaimed as Mozambique's most spectacular shore entry **snorkelling** site. At low tide it is possible to walk along the reef to the 3 m-deep pools, which sport 22 species of coral and an amazing variety and abundance of tropical fish.

On the seaward side of the reef a 30 m drop-off creates excellent conditions for **rock and surf angling** and among the commonly caught species are mata-hari, kingfish, pompano, stumpnose and bonefish. **Gamefishing** is, likewise, outstanding and catches include black marlin, sailfish, kingfish, rainbow runner, prodigal son and tuna.

Accommodation ranges from camping sites and *baracas* (reed huts with waist-high walls and cement floors) with communal hot water ablutions to four-bed and six-bed rondavels. There are also five reed and thatch fully equipped bungalows sleeping seven to eight people. Each bungalow has a kitchen, lounge and *en suite* bathroom.

A short way beyond the Coconut Bay/Guinjata Bay/Paindane turnoff you will reach the pleasant coastal city of **Inhambane** (see p 95). It has all the necessary amenities for visitors – a BCM bank, filling stations, *cabines públicas* (at the

TDM office in Avenida Eduardo Mondlane), a fish factory (Pescom) and one of the best municipal markets along the coast.  Among the restaurants to try are **Restaurante Maçaroca** (opposite the BCM bank) and the **Ti Jamu Snack Bar** which overlooks the bay and specialises in shellfish and chicken dishes. Fresh bread and delicious pastries can be bought at **Pastelaria Moçambicana**.

Accommodation in Inhambane is available at the **Inhambane Hotel**, which sees few tourists as they inevitably head for the more popular resorts at Praia da Barra and Praia do Tofo described below. Budget travellers and backpackers can head for **Pachiça Backpackers Hostel** which offers accommodation on the beachfront. The hostel is a few hundred metres beyond the jetty on the right-hand side of the road.

To get to Praia da Barra, turn right into Avenida da Independência (opposite the jetty) and follow it to the railway station where you turn right. Take the second turnoff to the left, cross the railway line, and continue on tar along a scenic drive through coconut palms. About 15 km beyond the airport turnoff you will reach the signposted track to Barra Reef and Barra Lodge. The first 2,2 km of the road can be negotiated in a sedan car, but the remaining 5 km to Barra Reef is a track with deep sand, suitable only in four-wheel drive. Guests of Barra Lodge can leave their vehicles at the signposted parking area, from where they are transferred to the lodge.

Sheltered by a high forested dune, **Barra Lodge** is situated on a long sandy spit, bounded by kilometres of unspoilt beaches and a mangrove estuary, with coconut trees providing a tropical beach atmosphere.  There are several excellent reefs nearby, offering **diving** from 9-40 m. The inshore reefs support a variety of small tropical fish, while a rich diversity and abundance of gamefish can be seen on the deeper reefs.

A 100 m drop-off, 6 km out to sea, provides excellent conditions for **angling** and to date some 22 species of gamefish have been caught in the area. Among these are sailfish (average 35 kg), kingfish (average 8 kg), marlin, king mackerel, barracuda, wahoo and yellowfin tuna.

Barra Lodge offers accommodation in self-catering cottages with a lounge, dining room, two bedrooms with six single beds and a bathroom with shower and toilet. The kitchen is equipped with a two-plate gas stove, fridge, crockery, cutlery and cooking utensils. Bedding is provided and the cottages are serviced daily. A more basic and less expensive option is the *casitas,* which have two beds and an *en suite* shower and toilet. Bunk houses catering for backpackers and camping sites are also available. The main complex has a restaurant offering a choice of fresh seafood meals and a bar.

The resort offers a wide range of activities including snorkelling, day trips on board a 10 m catamaran yacht, fishing charters, dhow trips and scuba diving. There is a fully equipped dive centre and Resort, Open Water 1 and Advanced NAUI diving courses are offered by Barra Lodge Dive Charters (see p 58 for addresses of dive services).

Also on offer are horseriding on the beach, microlight flights, quad bike safaris through the coconut plantations, and water-skiing, as well as parasailing and sailing on Hobiecats and Lasers in the bay area.

The owners of Barra Lodge also plan to build another resort, Flamingo Bay, on an island about 2,5 km west of the lodge. Accommodation will consist of reed A-framed self-catering units and bungalows built on stilts in the estuary.

Barra Reef, a few hundred metres beyond Barra Lodge, is geared at families and facilities include tastefully furnished self-catering brick and thatch chalets, comprising a kitchen, bedroom sleeping two people and *en suite* facilities. The camp sites, set among coconut palm trees, are served by clean ablutions with hot and cold water. A restaurant is planned for a later stage.

Activities include **diving** and **fishing** charters. A 10 m yacht is available for charters to Linga Linga (see p 98) and for **snorkelling** excursions. Also planned are **walks** in the mangrove swamps at low tide and **canoeing** on the estuary at high tide.

To reach Tofu, backtrack for 7 km and at the junction turn left and follow a tar road for just over 6 km. Less than 1 km before reaching Tofo you will see the signposted turnoff to the rustic **Turtle Cove**, which is 300 m off the road. Run by surfing enthusiast Nick Tasioulas, the resort is a mere 500 m from Tofinho and is popular with surfers and backpackers. It offers camp sites, dome tents, bungalows, a restaurant serving excellent meals and a bar. Surfboards, snorkelling gear and spearguns can be hired.

The turnoff to Albatroz and Casa Barry is signposted about 400 m further on. Situated high on a dune with views over Tofo

Bay, **Albatroz** offers accommodation in fully catered or self-catering chalets sleeping six people, a restaurant and bar. Fishing charters and other activities can be arranged.

The turnoff to **Casa Barry** is signposted a short way on. Built among causerina trees a stone's throw from the beach, accommodation consists of fully-equipped A-frame shelters with grass roofs and reeds. There is also a restaurant and bar, as well as camp sites with cold water showers.

From Casa Barry it is a 1,7 km drive to **Tofinho**, a rocky headland renowned for its excellent surfing, just south of Tofu. The track ends at a large pyramid-shaped monument erected in honour of the nationalist movement Frelimo. The monument originally bore the fist of freedom, but this was vandalised a number of years ago.

A short walk from the monument brings you to the spot where Frelimo nationalists were tortured by the Portuguese Secret Service and then dumped into a gully linked to the sea. The bones of some of these unfortunate victims were displayed at the spot in a glass cage until a few years ago, but this has since been removed.

At **Praia do Tofu** the coastline forms a wide sweeping bay which is popular with sunbathers, surfers and anglers. Its only drawback is that it lies right up against Lagoa Pembane, a large coastal lake which attracts swarms of mosquitoes.

Accommodation options at Praia do Tofu include rooms at the **Clube Ferroviário** and **Nordin's Lodge**, four self-catering beachfront chalets, sleeping four people each. Situated right on the beach, the **Hotel Marhinos Moçambique** reopened in mid-1999 and has rooms at reasonable rates, a restaurant and bar. Snorkels and goggles are available while scuba diving and angling can be arranged at extra cost. Excellent meals can be enjoyed at the **Restaurante Ferroviário** which has an extensive menu featuring fish and meat dishes.

ROUTE 4

INHAMBANE TO INHASSORO

DISTANCE: 480 km **TIME**: 2 days plus **ROAD CONDITIONS**: Tar, except for sandy track to Morrungulo and Pomene. **FUEL**: Inhambane, Maxise, Vilankulo, at E.N. 1 turnoff to Inhassoro **LINKING ROUTES**: Routes 3 and 5

From Inhambane, backtrack to Lindela on the E.N. 1 and turn north, continuing for 26 km to the town of **Maxise** (pronounced Masheesh). Situated on the western shores of Baia de Inhambane, economic activity centres around fishing and the processing of copra, the white flesh of the mature nut of the coconut tree which is used to make coconut oil.

Maxise has a BCM bank, filling station, a variety of shops and several restaurants. The best accommodation is at **Campismo de Maxise**, situated on the beachfront as you enter the town. Options range from two-bedded brick and thatch bungalows with hot water showers and two-bedded beach houses with communal hot water ablutions to camp sites with fireplaces and power points and small sites for backpackers, with hot water ablutions. There is also an on site restaurant which offers excellent meals. Another restaurant well worth a try is the **Stop Snack Bar**, an open-air restaurant with a magnificent view over the bay.

A popular outing from Maxise is a **dhow trip** to Inhambane where you can explore the town on foot and enjoy a meal before making the return journey. Ferries leave every 10-15 minutes from about 05:30 or 06:00 in the morning until dark and can take anything from just over 30 minutes to two hours, depending on the wind. Another option is to take a day trip to Linga Linga (see p 97).

Heading north along the E.N. 1, the next town you pass through is Morrumbene and 40 km on you reach the village of **Massinga**, where beautiful clay pots can be bought at the market. **Restaurante Dalilo** is well-known for its peri-peri chicken and at night for its disco, equipped with what must be the most sophisticated equipment north of Maputo.

The turnoff to Morrungulo is signposted about 8 km north of Massinga and you will reach the bay after travelling through coconut plantations for 13 km. The track is best negotiated in a four-wheel drive vehicle.

The reefs off **Morrungulo** offer excellent **diving** and attractions include 14 species of nudibranches, four species of firefish and rare species such as bar-tailed flathead and royal angelfish. Among the numerous diving spots are **Baixo Silvia**, a 14,5 km-long reef with depths from 10-23 m and the 8,5 km-long **New Year's Reef**. Other interesting sites are **Caves and Overhangs** with its network of tunnels through the reef, and the **Coral Garden of Ede**n where nine species of hard coral can be seen.

The **Morrungulo Resort** is situated just off the beach under a grove of coconut palms. The self-catering chalets have two bedrooms sleeping four persons, a fully equipped kitchen with a two-plate gas cooker and deep freeze, a living room and hot water shower. Visitors can also opt for *baracas* (a thatch-roof structure with waist-high reed walls and a cement floor) with power points, *casitas* (double-storey *baracas*), or grassed camp sites with communal hot water ablutions.

Island Style Diving, South Africa tel (011) 791-2634/5/6/7, fax 791-0337, offers full CMAS 1 Star courses with international certification, airfills, equipment hire, scuba and snorkelling trips and fishing charters. The dive camp has two self-catering five-bed units with a fully equipped communal kitchen and shower and an eight-bed chalet with four bedrooms, fully equipped kitchen and two showers.

Excellent boat **angling** can be enjoyed off the coast of Morrungulo and among the species to be caught are king mackerel, four species of kingfish, barracuda, wahoo, yellowfin tuna, bonito and sailfish. Boat charters and equipment can be arranged through Island Style Diving.

About 250 m north of the Morrungulo turnoff, the E.N. 1 veers to the left. As you enter the bend you will notice a track continuing straight ahead; this is the route to **Pomene**. The 69 km-long track is, however, in very poor condition and will deter all but the most determined. The coastal woodlands and dune vegetation in the area fall within the **Reserva de Pomene** (Pomene Reserve).

Sheltered by a rocky headland, **Pomene** lies in the curve of a gentle bay which ends in a sandspit, named Barra Falsa by the early Portuguese navigators. Options for divers include **Baixo Silvia**, the **Pomene Wall** (10-20 m) and some outstanding diving at the 7 km-long **Zambia Reef,** about 18 km north of Pomene.

The beach offers good **swimming** and hours can be spent exploring the potholes and pools that are exposed at low tide on the rock shelf just below the resort. The dilapidated Pomene resort, which fell into disrepair during the civil war, has been acquired by Pestana Hotels and will be rebuilt completely.

Continuing north along the E.N. 1 from the Pomene turnoff, the road winds through cashew nut plantations interspersed with coconut palms, passing through the old Portuguese settlement of Mchachengue after 15 km. About 65 km on you pass through the village of Mapihane and after another 31 km reach the turnoff to Vilankulo (previously Vilanculos). From the turnoff it is a 19 km drive along a narrow but good tar road to the coastal town of **Vilankulo**, the springboard to Magaruque and Benguerra islands, 10 km and 15 km away respectively (see pp 93-4 and 91-3).

If you are not bound by a tight time schedule, contact Margie Toens of **Paraiso Services** (which is well signposted) on arrival. Her service is aimed at adventurous travellers and she will advise you on accommodation and transfers to the islands by speed boat or dhow.

Vilankulo offers a variety of accommodation options, among them **Casa Josef's** rustic reed huts and the well-known **Hotel Dona Ana**, both on the beachfront. The hotel was built by the well-known Portuguese entrepreneur, Joaquim Alves, who had extensive business interests in Vilankulo and the Arquipélago do Bazaruto, and named after his wife. There is also a *campismo* (camp site) just off the beach which we were warned against staying at because of several incidents of theft.

A few kilometres north of the town is **Aguia Negra**, a resort offering accommodation in A-frame chalets. Other amenities include a restaurant and bar and a swimming pool. Activities range from deep-sea fishing and cruises to the islands on board a luxury yacht to diving, parasailing and water-skiing.

A short way on, the luxurious and stylish **Vilanculos Lodge** comprises 10 tastefully furnished chalets, on ironwood stilts, set among the coastal bush. Boardwalks connect the chalets to the restaurant and bar overlooking the sea. There is also a swimming pool and pool deck. Activities include island hopping boat trips, deep-sea fishing and diving, yacht cruises, sailing, windsurfing, paddle-skiing and canoeing.

Another option, **Baia do Paraiso**, is reached by taking the airport turnoff near the entrance to the town. After 2 km turn

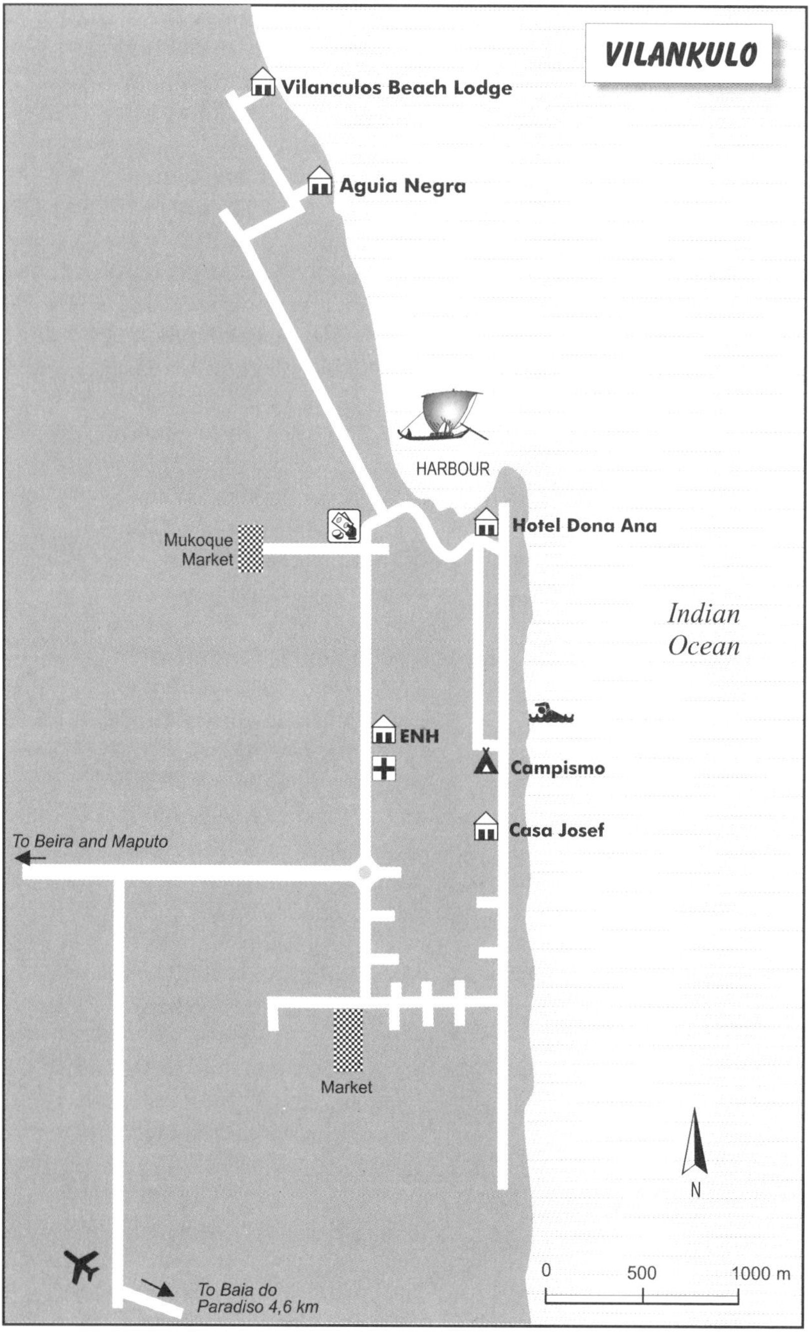
VILANKULO
Vilanculos Beach Lodge
Aguia Negra
HARBOUR
Mukoque
Market
Hotel Dona Ana
Indian
Ocean
ENH
Campismo
Casa Josef
To Beira and Maputo
Market
N
0
500
1000 m
To Baia do
Paradiso 4,6 km

left and continue for 4,6 km along a sandy track to the resort, which lies on a high dune with magnificent views across the sea to Benguerra Island. Accommodation comprises A-frame chalets sleeping six people. Chalets sleeping two to four people are planned. A restaurant with bar is also available and visitors can choose accommodation on a full board basis, or self-catering. Activities range from snorkelling off Bangue Island and diving to fishing trips and boat hire.

Vilankulo International Airport is 5 km from the town centre and is serviced by regular SabinAir flights from Maputo and SA Airlink flights from Nelspruit in South Africa's Mpumalanga Province (see pp 46 and 56). Amenities include a BCM bank, filling station, several restaurants, a variety of shops and *Mercado Central.*

From Vilankulo, backtrack to the E.N. 1 where you turn right, and continue for 49 km to the signposted turnoff to **Inhassoro**. This coastal village is reached after a 14 km journey on a narrow tar road. Much smaller than Vilankulo, it is a long-standing favourite with anglers and the gateway to Ilha da Bazaruto which lies about 28 km offshore.

The **Hotel Seta** is situated right on the beach amidst a grove of large shady trees. Accommodation is available in two-bedded bungalows and there is also a thatched central complex with a restaurant, designed without windows to allow the sea breeze to cool down the interior, and a bar and patio with a view across the sea. The adjacent camp site has hot water showers and is popular with angling enthusiasts. There is a shop and restaurant at the **Complexo Salema** which also has basic accommodation. It is reached by turning right after passing the Hotel Seta and continuing for about 1 km to the bus terminus.

8

CENTRAL MOZAMBIQUE

Mozambique's three central provinces – Sofala, Manica and Tete – hold considerable scope for adventure travellers, trailists, mountain climbers and birding enthusiasts. Among its attractions are the mountainous highlands bordering on Zimbabwe – a paradise for birders and trailists, Parque Nacional da Gorongosa with its wild scenery and Monte Gorongosa, where one of southern Africa's most elusive birds is to be found. Adventurous mountaineers will find the challenge presented by the monte-ilhas, *or inselbergen, of northern Manica Province hard to resist, while Cahora Bassa offers exciting tiger fishing possibilities. The region is, however, not as well developed from a tourism point of view as the three southernmost provinces.*

Bounded in the east by the white beaches of the Indian Ocean, the Rio Save in the south and the Rio Zambeze in the north, Sofala Province is characterised by coastal plains covered by miombo woodlands and a narrow band of dune forest along the coast. Further inland, along its western boundary with Manica Province, the plains rise gradually to the uplands of the Planalto de Chimoio where it merges with Zimbabwe's Eastern Highlands. Here there are montane evergreen forests and grasslands. To the north, Manica Province borders on Tete Province which is bounded by three countries – Zimbabwe, Zambia and Malawi. Mopane and baobab savannas are characteristic in the south of Tete Province, while dry deciduous miombo and deciduous miombo woodlands occur in the north.

The largest cultural groups of Sofala Province are the Sena and the Shona; the latter are the dominant group in adjoining Manica Province. Manica is also home to the Sena and the Nyungwe, while the Nyanya, Nyungwe and Sena cultural groups live in Tete Province.

Economic activity in Sofala Province centres around the production of citrus fruit, cashew nuts and sugar, while the Indian Ocean is a rich source of fish and the famous Beira prawns. Manica Province is the country's second largest producer of citrus fruit, with coal mining the most important economic activity in Tete Province.

The region has a long history of coastal trading and reports by Islamic travellers provide evidence that trade centres were already established along the coast of the "Land of Sofala" by the 10th century. Surprisingly, no material dating to before the 16th century has been found at the settlement of Sofala, some 40 km south of Beira. Built on dunes that were constantly lashed by the sea, much of the town was inundated in the 18th century. However, a significant archaeological site was discovered in 1977 at Chibuene, some 250 km further south, in Inhambane Province. These coastal trade centres were linked to the interior along ancient trade routes to the Monomotapa chieftaincy with its gold mines. Africa's fourth largest river, the Rio Zambeze, provided easy access to Tete, which was an important river port by the end of the 15th century, and Zumbo further upstream.

Control over Manica and Sofala provinces was established in 1891 when a concession over the area was granted to the Companhia de Moçambique. The area was incorporated into the Portuguese administration only in 1942 when the charter expired.

Tete Province fits like a piece of a jigsaw puzzle between three former British territories and provides an interesting study of how the boundaries of Africa were drawn following the "Scramble for Africa" by European powers. Portugal's territorial claims over the area were finally recognised in 1891 when Britain and Portugal signed a treaty.

Barragem de Chicamba (Chicamba Dam)

7

A deep, narrow gorge a few kilometres downstream of the confluence of the Rio Messica and the Rio Revué provided an ideal site for the construction of the Barragem de Chicamba (Chicamba Dam), one of only three large dams in Mozambique. Behind the 125 m-high wall, water was pushed back for several kilometres, flooding the courses of the Messica and Revué rivers, as well as numerous small rivers, to create an irregularly shaped dam with many small bays and inlets. Built as a water storage dam to supply Chimoio and to exploit the agricultural potential of the area, the dam also has a hydro-electric power station with a capacity of 38 MW. Following the development of Casa Msika (see route 7) it has also become a popular stopover with tourists travelling from Zimbabwe to Beira and has an outstanding reputation for bass angling.

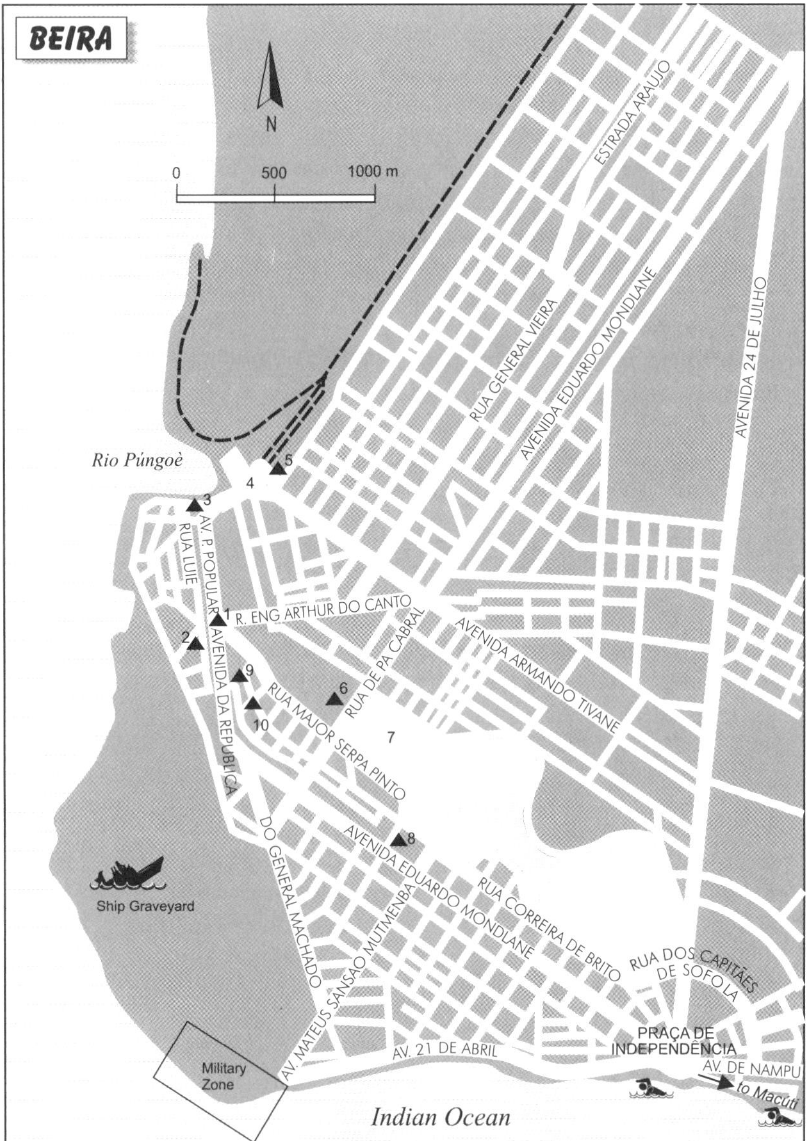

▲ **Places of Interest**

1 Praça do Metical
2 Casa Portugal
3 Casa Infante Sagres
4 Praça dos Trabalhadores
5 Estação dos Caminhos de Ferro
6 Casa dos Bicos
7 Clube de Golfe
8 Cathedral de Nosso Senhora de Rosario
9 Praça do Minicipio
10 Mercado Central

Beira

5

Beira, Mozambique's second largest city, lies on the northern banks of the delta formed by the Rio Púngoè and the Rio Búzi. Here the Mozambican coast swings sharply to the northeast to form a sweeping bay, ideally suited for shipping. Originally known as Aruângua, the city developed around a base established here by a Portuguese official, Joaquim Carlos Paiva de Andrade, in 1884.

The importance of the settlement grew in 1892 when it was decided to shift the capital of Sofala Province from the ancient trading town of Sofala to Beira. Its subsequent growth is largely due to the decision to build a harbour and a railway line to the interior. In 1898 the railway line to Umtali (now Mutare) in the former Southern Rhodesia was completed and the harbour facilities on the northern banks of the Rio Púngoè estuary were expanded and improved.

The port was owned by the British South Africa Company until 1949 when it became Portuguese state property; together with the railway line it provided a vital link to Southern Rhodesia. Following the declaration of UDI by Southern Rhodesia in November 1965, Beira made the world headlines when the British government sent a warship to blockade the port to prevent imports from reaching the landlocked country. Owing to its strategic importance the railway line became a target of Frelimo's struggle against Portuguese rule and later also came under frequent attack by Renamo rebels. This caused the port to come to a standstill for several years during the civil war and resulted in the economic decline of the city. In a bid to decrease the dependence of Southern African Development and Co-ordinating Conference member states on South Africa, the Corredor Beira project was launched in 1985. The US $500 million project included the dredging of the port's 200 m-wide entrance channel and the construction of container and oil terminals.

The name Beira was given in honour of D Luis Filipe, the Prince of Beira and son of one of the last Portuguese monarchs, who visited Manica and Sofala at the beginning of the century. A city with 300 000 people, Beira's architecture is a curious mixture of high-rise buildings interspersed by British and Portuguese architectural styles, a heritage it owes to the fact that the port was a British possession until 1949. The commercial sector is centred around the old town with its narrow streets, while the residential area is characterised by wide *avenidas* (avenues).

Beira owes much of its fame as a popular holiday destination to its inviting beaches and prawns. Long stretches of white beach hug the coast along Avenida das FPLM and **Macúti beach** offers excellent swimming. The beach and the upmarket suburb is named after a trawler, the *Macúti*, which was wrecked nearby in 1917 and later towed here to stop the erosion of the beach in front of the lighthouse.

A walking tour

Numbers on the map on p 128 correspond with those in the text. A convenient starting point for a tour of the city's sights is the **Praça do Metical** (1), a square appropriately named after the country's currency, as there are several banks in this area. Unlikely to escape attention is the nearby **Casa Portugal** (2), or Portugal House. Its architecture is typical of the Portuguese building style of the early 1900s and it is easily recognised by the red brick exterior. From the square travel down Rua Luis Inacio and then turn right, continuing to the Largo Infante Sagres at the end of Avenida Poder Popular where the **Casa Infante Sagres** (3) is the most conspicuous building. The neo-classical double-storey building with arched windows on the ground floor and colonnades on the first floor now serves as the headquarters of the Manica Company.

A short distance further the **Praça dos Trabalhadores** (4) (Workers' Square) and the **Estação dos Caminhos de Ferro** (5), or Railway Station, are reached. Completed in 1966 at a cost of over R1 million, the station building features a concave-shaped concrete roof, with a fish pond forming the focal point of the main hall.

From the station, go down Avenida Armando Tivane and then right into Avenida Eduardo Mondlane. Keep an eye out to the right for the pointed roofs of the **Casa dos Bicos** (6) at the city's showgrounds. The defunct 18-hole **Clube de Golfe** (7) (Golf Club) opposite the showgrounds dates back to 1907. Turn left into Rua Major Serpa Pinto and continue to the **Cathedral de Nosso Senhora de Rosario** (8) (Cathedral of Our Lady of the Rosary) in Avenida Eduardo Mondlane. The cathedral, built partially from dressed stone from the 16th century Forteleza de Sofala, was completed in 1925, 18 years after work started.

From here, head for the **Praça do Minicipio** (9), or Municipal Square, with its central water feature and palm trees. Dominating the buildings overlooking the square is the imposing three-storey Municipal Building. Diagonally across from the square, between Rua Correiro de Brito and Rua Jaime Ferreira, is the **Mercado Central** (10) or central market, where fresh fish, fruit, vegetables and arts and crafts are sold.

Where to eat in Beira

Restaurante Arcadia, 200 Rua Poder Popular, tel (03) 33 22 66. Better known as Johnny's Place, the Arcadia has been a popular restaurant for over four decades.

Restaurante Biques, Avenida das FPLM, tel (03) 31 30 51. Located on the beach, part of this large thatched restaurant overlooks the sea. Popular with South African visitors, it has an extensive menu featuring seafood and continental dishes.

Restaurante O Zequinhas, Avenida das FPLM, tel (03) 31 30 93.

Restaurante Pic-Nic, 115 Rua Costa Serrão, tel (03) 32 65 18. Situated in the city centre, Pic-Nic offers an extensive menu, good food and fast service. One of Beira's most popular restaurants, booking is essential.

Restaurante The Cutty Sark, 296 Avenida das FPLM. tel (03) 31 30 37. Located on the beachfront in Macúti suburb, the complex has an excellent restaurant, swimming pool, sauna and a popular disco.

Where to stay in Beira

Hotels

Hotel Embaixador, Rua Major Serpa Pinto, tel (03) 32 31 21. This four-star hotel is located in the town centre.

Hotel Moçambique, 3 Rua do Bagamoyo, tel (03) 32 50 11. Situated in downtown Beira, this four-star hotel was refurbished in 1998. It offers air-conditioned rooms with satellite TV and telephone, a restaurant and nearby swimming pool.

Hotel Tivoli Beira, 363 Avenida de Bagamoio, tel (03) 32 85 70. A three-star hotel refurbished in 1998.

Hotel Miramar, 157 Rua Vila Boas Trução, tel (03) 32 22 83. A two-star hotel close to the beach in the Ponté-Gêa area.

Guesthouses

Residencial Infante, Avenida Jaime Ferreira, tel (03) 32 30 42.

Camp sites

Biques Camping, Avenida das FPLM. A pleasant camp site situated under causerina trees right on the beach near the Macúti lighthouse. Amenities include a restaurant with a good selection of meals, a busy bar and hot water ablutions.

Clube Náutico, Avenida das FPLM, tel (03) 31 30 93. Camp sites with cold water ablutions and basic huts with sand floors and electricity situated at the yacht club. There is also a restaurant.

Cahora Bassa

Over countless aeons the Rio Zambeze carved an awesome gorge through the rugged mountains about 130 km upstream of Tete. Here the Zambeze tumbled down a series of wild white-water rapids and in the days when the river served as a highway into the interior of southern Africa this was as far as vessels could navigate. The rapids became known as Kebrabassa, a Chewa name meaning "the end of the work", for the rapids heralded the end of the labours of the paddlers recruited by the early traders. The name later became corrupted to Cahora Bassa.

The idea of harnessing the waters of the Zambeze was first investigated by the Portuguese in the late 1950s and Cahora Bassa, about 500 km downstream of Kariba Dam, proved to be the ideal site. The contract for the construction of the dam was awarded in 1969 to Zamco, a consortium of companies from South Africa, Italy, France and West Germany, and construction began soon afterwards. A coffer dam was built above the site of the proposed dam wall and water was diverted through two large tunnels excavated through the slopes of the ravine.

Frelimo was vehemently opposed to the project which it viewed as a symbol of colonial exploitation. Despite an international campaign against the dam and threats to sabotage it, the project was completed in 1977. It comprises the storage dam with its 160 m-high wall and a capacity of 52 000 million m^3, a hydro-electric power station with five turbines capable of generating 2 000 MW and two 1 400 km-long power lines to Irene, near Pretoria in South Africa. It is the second largest such scheme in Africa and among the 10 largest in the world. The Portuguese government owns 82 per cent of the shares in the power station and the Mozambican government holds the remaining 18 per cent.

One of the largest construction projects of its kind in the world at the time, some 210 000 m^2 of rock were excavated for the foundations of the 303 m-long double curved concrete arch wall, while 450 000 m^2 of concrete were used on the project. When full, the water dams up for 270 km behind the wall and covers a surface area of 2 660 km^2. To the west of the wall the dam is confined to a 200 to 300 m-wide strip of water for 35 km and then branches out into a 30 km-long eastern basin which is bounded in the west by a number of islands. Then follows an 80 km-long central basin and finally the western basin.

Electricity was transmitted to the South African electricity utility, Eskom, on a fairly regular basis until 1980. As a result of increasing acts of sabotage by Renamo rebels the supply agreement was later suspended and after October 1983 no power was transmitted to South Africa from Cahora Bassa. Following the signing of the Nkomati Accord in March 1984 (see p 8), the Cahora Bassa Agreement providing for the delivery of power to South Africa was signed two months later. Because of sabotage attacks by Renamo the infrastructure could, however, only be rehabilitated after the 1992 peace accord. Repairs to the power station's infrastructure, including more than 2 000 damaged electricity pylons, cost about US $137 million and the flow of power to South Africa was restored in 1997; but an agreement on the tariff for electricity could not be reached. An agreement was also reached with the Zimbabwean electricity utility, ZEZA, for the supply of 500 MW to that country and a transmission line was built from Songo to Bindura in Zimbabwe.

Contrary to expectations, some kapenta (a small pelagic fish introduced into Lake Kariba from Lake Tanganyika in the 1960s) survived the turbines of Kariba and established a healthy population in Cahora Bassa. Realising the potential of Cahora Bassa as a source of inexpensive protein, several Zimbabwean companies began the commercial exploitation of kapenta in the second half of the 1990s. The rigs, with their large circular nets, take to the water at sunset and the fish are lured to the surface by bright lights and then scooped up.

September to December is usually the best time for kapenta fishing and a rig can catch up to 1 000 kg of kapenta a night. The vessels return to the shore at sunrise and the kapenta are then dried before being marketed.

The lake is also fast gaining popularity as a superb angling destination. Tiger fish average around 4-5 kg, although specimens of 8, 10 and 14 kg have been landed. Other species to be caught include bream, eastern bottlenose, chessa, vundu and brown squeaker.

Monte Gorongosa

Along the eastern edge of the Planalto Chimoio the granite massif of Monte Gorongosa rises to a height of 1 862 m, making it the fourth highest peak in the country. Lying within the path of the moisture-laden coastal winds, the slopes of the mountains are clothed in magnificent forests of fig trees, yellowwoods, red mahogany and lemonwood. Numerous streams trickle down the damp slopes, which also support a rich variety of mosses, ferns and delicate orchids. On the summit the vegetation is a patchwork of montane grasslands, proteaveld and rocky outcrops that provide a habitat for sagewood, wild peach and tree-fuchsia.

Monte Gorongosa is the only place in southern Africa where the green-headed oriole, one of the sub-continent's rarest birds, occurs, and it is a must for avid birders. Other species you might tick include blue-spotted dove, silvery-cheeked hornbill, eastern honeyguide, white-breasted alethe and Chirinda apalis. The mountain is also a paradise for trailists, with numerous exciting possibilities. Birders and trailists should be fit though, as the terrain is difficult and the going tough.

The best way to see the elusive green-headed oriole, or to explore the mountain on foot, is to hire guides and porters from *Senhor* Pedro Chichone, who has a small base camp at the foot of the mountain.

Parque Nacional da Gorongosa

At the time of Mozambique's independence the Parque Nacional da Gorongosa was the flagship of the country's conservation areas. Proclaimed as a game reserve covering

100 000 ha in 1921, it was subsequently enlarged and at a later stage reduced to its current size of 377 000 ha.

Bounded by the Rio Urema in the east and Monte Gorongosa in the west, it lies at the southern end of the Great Rift Valley which is about 40 km wide here. At the lowest point of the valley the Rio Urema forms a lake which increases from 10 km^2 to over 200 km^2 during the summer floods. The park's vegetation is a mosaic of miombo woodlands, seasonally in-undated floodplains and termitaria islands dotted with palm trees, fever tree parklands and baobabs.

Until the late 1970s Gorongosa was regarded as one of Africa's great game parks and its prolific wildlife included more than 12 000 buffalo, 7 000 blue wildebeest, 3 500 hippo, 3 000 Burchell's zebra, 3 000 waterbuck and 2 500 elephant. Years of bloody civil war changed all of this, especially as the Gorongosa area was once the stronghold of the Renamo rebel movement. The rebels first attacked the park headquarters in 1981, and occupied the park the following year. For the next seven years control over the park changed several times and government forces pounded rebel positions with aerial bombardments on a number of occasions. The Renamo camps were finally overrun by government forces in 1989.

A survey conducted by the World Wide Fund for Nature in 1994 revealed that there were only 108 elephants left, with the waterbuck population down to 129. No buffalo, hippo, blue wildebeest and eland were counted.

A rehabilitation programme was launched in 1995 and with conservation policies in place game numbers will slowly increase, although certain species need to be reintroduced. Given sufficient time Gorongosa could regain its former status as one of Africa's great game parks.

The park does offer some worthwhile birding though. Large flocks of flamingoes and waterfowl are attracted to the seasonal vleis and Lake Urema; crowned cranes occur on the floodplains, while the miombo woodlands support a rich diversity of species.

ROUTE 5

INHASSORO TO BEIRA AND QUELIMANE

DISTANCE: 990 km **TIME**: 2 days plus **ROAD CONDITIONS**: Inhassoro to Beira 475 km tar; Dondo to Rio Zambeze 224 km rough track requiring 4x4, 17 km tar; Rio Zambeze to Quelimane 205 km tar **FUEL**: Inhassoro junction with E.N. 1, Pande, Beira, Quelimane **LINKING ROUTES**: Routes 4, 6, 8

From Inhassoro (see p 125 and route 4), backtrack for 14 km to the E.N. 1 where you turn right. The road now veers inland to skirt the numerous small lakes and marshes along the coast, passing through attractive deciduous miombo woodlands. After about 63 km you will notice a small church on your left and a large baobab with a nearby map of Sofala Province to the right of the road.

The 1 km-long bridge across the Rio Save into Sofala Province is reached after about 900 m. Further along the vegetation changes to mopane and silver cluster-leaf before giving way to a mixture of acacia, marula and palms. After about 163 km you cross the Rio Búzi and 12 km further the Rio Revué, which has been dammed further upstream to form the Barragem de Chicamba (see p 127). After another 83 km you join the E.N. 6 at Inchope and link up with route 6 (see p 141). Beautiful woodcarvings of animals and household goods can usually be bought from craftsmen at the junction.

Turn right onto the 'E.N. 6 and continue past **Dondo** to reach **Beira** (see p 129), the capital of Sofala Province, about 128 km after joining the E.N. 6. Mozambique's second largest city, Beira has all the shops and services that a tourist might require.

The city is served by regular scheduled LAM flights from Maputo and Virginia buses run daily between Maputo and Beira. Public buses also service the route between Beira and Chimoio.

Although the distance from Beira to the Rio Zambeze is a mere 269 km, the road north of Dondo is in an exceptionally poor state, with loose sand replaced further north by a seemingly endless succession of dips. You should, therefore, allow at least seven hours for this section. Also bear in mind that there are no accommodation facilities anywhere along the route and once across the Rio Zambeze it will take you another four to five hours to complete the 203 km journey to Quelimane (see p 138). A very early start is, therefore, recommended.

From Beira backtrack for 28 km to Dondo and a short way on turn right onto the E.N. 213, a gravel road that soon disintegrates into a narrow sandy track despite the fact that it is the main north-south link. The track meanders through magnificent tall miombo woodlands along a sandy ridge of the Cheringoma Plateau that bounds the Rift Valley to the east. These woodlands are the habitat of several noteworthy bird species that are difficult to spot elsewhere in southern Africa (see p 18) and the area is highly recommended for keen birders. Although demining has taken place, care should be taken by visitors.

Running parallel to the track is the remains of the Trans Zambezia railway line which was built from Beira to the southern bank of the Rio Zambeze between 1920 and 1922. The line was a frequent target of Renamo rebels during the civil war and after about 26 km you will pass several derailed goods trucks to the right of the road, and 18 km further on abandoned tanks serve as a further reminder of the frequent attacks they carried out in the area.

The old Portuguese settlement of Semacuenza is passed 1,7 km on and 13,7 km later you will pass more derailed goods trucks. A signpost indicating the eastern boundary of Parque Nacional da Gorongosa (see p 134) is reached after 17,7 km. Before attempting to approach the park along this route, it is recommended that you enquire whether the bridges across the Rio Urema and Rio Púngoè have been rebuilt. After another 9 km the settlement of Muanza is reached.

Continuing through miombo woodlands, you reach Condué about 23 km north of Muanza and the settlement of Inhaminga 44 km on. Further along you pass through the settlements of Inhamitanga, where the road starts descending gradually to the Zambeze Valley. You then reach Matondo and after travelling for about 222 km on one of the country's worst roads and on the verge of despair, you join a reasonably good tar road which is followed for about 18 km to Caia on the southern bank of the Rio Zambeze. From here the railway line continues upstream along the southern bank of the Rio Zambeze to Vila de Sena, where a bridge provides access to the northern bank. From it one line continues to the Moatize coal mine, while the other line runs to Blantyre in Malawi. Built in 1932-33, the 3 800 m-long bridge was the second longest in the world at the time. It was destroyed by Renamo in 1983 and rebuilt after peace returned to Mozambique.

The final 2 km to the river is a gravel road that winds across the floodplains. If luck is on your side you will find the ferry (100 000 Mt toll fee) on the southern bank and you might not have to wait too long. It is a good idea to reverse your vehicle onto the ferry to enable you to drive straight off when you reach the northern bank.

From the Rio Zambeze, the southern boundary of Zambezia Province, the road remains inland for the first 106 km before curving gently towards the coast. The small settlement of Nicuadala, 164 km beyond Rio Zambeze, marks the turnoff to the coastal city of Quelimane, 37 km further along a good tar road which was rebuilt in 1998-99. The road winds across coastal grasslands and as you approach Quelimane the scenery becomes increasingly dominated by coconut palms.

Quelimane, the capital of Zambezia province and an important port city, lies on the northern banks of the Rio Cua Cua. An Islamic trading centre was already established along the coast here when the first Portuguese navigators arrived in the late 1400s. It was linked to Muslim trade centres further north along the east coast of Africa and to the interior by ancient trade routes.

In January 1498 the Portuguese navigator Vasco da Gama landed at Quelimane when searching for a sea route to India. Da Gama planted a *padrão* that withstood the ravages of time for nearly 450 years until it was swept away by the river. Before continuing his journey, Da Gama carried out repairs to his vessels and the crews were given time to recover from scurvy. He named the river in which he had anchored the Rio dos Bons Sinais, or the River of Good Omens.

Lured by reports of gold in the interior, the Portuguese had established a settlement at Quelimane, about 16 km upstream from the mouth of the Rio Cua Cua, by 1540. However, almost a century later the settlement consisted of little more than a dozen or so straw houses along the river and a fort.

The fortunes of the settlement improved when the Zambeze became an important trade route to the interior during the 1700s. Although the Rio Zambeze was navigable for 200 km, access through the sprawling delta with its ever-changing channels and sandbanks was difficult. Safe and easy access to the Zambeze was, however, possible by using a channel which linked the Rio Cua Cua to the Zambeze during the flood period. As a result Quelimane developed as the main springboard into the interior by the middle of the 18th century.

Towards the end of the 1700s Quelimane became an important port from where slaves were exported to Mauritius, Réunion, Madagascar, Cuba and Brazil. The slave trade also resulted in an increased demand for food and in the early 1800s a variety of crops was grown commercially, among them wheat, maize, millet and vegetables. The town received a further boost when Quelimane became a separate captaincy with its own customs house in 1812. As a result, ships no longer had to call at Ilha de Moçambique to pay customs duties and to register their cargoes.

Despite its long history stretching back more than 500 years, the only noteworthy historical building is the **Catholic Cathedral.** Built more than two centuries ago, the church with its twin towers, tile roof and white walls faces the Rio Cua Cua.

Quelimane has two banks (BCM and Standard Totta), filling stations, a TDM *cabine pública* at the corner of Avenida Samora Machel and Avenida Filipe Magaia, a variety of shops, *Mercado Central* (central market) and restaurants. Accommodation in Quelimane ranges from the popular **Pensão Ideal** in Avenida Samuel Magaia and the **Hotel 1 de Junho**, which both offer good, clean accommodation at reasonable prices, to the decidedly upmarket **Hotel Chuabo** in Avenida Samora Machel.

The city is served by regular scheduled LAM flights from Maputo, but due to the poor condition of the road there is no bus service from Beira, although covered trucks do make the journey. For backpackers the best option would be to enquire about transport at Dondo, 28 km west of Beira. Travellers heading south from Quelimane to Beira should ask about transport at Nicaudala.

The most popular beach, **Praia de Zalala**, is reached by travelling north along Avenida Julius Nyerere. On leaving the city centre, the tar road gives way to a stretch of gravel, but after about 1 km you will be back on a narrow tar road winding through extensive coconut plantations. The first plantations in and around Quelimane were established in the closing years of the 1800s and the early 1900s and once ranked with the largest in the world. Among the many products derived from the coconut are coir and copra, the base of coconut oil. The province is the country's main producer of copra, the dried kernel of the coconut, and in 1971 over 7,5 million trees were registered in the province.

After travelling through coconut plantations for 33 km the tar road ends. Turn right here to reach the **Complexo Turistico Kass-Kass** a short way on. Amenities include four-bedded bungalows and a restaurant with bar. Camping is permitted alongside the beach under causerina trees used as roosts by large numbers of crows. There are no amenities, but the owner of the complex will let you use the restaurant's toilet facilities.

ROUTE 6

BEIRA CORRIDOR – MACHIPANDA TO GORONGOSA AND BEIRA

DISTANCE: Machipanda to Beira 300 km and 280 km optional detour to Parque Nacional da Gorongosa and Monte Gorongosa **TIME**: Machipanda to Beira 3,5 hours, or several days if optional detour is taken. **ROAD CONDITIONS**: Machipanda to Beira 300 km good tar; Inchope to Parque Nacional da Gorongosa and Monte Gorongosa 130 km potholed tar and 150 km gravel tracks **FUEL**: Chimoio, Beira **LINKING ROUTES**: Routes 5 and 7

The Beira Corridor is an important link between landlocked Zimbabwe, Zambia and Malawi and the port city of Beira and has hence been a major trade route between the interior and the coast for centuries.

At the Machipanda border post (06:00-18:00) you enter Manica Province, and after 31 km reach the town of **Manica** with the Vumba Mountains forming an impressive backdrop. Gold has been mined in the area for centuries and Muslim traders, based at Sofala, established trade routes to the gold fairs that were held here. In 1575 a Portuguese military expedition was sent to Manica to conquer the gold mines, but the idea was abandoned in favour of a treaty that would allow the

Portuguese access to the gold fairs. Of interest in Manica is the **Geology Museum**, which contains a large collection of rocks and minerals and the plant where spring water from the Vumba Mountains is bottled under the name of Agua Vumba.

Continuing further east, the road traverses the gently undulating Planalto de Chimoio. About 23 km beyond Manica you will see the signposted turnoff to **Casa Msika** (see route 7) and 10 km on you pass the turnoff to **Barragem de Chicamba** (Chicamba Dam) (see p 127 and route 7).

Continuing along the E.N. 6, the turnoff onto the E.N. 102 to Tete is reached after 13 km and a further 23 km on you reach **Chimoio**. Formerly known as Vila Pery, Chimoio is the capital of Manica Province and an important commercial, transport and agricultural centre.

In the early 1970s Frelimo intensified its infiltration of the centre of the country, attacking farms and the Beira railway line. This, combined with the more open terrain, prompted the Portuguese to establish a cavalry unit at Vila Pery.

A well-known natural feature of the area, **Cabeca do Velho**, or the Face of the Old Man, can be viewed from the *Mercado Central* (central market) in Chimoio. The enormous granite outcrop resembles the head of a man lying down with the eyes, nose, mouth and chin clearly delineated.

There are several shops, supermarkets, *Mercado Central* (central market), filling stations, two banks (BCM and Standard Totta) and a TDM office in Chimoio. Accommodation ranges from the **Executive Manica Hotel** just off the E.N. 6 on the western outskirts of the town and the **Hotel Moinho**, which resembles a windmill, off the E.N. 6 on the eastern outskirts of the town, to the **Flor de Volga** which is a good option for budget travellers.

One of the most popular restaurants, the **Maua**, is situated in the Feira Popular off the E.N. 6 bypassing the town. It offers a varied menu featuring seafood dishes and Mozambican fare. The restaurant in the **Hotel Moinho** offers a wide selection of good meals, while **Restaurante Bar Sport Clube**, next to the soccer field in Avenida 25 de Setembro, is one of the best options in the town centre. The nearby **Restaurante Concorde** in 155 Avenida Dr Araujo de Lacerda has a fair selection of meals at reasonable prices.

Chimoio is accessible by Virginia bus from Beira and Tete, or by train on the Beira to Mutare railway line.

East of Chimoio the road winds gradually down to the coastal plain, crossing the Beira railway line, built between 1896 and 1898 to connect the then Southern Rhodesia to the coast. Financed and controlled by foreign interests, the line and the port of Beira became in effect a British enclave within Mozambican territory until the railway line was bought by the Portuguese government in 1948 and the port of Beira in 1949.

In the 1970s, when Frelimo began infiltrating the central provinces, the railway line, road and farms in the area came increasingly under attack. Armed militiamen and commandos were posted on trains and as the railway line provided a vital economic link between what was then known as Southern Rhodesia and the coast, Rhodesian troops were deployed to protect it.

The railway line, oil pipeline and road later also became the targets of frequent attacks by Renamo rebels, prompting Zimbabwe to send 10 000 troops to guard the corridor. In 1985 the strategic importance of the railway line prompted the Southern African Development and Co-ordinating Conference (SADCC) to rehabilitate the line to make Zimbabwe, Zambia and Malawi less dependent on exports through South Africa.

About 22 km beyond Chimoio you pass the railway settlement of **Gondola** where several old steam locomotives can be seen. **Inchope**, at the junction of the E.N. 6 with the E.N. 1 north and the E.N. 1 south, is reached after 42 km.

To reach **Monte Gorongosa** and **Parque Nacional da Gorongosa** (see p 134), turn left at Inchope and continue for 42 km along a potholed tar road to the park turnoff. If you are headed for the park, turn right and continue for 11 km to the park entrance. Chitengo park headquarters is another 17 km further.

To reach Monte Gorongosa, ignore the turnoff to the park and continue for another 22 km to the town of Gorongosa, where you should ask for directions to *Senhor* Pedro Chicone's rustic camp, Vunduzi, at the base of the mountain. Guides and porters can be arranged here for trips up the mountain.

The E.N. 6 now traverses grasslands and the floodplains of the Rio Púngoè, passing the Mafambisse sugar mill. Rehabilitated in 1997, it is one of five sugar mills that made Mozambique the fourth largest producer of sugar in Africa prior to independence. Further along you reach the E.N. 213 to Quelimane (see route 5) and a short way on the village of

Dondo. After about 28 km you reach Beira (see p 129), the capital of Sofala Province.

ROUTE 7

ESPUNGABERA TO TETE AND CAHORA BASSA

DISTANCE: 1 235 km **TIME**: 2 days plus **ROAD CONDITIONS**: Espungabera to Casa Msika 209 km gravel requiring a 4x4 or vehicle with high ground clearance, 26 km tar; Casa Msika to Tete 10 km gravel, 340 km good tar; Tete to Cahora Bassa and back 300 km gravel, 240 km good tar, 12 km potholed tar **FUEL**: Catandica, Tete **LINKING ROUTES**: Routes 6 and 10

This scenic route is best tackled in a four-wheel drive vehicle, or a rugged vehicle that will stand up to corrugated roads. In the rainy season it might prove to be a testing route and is, therefore, best travelled during the dry winter months. As it is a long day's drive to the first overnight stop, it is advisable to sleep at Chirundu in Zimbabwe, 11 km from the Mt Selinda border post.

After clearing immigration and customs at Espungabera, take the road branching off to the left a few metres before the control post. From here the road descends steeply through spectacular semi-deciduous miombo woodlands for 9 km, with the eastern slopes of the Chimanimani Mountains dominating the scenery to the west.

About 33 km beyond the border post you pass the settlement of Dacata and 15 km on reach Gogoi, where a 16 km stretch of tar road provides relief from the bumpy gravel road. A few kilometres on you pass through a magnificent tract of msasa forest and then passed an abandoned tank that serves as a reminder of the country's civil war. About 101 km beyond Espungabera you reach the Rio Lucite which is crossed by means of a ferry (50 000 Mt toll fee). Turn left after crossing the river and follow the winding road steadily uphill, passing through beautiful montane forest before reaching a village, 77 km beyond the Rio Lucite. Take the road signposted to

Rotunda and as you travel west the scenery is dominated by Monte Binga, at 2 436 m the highest point in Mozambique, with the Chimanimani Mountains further south. The small settlement of Mavita is reached after 17 km and from here you continue to Rotunda, a settlement close to the Zimbabwean border.

Turn right at the western outskirts of Rotunda and after 36 km you will reach a T-junction where there used to be an old Portuguese trading store. Turn right here and after 19 km the Barragem de Chicamba (see p 127) comes into view. From here it is a further 6,7 km to the dam wall where there is a lay-by with a fine view over the dam. The road then descends to a bridge across the river below the dam wall and then climbs steeply out of the valley. About 600 m beyond the bridge a turnoff to the left leads to another good viewpoint over the dam and 14 km on you reach the E.N. 6. Turn left here and drive for just short of 10 km to the signposted turnoff to **Casa Msika**, a popular holiday resort.

The resort, reached about 5 km from the turnoff, is popular at weekends with residents of nearby Chimoio and is also ideally situated for those travelling from Zimbabwe to the coast.

On a tract of unspoilt land between the Rio Messica and the Rio Revué, the resort is owned by Peter Thornicroft, who obtained the land in 1984 to develop a fishing camp and a crocodile farming operation. The vegetation is an interesting mixture of species including bauhinia, *Brachystegia*, msasa, kiaat, monkey orange and bushwillows. This, combined with the dam and the scenic granite outcrops, attracts a diversity of birds and a few hours of birding will be well rewarded.

The resort comprises of 12 two-bed rooms with *en suite* facilities, nine chalets sleeping three to six people and basic camp sites. When the dam is full, the restaurant, bar and swimming pool on the edge of the dam are virtually surrounded by water. Worthwhile visiting is the crocodile farming operation where about 1 000 crocodiles are bred for their skins, which are exported mainly to the Far East.

From Casa Msika backtrack to the E.N. 6; turn right and head towards Chimoio for 23 km to the signposted turnoff to Tete. Turn left here and head north through miombo woodlands punctuated by spectacular granite outcrops. About 60 km beyond the turnoff a plank bridge provides access across the Rio Púngoè and after another 60 km you reach the village of Catandica. Continuing further north, you reach Guru, a large settlement with thatched traditional huts. The vegetation now changes markedly from miombo woodlands to a savanna with baobabs, candelabra trees, marula, knobthorn and acacias before giving way to mopane savanna.

At Changara the route links up with the E.N. 103 from the Nyamapanda border post – the Tete Corridor linking Zimbabwe and Malawi. In the 1970s the road was frequently mined and attacked by Frelimo soldiers and Portuguese troops referred to it as the "road to hell". Travelling was only possible under the protection of armed convoys that came under frequent attack. The corridor later also became a target of Renamo rebels, earning it the name "Gun Run".

About 71 km on you pass the turnoff to Songo and Cahora Bassa (not signposted) on your left and after another 24 km you reach **Tete** on the southern banks of the Rio Zambeze, Africa's fourth largest river. Situated about 650 km upstream of the river mouth, Tete lays claim to two dubious distinctions: one of the hottest towns in the country and with the highest incidence of malaria. Average annual temperatures are above 26 °C and in midsummer temperatures of 40 °C are not uncommon.

With a population of 50 000, Tete is the capital of the province of the same name and an important transport centre along the Tete Corridor linking Zimbabwe and landlocked Malawi. The city experienced a major economic boost in the 1970s when Cahorra Bassa was built, but the decline that set in when the Portuguese left after independence has left once graceful homes close to the river in ruins. Other than as a convenient stopover for travellers heading to and from Zimbabwe, Malawi and Niassa Province, the town holds little of interest to tourists.

It has been suggested that Arab traders could have established a trading centre in the vicinity of Tete in the 13th century and towards the close of the 1400s it was an important river port. In 1531 the abandoned Muslim trading post was occupied by the Portuguese, who built a fort on the banks of the river in 1575-76 to protect their interests. The importance of the settlement received a boost in 1767 when the seat of government of what was known as the Rivers of Sena settlements was moved from Sena to Tete.

Of historical interest is the waterside **fort** near the flyover as you enter the city. Built in about 1576, the fort was in ruins by

1836 and rebuilt the following year. In the early 1900s, the Governor of Tete suggested that it be demolished; the suggestion was fortunately turned down and the fort was then used as a vehicle storage depot. It was not until 1942 that the walls were rebuilt and today it serves as a centre for orphans of the civil war. Another old **fort** where slaves were once traded can be seen on the southern outskirts of the town near the municipal market in Avenida 25 de Junho. Among the few other places of interest are the disused **Roman Catholic Cathedral** and a curious dome-shaped structure on the banks of the river. Now in ruins, the building formerly served as a **hydrological and meteorological station**, while the square tower housed a lighthouse to warn ships of sandbanks and islands in the river.

Facilities in Tete include two banks (BCM and Standard Totta), a TDM office in Avenida Liberdade, filling stations, a variety of shops and the *Mercado Central* (central market) where fresh fruit and vegetables can be bought.

Regular scheduled LAM flights link Tete with Maputo, Beira and Quelimane. The city is served by a daily bus service between Harare and Blantyre and Virginia buses operate to Chimoio and Beira from the terminal in Avenida 25 de Junho.

There are several accommodation options in Tete. **A Pescina** in Avenida Liberdade on the banks of the Rio Zambeze offers small but pleasant air-conditioned rooms with showers and a restaurant. Camping is permitted in the courtyard which features a swimming pool that is apparently only filled during the summer months. The complex also has tennis courts. **Pensão Alves Melo** has large air-conditioned rooms with separate bathrooms in a large building resembling a warehouse. There are also two hotels: the centrally located five-storey **Hotel Zambeze** in Avenida Eduardo Mondlane, and the **Hotel Kassuende** on the southern outskirts of the town along Avenida 25 de Junho.

In Avenida Liberdade on the banks of the Rio Zambeze, **Restaurant Freitas** is a popular eatery with a wide selection of meals and a shady terrace overlooking the river. At the nearby **A Pescina** meals are served in a covered area with ceiling fans and a TV. The menu features a variety of dishes at reasonable prices, but unfortunately the restaurant does not have a view over the river. Two other options, further upstream, are the **Esplanada Almeida** and the **Complexo Turistico Jemba** in **B°** Francisco Manyanga. The **Restaurante Melo** is a popular, bustling establishment in a covered courtyard and has a disco at weekends.

To visit Cahora Bassa you must obtain a permit from the Hidroelectrica De Cahora Bassa (HCB) office in the SOMAC building in Avenida da Independência (tel (052) 2 27 88). Guided tours of the complex are usually conducted on Wednesdays, but can also be conducted on other weekdays, subject to the availability of a guide.

From Tete backtrack along the E.N. 103 for 24 km and turn right (not signposted); continue along a tar road that strikes northeast through a savanna of mopane, baobabs, leadwood and knobthorn. As you approach Songo the landscape becomes more mountainous and 116 km beyond the turnoff from the E.N. 103 you reach a police control post where you will be required to show your permit.

For the next 5 km the road winds steeply upwards to **Songo**, which lies on top of the mountains. The village was used as a construction camp during the building of the Cahora Bassa scheme and today houses employees, including 300 families from Portugal, of HCB. Interestingly, the village and the hydro-electric scheme are virtually Portuguese territory and Songo has its own international airport.

As you approach the control post you will notice a tar road leading off to the left, with controlled access through a boom. Just over 11 km along this road you reach the signposted turnoff to Phil Bezuidenhout's **Ugezi Tiger Lodge**. Accommodation is provided in rock and thatch A-framed chalets with *en suite* facilities, or in four-bed safari tents served by hot water ablutions, either on a full board basis or self-catering. Opened in November 1997, Ugezi offers boat hire, a sundowner cruise and night fishing from a kapenta rig. The best months for tiger fishing, from September to January, unfortunately coincide with the hot season.

For a different perspective of the dam, continue for 4,4 km beyond the Ugezi Tiger Lodge turnoff and stop to view the narrow gorge and the dam wall. The tar road continues to Songo, but as there is a control post further on through which you will not be allowed without a permit, turn around and backtrack for 15 km to the boom gate.

To reach the shores of Cahora Bassa, backtrack for about 2 km from the boom gate and then turn right onto a potholed gravel road that a short way on changes to potholed tar. After meandering through the mountains for about 12 km you will join the all-weather gravel road to Mágoè. Turn right here and continue for 24 km to Nchapiriri village. As you are about to leave the village, turn right and drive past the settlement of **Chicoa**, visited in the 1570s by a Portuguese expedition investigating rumours of silver being mined here. Not only did the search prove fruitless, but the expedition members were all massacred. Rumours about silver persisted and in 1614 a Portuguese trader from Tete journeyed to Chicoa, but again the mission met without success.

There are about half a dozen kapenta operations along the lake shore, which is reached 20 km after the Nchapiriri turnoff. Several of them were in the process of setting up tourism resorts in 1989 and it might be worthwhile making enquiries.

From Mchapiriri another option is to continue for 47 km to the outskirts of Daque village, where a signpost indicates a turnoff to the right to the **Daque Tchuma Tchato**, a community conservation programme based on the Zimbabwean CAMPFIRE model. After 9 km the track ends at a small rest camp built on the shores of Cahora Bassa. The rest camp comprises of three rustic reed and thatch huts each sleeping two, a communal cooking/dining area and basic ablution facilities. There are, however, no other facilities.

The Daque Chuma Chato was established in June 1997 and although game is not abundant elephant, buffalo, lion, leopard, sable, kudu, impala and Burchell's zebra still occur in the area. With proper conservation measures in place, however, the animal populations are likely to increase and in a few years the area could offer a superb wilderness experience.

West of Mágoè, the Daque Chuma Chato borders on the **Bawa Chuma Chato** which extends westwards and southwards to the Zimbabwean border. Established in 1995, Bawa was Mozambique's first community-based conservation area, but at the time of writing there were no facilities.

Backtrack to the E.N. 258 where you turn right and after 55 km you will reach a turnoff to Marara. After following a rather bumpy track for 9 km, with numerous detours around bridges that were destroyed in the civil war, the mission station of Marara is reached and about 27 km on the **Boroma mission church** comes into view. Perched on a hill on the southern banks of the Rio Zambeze, the magnificent church has a commanding view over the surrounding countryside.

The mission was established in 1885 by the Jesuits and the church with its Luso-Jesuit architecture was completed in 1900. The first Father Superior was a German Jesuit priest named João Baptista Iller. The Jesuit brother who painted the ceilings is said to have fallen to his death just when he was about to complete his work.

Despite its sad state of neglect, the building, with its beautifully painted ceiling and exquisite woodwork behind the altar of prominent Jesuit leaders, has retained its atmosphere of sanctity. In 1995 the mission was taken over by the Catholic Church, but most of the buildings serve as classrooms and hostel accommodation for a state school.

From Boroma it is a 26 km drive along a gravel road with a good surface back to Tete.

9

NORTHERN MOZAMBIQUE

From the baobab-lined shores of Lago Niassa the vast miombo woodlands of northern Mozambique extend seemingly forever eastwards to the Indian Ocean town of Pemba. In between lies some of the wildest countryside to be found in Mozambique. Owing to their remote location, the northern provinces of Zambezia, Nampula, Niassa and Cabo Delgado see few visitors, but those who do take time to visit this region will not be disappointed.

Among the region's attractions are the untouched shores of Lago Niassa, the herds of game of Reserva do Niassa and the magnificent white, palm-lined beaches of Pemba. The marvellous coral reefs and islands of the Arquipélago das Quirimbas, off the coast of Cabo Delgado, are among Africa's least explored areas. In Nampula Province the sheer cliffs of the monte-ilhas *offer rock climbers exciting possibilities, as does Namúli, at 2 419 m the second highest point in the country. Also of interest are the historic trading settlements of Ilha de Moçambique and Ibo that overshadowed Lourenço Marques (now Maputo) for centuries.*

The landscape is characterised by a narrow coastal plain that is replaced about 30 km inland by the Planalto Moçambicano and further west by the Planalto de Lichinga, that rises steeply above Lago Niassa. Extensive miombo woodlands, ranging from semi-deciduous miombo in the highlands of Gurué to deciduous miombo and dry deciduous miombo along the Lugenda and Lúrio rivers, dominate the vegetation.

Agricultural production is largely based on subsistence farming of cotton and mandioca, while small-scale livestock rearing also takes place. Along the shores of Lago Niassa freshwater fishing is an important economic activity, while the ocean off Cabo Delgado Province is a rich source of rock lobster, prawns and fish. Over the next few years the economy of towns along the 615 km-long Nacala railway line is likely to benefit substantially from the Nacala Development Corridor launched in 1998 to provide an efficient transport link between Malawi and the port of Nacala.

Niassa is one of the most sparsely populated provinces in the country, with a density of just under six people per square kilometre, compared to the national average of 19. The Makua is the dominant cultural group in the north of the country. Other groups include the Nyanya and the Yao of western Niassa Province and the Makonde of Cabo Delgado Province (see route 9). Zambezia province is the home of the Lomwe, Chuabo, Marende and Sena cultural groups.

Once the capital of Portugal's east African colony, Ilha de Moçambique, and the Arquipélago das Quirimbas further north, played important roles in the ancient trade networks established by Muslim traders. By the 1530s Portuguese settlements were restricted to the coast and the first attempts to establish control over the interior were made in the 17th century by granting prazos, *or crown estates, along the Zambeze valley. Control over Niassa and Cabo Delgado was only established in 1894 when a concession for the territory north of the Rio Lúrio was granted to the Companhia do Niassa. In more recent historical times, Cabo Delgado Province was at the forefront of Frelimo's resistance to Portuguese colonialism.*

Arquipélago das Quirimbas

9

Also known as the Ilhas do Cabo Delgado, the Arquipélago das Quirimbas comprises some 32 coral islands, islets and rocky outcrops strung over a distance of 250 km off the north coast of Mozambique. Although the archipelago owes its name to Ilha Quirimba, the best known island is **Ilha do Ibo**, about 5 km to the north.

Owing to their strategic location, the islands played an important role in the trade along the east coast of Africa for centuries and featured prominently in the rivalry for trade supremacy. By the time the Portuguese arrived at the Quirimbas, Muslim traders were already well established in the archipelago. Quirimba supplied highly prized cowries, while Amisa, the largest island in the archipelago, was renowned for its weaving industry that produced maluane cloth. The Portuguese, hence, first came to know the archipelago as the Maluane Islands.

To break Muslim control over the gold trade and to prevent the traders from reaching the centres further south along the coast, the Portuguese attacked Ilha Quirimba in 1522. Buildings were razed to the ground, boats lying at anchor in the harbour were set on fire and a large quantity of loot taken.

Land grants were given to Portuguese, who built magnificent mansions on Quirimba, Matemo and Quisiva, while a fortified settlement was established on Ibo. By the early 1600s the archipelago supplied a variety of agricultural produce and animals to meet the growing needs of Ilha de Moçambique.

Rivalry for control over the coastal trade persisted and in 1670 the archipelago was attacked by Omani Arabs. Ibo's economic importance grew steadily in the second half of the 18th century and in 1763 it received municipal status. A fort was erected in the 1770s and, as the settlement expanded, a church and a warehouse were built. In 1786 a customs house was erected and work on a star-shaped fort, similar in design to the one on Ilha de Moçambique, began in 1791 on the northern shores of the island.

By the 1800s *prazos* had been granted on all the large islands, with the powerful Moraes family holding leases over four islands. In the meantime Ibo had become a major centre in the slave trade and from 1839 to 1842 some 4 900 slaves were exported from it.

In 1897 Ibo was incorporated into the concession of the Companhia do Niassa, which was granted a charter in 1894 over the land north of the Lugenda River (the present-day Cabo Delgado and Niassa provinces). The town served as the company's headquarters until 1904 when Porto Amelia (later Pemba) was founded, a move that set in motion the inevitable economic decline of this once important harbour town.

Abandoned to the elements when the Portuguese fled the country after independence in 1975, the once stately mansions began disintegrating and trees and shrubs steadily regained their rightful place, to create the atmospheric ruin town that historic Ibo is. After disembarking at the harbour, make your way to the southwestern corner of the island, which is commanded by the **Igreja de Nosso Senhora de Rosario** (Church of the Lady of the Rosary). The lovely old building faces onto the town square and is only a few metres from the water's edge. Alongside the church is an old **fort**, completed in 1770.

From the fort, make your way northwards past some magnificent old mansions to the imposing star-shaped **Fortaleza de São João Baptista**, that could house 300 troops. Built in 1791, its design resembles the fort at Ilha de Moçambique, although it is on a smaller scale. During the liberation struggle, it was used to incarcerate Frelimo activists and is reputed to be haunted by the spirits of those who died in detention. Inside the fort you can watch traditional silversmiths using ancient methods to craft jewellery from melted down Portuguese coins.

From the fort, a road leads through the old part of town to the *Mercado Central* (central market) and yet another **fort**, built in 1847. Backtrack to the market and then make your way back towards the harbour until you reach the **Trabalhadores (Workers') Monument**. There are some silversmiths close to the monument and if you follow the main road to the left you will reach the old Portuguese cemetery.

In addition to experiencing the island's rich history, a **snorkelling trip** by dhow to the coral reefs to the north and east of the island is a must. The reefs are pristine and the habitat of a rich diversity of coral and brightly coloured tropical fish.

Accommodation on Ibo is available near the star-shaped fort at **Casa Janine**, an establishment run by a French woman who has lived on the island for several years. Although the shops on the island are poorly stocked and the central market has little to offer, fresh seafood can be bought cheaply when the boats come in.

Ibo is accessible either by dhow (see p 18) or you can arrange a flight through Luis Faria of E.G.E.S. (Empresa de Prestação de Serviços) in Pemba (tel (072) 34 31, fax 22 49).

Ilha de Moçambique

8

It is hard to imagine that this historic island, with its narrow streets lined by flat-roofed double-storey houses, warehouses, ornate bandstand and town squares, was once the capital of Mozambique. Years of economic decline and the flight of Portuguese settlers after independence have reduced once majestic buildings to empty shells; fig trees have pushed over walls and the plaster has peeled off many buildings. The island is also hopelessly overcrowded, a legacy of the civil war when people from the mainland sought refuge here. Despite the general decay and dilapidated state of most of the buildings, the island has a vibrant atmosphere and a charm of its own.

Ilha de Moçambique's rich architectural heritage reflects a combination of Portuguese building styles influenced by Arab and Indian architecture and local building traditions. This, together with its historical importance in the maritime history of the Indian Ocean, prompted UNESCO (United Nations

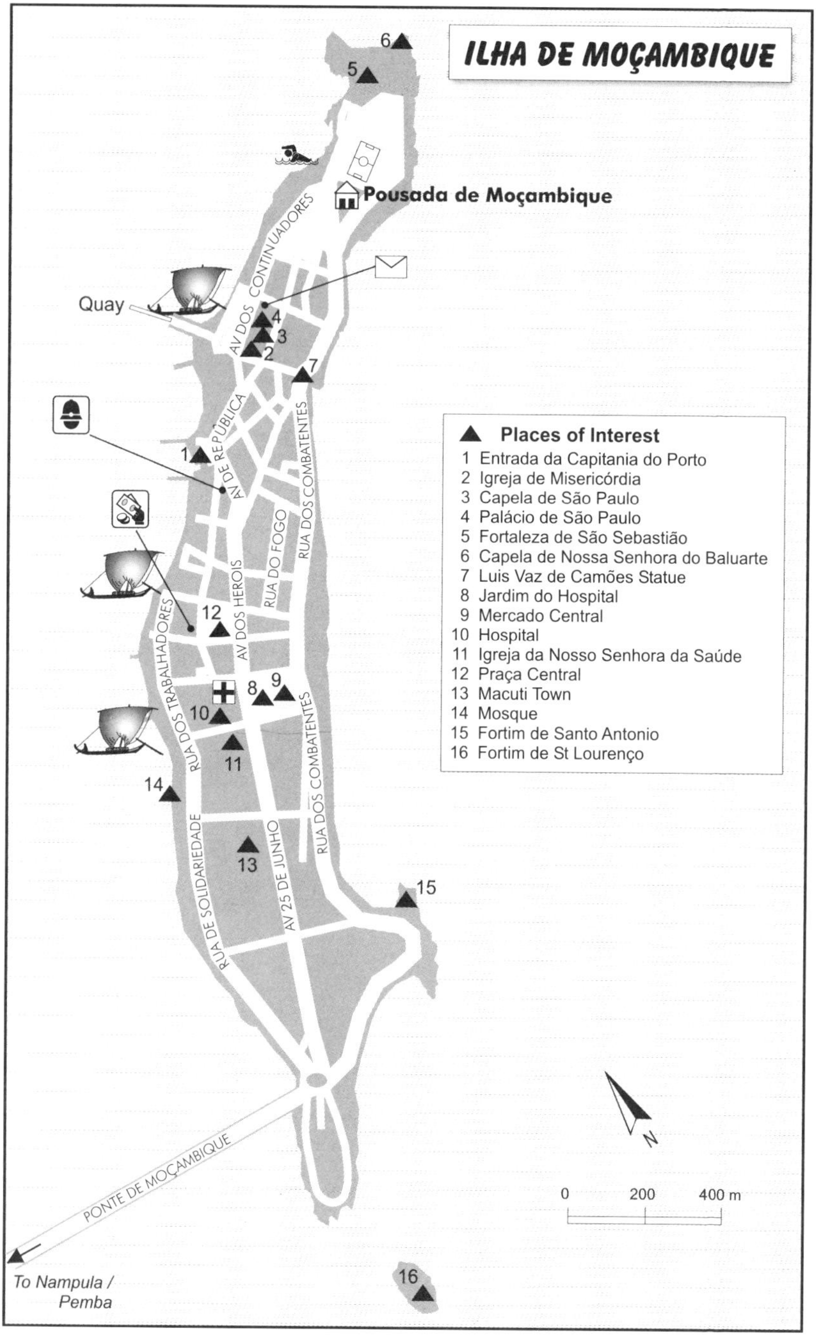
ILHA DE MOÇAMBIQUE
Pousada de Moçambique
Quay
AV DOS CONTINUADORES
AV DE REPÚBLICA
RUA DOS COMBATENTES
RUA DO FOGO
AV DOS HEROIS
RUA DOS TRABALHADORES
RUA DE SOLIDARIEDADE
AV 25 DE JUNHO
PONTE DE MOÇAMBIQUE
To Nampula / Pemba
N
0 200 400 m
Places of Interest
1 Entrada da Capitania do Porto
2 Igreja de Misericórdia
3 Capela de São Paulo
4 Palácio de São Paulo
5 Fortaleza de São Sebastião
6 Capela de Nossa Senhora do Baluarte
7 Luis Vaz de Camões Statue
8 Jardim do Hospital
9 Mercado Central
10 Hospital
11 Igreja da Nosso Senhora da Saúde
12 Praça Central
13 Macuti Town
14 Mosque
15 Fortim de Santo Antonio
16 Fortim de St Lourenço

Educational, Scientific, and Cultural Organization) to designate the island a World Heritage Site in 1991. In September 1997 UNESCO announced an ambitious project, and launched a fund, to restore the island to its former glory at an estimated cost of US $11 million.

With a length of 3 km and a width of 200-500 m, the coral island of Ilha de Moçambique lies at the entrance of the sheltered, 10 km-wide Baia de Moçambique. To its south lies Ilha St Lourenço, almost entirely occupied by a fort, with Ilha de Goa to the east and Ilha de Sena to the southeast.

It is almost certain that Ilha de Moçambique was used by Muslim traders as early as the 10th century, by which time the "Land of Sofala" further south was already an important Arab trade centre. In February 1498, when Vasco da Gama landed at the island while searching for a passage to India, trade was in the hands of a sheik who ruled in the name of an Arab king.

Eager to control the lucrative coastal trade, the Portuguese, with their superior military power, expelled the Muslims and established a trading station on the island in 1507. In the following year a small fort, São Gabriel, was built to protect the island which soon developed into an important stop on the sea route to India, a trade centre and a naval base.

The importance of Ilha de Moçambique began to decline when the focus of trade shifted to Quelimane and in 1898 it suffered a further setback when the capital was transferred to Lourenço Marques (now Maputo). Its economic significance waned even further when the port of Nacala was opened in 1951 and following the exodus of Portuguese settlers the stone-built town degenerated into a state of decay.

A walking tour

The best way to experience the island's atmosphere is to take a leisurely stroll along its narrow alleyways, starting from the police station, a 20th century building with a neo-classical style, at thc **Praça João Belo**. Numbers on the map on p 154 correspond with those in the text. The first building of note is the **Entrada da Capitania do Porto** (1) (Entrance Gate to the Port Captain's Offices). Stroll down Avenida da República, a narrow avenue hemmed in by double-storey buildings until its junction with Rua Tristão de Cunha. This is the heart of the old town where most of the buildings were concentrated until the mid-1750s.

Diagonally across the street you will see the **Igreja de Misericórdia** church (2) run by a Portuguese religious organisation, the House of Mercy. The **Museu de Arte Sacra** (Museum of the Sacred Arts) is housed in the hospital wing of the church and among the exhibits are a wood engraved panel of a pulpit in the same style as the pulpit in St Paul's chapel and a 17th century sculpture of Santa Isabel, Queen of Portugal and patron saint of the Church of Mercy. Also on display are a statue of St Francis, a silver case from the Holy Reserve, chalices, a silver lamp for the Blessed Sacrament and a 17th century chased leatherware case for carrying the Blessed Sacrament in burial processions. The building dates back to 1635, but the pediment was added in 1700. The **Capela de São Paulo** (3) in nearby Avenida dos Continuadores features a magnificent gilded altar piece and a hand-carved pulpit of Luso Indian origin dating back to the middle of the 17th century. The tower dates back to 1864.

Adjacent to the church is the ornate **Palácio de São Paulo** (4), an imposing red brick building. It was built in 1674 as a Jesuit convent on the site of an earlier Jesuit monastery destroyed by fire when Omani Arabs attacked the island in 1670. After the Jesuits were expelled from Portugal and its colonies in 1759, the building was modified to serve as the residence of the Governor-General, a purpose it served until 1898. Subsequently it has been used, among others, as the residence of the District Governor until 1933 and an overseas residence for the Portuguese President and ministers.

The palace consists of some 20 large rooms, including several bedrooms with four-poster beds, and a large banqueting hall decorated with a striking mural. The rooms were lavishly furnished with exquisite carpets, delicately carved furniture from Goa and Portugal's colonies in the east, Chinese porcelain and numerous paintings. The steps in the courtyard are graced by beautiful statues. The museum is open Wednesdays to Sundays from 08:00-12:00 and again from 14:00-17:00.

Continue along Avenida dos Continuadores to the **Fortaleza de São Sebastião** (5) at the northernmost tip of the island. Construction of the fort began in 1558 and although most of the work was done by 1583, it was not until 1620 that the building was finally completed. The fortification was heavily guarded by a large battery of cannons and successfully withstood successive attacks by the Dutch in 1607 and 1608 and Omani Arabs in 1670. Many of the cannons on the battlements bear dates of 1823 and 1824. Other interesting features include another church inside the fort, the old hospital and three huge underground water reservoirs. The reservoirs were filled by rainwater draining off the inward sloping roofs and are today still used by the islanders as a source of water.

The northern extremity of the island served as an artillery bastion until it was replaced by the **Capela de Nossa Senhora do Baluarte** (6) (The Chapel of Our Lady of the Bastion). Built in 1522, it is the oldest extant European building in the Southern Hemisphere. An interesting feature of the chapel, with its Manuelino architecture (a building style commonly used during the late Portuguese Middle Ages), is the narrow crucifix-shaped windows in the nave. Also of interest are a number of plaques commemorating those who have passed away and human bones kept in a box.

From the fort take the road that winds along the southern shores of the island, where affluent inhabitants built their villas in the late 1800s. Continuing along the Rua dos Combatentes you reach the **statue of Luis Vaz de Camões** (7). The 16th century Portuguese poet, who wrote *The Lusiads* in 1572, spent three years in Mozambique while on his way back from India to Portugal. Continue along the coastal road until you reach the **Jardim do Hospital** (8) (Hospital Park). Turn right down the street along the western end of the park, which has the **Mercado Central** (9) (central market) as its focus. The market building, with small towers on its corners connected by iron railings, dates back to 1887, but is no longer in use.

Opposite the market is the **Hospital** (10) with its imposing colonnades in late classical Schinkel style. Built in 1877 it stands on the site of the earlier Convento de San João de Deus which was erected in 1681. To reduce the possible spread of infection, the hospital was divided into several buildings in 1880. Diagonally across from the hospital is the **Igreja da Nosso Senhora da Saúde** (11), a Catholic Church dating back to the early 1600s. It was beautifully restored in 1996.

Facing the hospital, turn right and walk down Avenida dos Heróis until you reach the **Praça Central** (12) (Central Square) with its bandstand and flame trees. From here it is a short way back to your starting point along Avenida Amilcar Cabral, stopping along the way to look at the interior of the beautifully restored Banco Comercial de Moçambique building.

Alternatively you can explore the "**macuti" town** (13), named after the palm leaves used to cover the roofs of houses. The town developed in and around the limestone quarries south of the hospital. From the eastern side of the square, walk up Travessa da Saudade and turn left into Rua dos Trabalhadores which winds along the coast to Largo do Celeiro where there is a fish market and dhow harbour. Continuing along Rua da Solidariedade, you pass a **mosque** (14), one of several on the islands and evidence of the Muslim influence along the northern Mozambican coast for centuries.

From here, make your way to the southern shores of the island where the **Fortim de Santo Antonio** (15) and the adjoining church are worth looking at. The existing fort dates back to 1820, when it replaced the original built in 1587. The church dates back to 1969 when it replaced one built in 1820, on the same spot where the first church was erected in the early 16th century.

About 250 m off the southern point of Ilha de Moçambique lies the small coral islet of Ilha de St Lourenço which can be reached by wading across at low tide. The first fortification on the island was built in 1588 to protect Ilha de Moçambique from attacks from the south, while the present fort, **Fortim de St Lourenço** (16) was built between 1695 and 1707 and altered in 1830.

A word of warning; the main motivation for visiting the island is to experience its rich history, architectural heritage and atmosphere. Do not expect to swim and enjoy beautiful clean beaches, two activities synonymous with the tropics, as the beaches are used as ablutions at low tide.

Lago Niassa

10

Originally named Lake Nyasa by the British explorer David Livingstone when he reached the lake in 1859, it was renamed Lake Malawi when Nyasaland became independent in 1964. In Mozambique and Tanzania though, the names Lago Niassa and Lake Nyassa continue to be used. In the 1950s the southern part of the lake was divided between Mozambique and Malawi and about 6 680 km^2, or a quarter of the lake, falls within the territory of Mozambique. Although situated in Mozambican territorial waters, Likoma and Chintheche islands are part of Malawi.

Lago Niassa is the southernmost of a string of lakes that lie within the Great Rift Valley's Western Rift stretching from Lake Albert southwards to the Zambezi Valley. Covering 26 000 km^2, the lake is 570 km long and 80 km at its widest point. With a depth of over 700 m north of Nkhata Bay (the lowest point is 230 m below sea level), it is the world's fourth deepest lake. It is also the 12th largest lake in the world.

The lake has a greater diversity of fish than any other freshwater lake in the world, most of them endemic. Estimates of the number of species vary considerably, but there are possibly as many as 1 000 species. Dominating the aquatic life are the cichlids which include *mbuna* – brightly coloured fish that live in the shallow waters along the lake's rocky shores and around offshore islands. There may be as many as 350 species of *mbuna* in Lago Niassa, but classifying the lake's fishes is not an easy task, as males and females of the same species are usually different colours. In addition, females may have up to four different colour forms. It has been suggested that the lake's incredibly rich diversity of species developed when Lago Niassa was isolated from other lakes in the Rift Valley between one and two million years ago.

The shores of Lago Niassa are undeveloped, except for the villages of Meponda, Metangula and Cóbuè where the people exploit the rich source of protein provided by the lake. Common catches include chambo, usipa (a whitebait species attracted to the surface at night with paraffin lanterns, or burning twigs), utaka and catfish. Catches are dried on wooden racks on the beach and sold further inland.

The untouched and wild shores of the lake provide an exciting alternative to the resorts along the shores in Malawi. Tourism facilities are for all practical purposes non-existent and adventurous travellers will have to be fully kitted out. Among the activities that can be pursued are kayaking, snorkelling, windsurfing and angling. September to April is best for angling and among the species you might hook are sungwa, ncheni or lake tiger, binga, sanjika and mpasa or lake salmon, a species known to put up a spectacular fight.

Pemba

8

Pemba, northern Mozambique's premier resort town, lies along the shores of Baia de Pemba, formed by a peninsula jut-

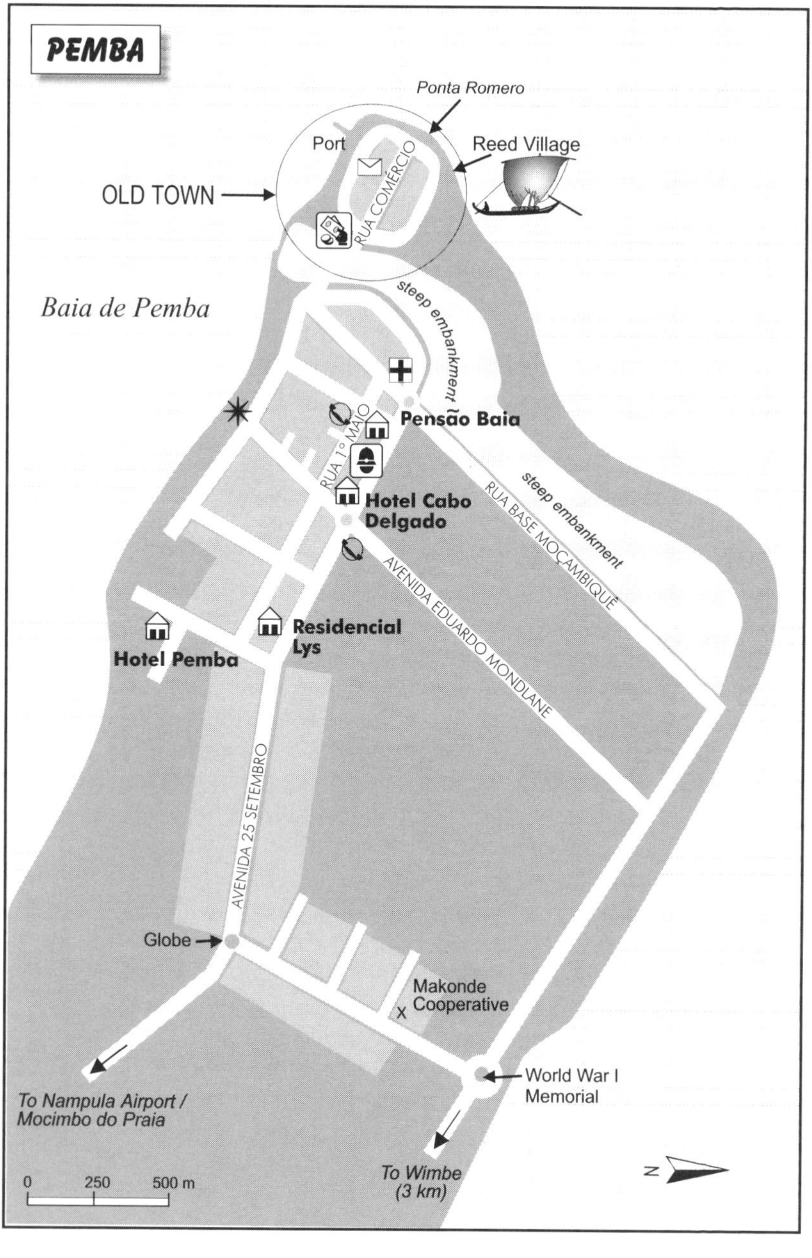
PEMBA
Ponta Romero
Port
Reed Village
OLD TOWN
RUA COMÉRCIO
Baia de Pemba
steep embankment
Pensão Baia
RUA 1° MAIO
Hotel Cabo Delgado
steep embankment
RUA BASE MOÇAMBIQUE
AVENIDA EDUARDO MONDLANE
Residencial Lys
Hotel Pemba
AVENIDA 25 SETEMBRO
Globe
Makonde Cooperative
World War I Memorial
To Nampula Airport / Mocimbo do Praia
To Wimbe (3 km)
0 250 500 m
N

ting north and the Londo peninsula which extends southwards. Access into the bay is through a narrow 2,5 km-wide channel between Ponta Said Ali at the southern end of the Londo Peninsula and Ponta Romero. With a length of 17 km and a width of 12 km at its widest point, Baia de Pemba is said to rank among the largest inland bays in the world.

Portuguese settlement at Pemba dates back to the second half of the 1850s when 36 settlers were granted land concessions here, but the project was short-lived. The town, originally named Porto Amelia in honour of Queen Amelia of Orleans and Braganca, was established in 1904 by the Companhia do Niassa. Prior to that date the company's headquarters were on Ibo, but as the harbour was only navigable by small vessels the company found it necessary to develop another port. During World War I, German U-boats were said to slip into the bay under cover of darkness to recharge their batteries and to take on supplies from the local population.

Pemba is a pleasant coastal town that has largely escaped the decay that most Mozambican towns suffered during the civil war, a blessing it owes to its remote location. It comprises a modern town, the *baixa* or old town in the vicinity of the harbour, and a reed-and-thatch village with a dhow harbour.

The most popular beach, **Praia de Wimbe**, lies about 3 km east of the town along the sweeping curve of the bay. The beach is protected by a coral reef that lies about 200 m offshore, creating safe **swimming** conditions and **snorkelling** possibilities. There are numerous dive sites, including exciting wall dives on the outside of the reef where there is a 300 m drop-off. Popular sites include **Londo Gardens** (12-25 m) which features beautiful coral and schools of large fish and **Caves**, a 36 m wall dive featuring overhangs, zigzag outcrops and potato bass. The main attractions of **Pete's Canyons** are large fan corals and Napoleon wrasses. Dive charters, angling trips and other water sports can be arranged through C I Divers, run by Pieter and Gi Gi Jacobs, based at Complexo Nautilus (see p 58).

Reserva do Niassa

11

Of all the conservation areas in Mozambique the Reserva do Niassa has the largest game populations. This has made it an obvious choice for a rehabilitation programme and the

Mozambican conservation authorities have been working on a management plan for the reserve in conjunction with a private company, Grupo Madal, since late-1995.

When it was proclaimed in 1962 the reserve covered 15 000 km^2 between the Rio Rovuma in the north and the Rio Lussanhando in the west, with the Lugenda River partly forming its southern boundary. In terms of the rehabilitation programme the Rio Lugenda will also form its eastern boundary; this will enlarge it by 7 000 km^2. Bordering the reserve will be a 13 000 km^2 buffer zone divided into five or six blocks, for which hunting concessions will be awarded. A number of lodges are planned and will cater mainly for fly-in tourists, due to the remoteness of the reserve. Activities will emphasise a total wilderness experience, rather than focusing on game-viewing and are likely to include guided walks.

The scenery of the reserve is dominated by miombo woodlands punctuated by spectacular granite outcrops, while magnificent riverine forests of mahogany and large sterculias occur along the major rivers. Interspersed between the miombo woodlands are open savannas and vlei areas.

One of the attractions of the park is that it is a sanctuary to four subspecies of large mammals, namely Boehm's zebra, the Niassa or Johnson's wildebeest, Johnson's impala and the *kondensis* subspecies of the waterbuck of southern Tanzania. Another species of interest is Lichtenstein's hartebeest which has a patchy distribution in southern Central Africa. The reserve is home to between 5 000 and 6 000 elephants, among them several large tuskers with ivory exceeding 45 kg. The sable population is estimated at between 3 500 and 4 500 animals and there are also substantial numbers of kudu, eland, buffalo and a variety of smaller antelope. The larger predators are represented by lion, leopard and wild dog.

Although relatively little is known about the birdlife of the area, **birdwatching** is another possibility as it is likely that several east African species reach the southern limit of their distribution in northern Mozambique.

ROUTE 8

QUELIMANE TO ILHA DE MOÇAMBIQUE AND PEMBA

DISTANCE: 1 270 km **TIME**: 3 days plus **ROAD CONDITIONS**: Quelimane to Namacurra 70 km tar; Namacurra to Mocuba 28 km gravel, 57 km tar; Mocuba to Alto Molócuè 185 km alternating between gravel and tar; Alto Molócuè to Rio Ligonha 112 km alternating between gravel and tar; Rio Ligonha to Nampula 100 km fair tar; Nampula to Ilha de Moçambique 178 km patched, but fair tar; Namialo to Pemba 335 km fairly good tar road **FUEL**: Quelimanc, Alto Molócuè (petrol unreliable), Nampula, Ilha de Moçambique, Pemba **LINKING ROUTES**: Routes 5, 9 and 11

From Quelimane (see route 5) backtrack for 37 km to **Nicuadala** where you turn right; continue for 32 km along a tar road to **Namacurra**. From here the E.N. 104 heads north along the valley carved by the Rio Licungo; the first 28 km is gravel and 5 km after joining the tar road you reach the abandoned Portuguese settlement of **Malei**. The remaining 52 km to Mocuba is on a good tar surface. At Mocuba the road swings northeast, ascending steadily through miombo woodlands to the Planalto Moçambicano. The first 100 km of the road from Mocuba to Alto Molócuè is tar in good condition, while the remaining 87 km alternates between gravel and tar.

Beyond Alto Molócuè a gravel road traverses undulating countryside with miombo woodlands and small granite outcrops. The next large settlement, **Alto Ligonha**, is reached 77 km beyond Alto Molócuè and the interesting castle-like building as you leave the town is unlikely to be missed. About 34 km after leaving Alto Ligonha you cross the Rio Ligonha, the southern boundary of Nampula Province.

Here you join a good tar road and 22 km further on pass through the village of Murrupala. The road then ascends gradually towards Nampula, the capital of Nampula Province. **Nampula** became the capital of the province of the same name in 1933, three years after the railway line from Ilha de Moçambique reached the town. During the liberation struggle, Nampula was the operational headquarters of the Mozambican Armed Forces.

Nampula is a pleasant, bustling city of some 200 000 people and an important railway and road junction. Encircling the city are striking granite outcrops that rise abruptly from the plains. The only places of interest to tourists are the cathedral, museum and Makonde co-operative. The **Cathedral de Nossa Senhora da Conceição** (Church of Our Lady of the Conception) with its large dome was also referred to by the Portuguese as Gina Lollobrigida, a name it owes to the cup-shaped structures on the roof. The **museum** in Avenida Eduardo Mondlane has an interesting collection of masks, musical instruments and other forms of typical Mozambican art. Also worth a visit is the **Makonde Co-operative** where you can see the craftsmen at work. It is situated behind the museum.

Nampula has filling stations, three banks (BCM, BIM and Standard Totta), a TDM office in Rua Monomotapa, a variety of shops, *Mercado Central* (central market) and a wide variety of restaurants. There are several accommodation options for travellers, among them the **Hotel Tropical** and **Pensão Marques** in Avenida Paulo Samuel Kamkama.

The city is linked by rail to Nacala and Cuamba, while LAM has regular scheduled flights. It is also served by buses from Cuamba, Nacala and Pemba.

From Nampula the main road continues north for 87 km to the village of Namialo where the E.N. 106 branches off to the north, while the road to Nacala and Ilha de Moçambique continues straight. After about 38 km you pass the turnoff to Monapo, which lies at the railway junction to Nacala and has a factory where cashew nuts can be bought. About 2,4 km on you turn right onto the E.N. 105, a good tar road, to Ilha de Moçambique.

After 24 km you will pass a signpost to the settlement of Mossuril, which lies on a peninsula to the north of Baia de Moçambique. The settlement is reached after 21 km along a gravel road and if you are interested in history, ask for directions to the **Igreja de Nossa Senhora de Remedios** (Church of Our Lady of Remedy), a beautiful church built by the Portuguese at the settlement of **Cabaceira** in the 18th century.

The main reason for making a detour to Mossuril, though, is the magnificent beach of **Praia da Chocas** at the northeastern end of the peninsula. The **Complexo Chocas Mar** offers rooms, a restaurant and camp sites and is a pleasant alternative to staying on Ilha de Moçambique.

Backtrack to the E.N. 105, turn left and continue for about 20 km to a signpost indicating the turnoff to the **Lumbo Military Cemetery**. Turn left here and follow a gravel road for 1 km to the cemetery where African, British, Indian and South African soldiers killed in the Battle of Lumbo during World War I are buried. Return to the main road, turn left and continue for just 3,6 km to the 3,5 km-long bridge linking the mainland with **Ilha de Moçambique** (see p 153). Built in 1966, it is a narrow single-lane bridge with frequent lay-bys to enable vehicles to pass each other.

The island has a filling station, BCM bank, TDM office, *Mercado Central* (central market) and fish market, but few shops. There are several restaurants with **Reliquias** in Avenida da República possibly the best option. It offers a good selection of meals at reasonable prices and also has a bar and a disco. Accommodation is limited to the **Hotel Pousada** which was closed for refurbishment in late 1998.

Ilha de Moçambique is served by regular LAM flights. It can also be reached by bus from Nampula to Monapo, or from Pemba to Namialo where you can catch a bus or *chapa* to the island.

From Ilha de Moçambique you will have to backtrack for 89 km to the village of Namialo, where you turn right onto the E.N. 106. The road traverses miombo woodlands with baobabs and magnificent star chestnut trees conspicuous as you continue north. Villa Nacaroa is reached after 65 km and the village of Alua is another 56 km further on. Beyond Alua the scenery is dominated by fascinating granite outcrops, baobabs, chestnut trees and groves of cashew nut trees. About 31 km beyond Alua you reach the Rio Lúrio which forms the southern boundary of Cabo Delgado Province.

Continuing north, you reach Metoro after 73 km. The settlement lies at the junction of the roads to Pemba and this is also where route 11 (Lichinga to Pemba) joins in. Turn right here to reach the turnoff to Macomia and Mocimboa da Praia 12 km further at the village of Sunate (also known as Silva Macua). From here, continue straight along the E.N. 106, a patched tar road in fair condition, except for a few bad sections at bridges. After about 17 km you will enjoy your first glimpse of the coastal plains and a few kilometres on the road begins its descent to the plains. As you approach Pemba, keep an eye out for the **Makonde Co-operative** under the trees to the right of the road, a short way beyond the turnoff to the airport. **Pemba** (see p 159) is reached 80 km beyond Sunate.

The largest city north of Nampula, Pemba has two banks (BCM and Standard Totta), a filling station, *Mercado Central* (central market), a variety of small shops and TDM *cabines públicas* (in Avenida 25 de Setembro, Avenida 1° Maio and Wimbe). Accommodation options in Pemba range from the **Hotel Pemba** in Rua Forças Armadas and the **Hotel Cabo Delgado** on Avenida Eduardo Mondlane to **Pensão Baia** in Avenida 1° Maio, a popular option for budget travellers and hence often fully booked.

The airport is about 5 km outside the city alongside the E.N. 106 and is served by regular scheduled LAM flights. Transnorte buses serve the route between Nampula and Pemba daily in both directions, departing from the terminus in Nampula at the traffic circle in front of the railway station. In Pemba you can board the bus either at the terminus near Pensão Baia, or the bus stop about 500 m beyond the Wimbe turnoff as you leave the city.

Not to be missed is the **scenic Marginal drive** which will also give you a good perspective of the new town and the *baixa*. Drive along Avenida 25 de Setembro and then turn left into Avenida Eduardo Mondlane, which is followed to a view-point overlooking Baia de Pemba. Turn right here and follow the palm-lined Marginal past an open area where a monument to the country's first president, Samora Machel, stands among the foundations of old buildings. A short way on, the road winds its way down a steep hill to the leafy old town with its modern harbour and a scenic reed village and dhow harbour. For pedestrians there are beautiful steps that lead down the steep embankment to the old town.

Pemba's most popular beach and resort area, **Wimbe**, is reached by taking the signposted turnoff at the stone globe of the earth as you enter the city. Turn right here and keep a look-out for the **Makonde Co-operative** 600 m further, to the left of the road underneath a large tree. A short way on you will reach a large circle with a monument commemorating those killed during World War I. Take the signposted road to Wimbe past the ruins of an old resort which has been earmarked for reno-vation. To the right of the road are large baobab trees that appear to have been planted in a straight line – a phenomenon that has been attributed to the seeds discarded by people along

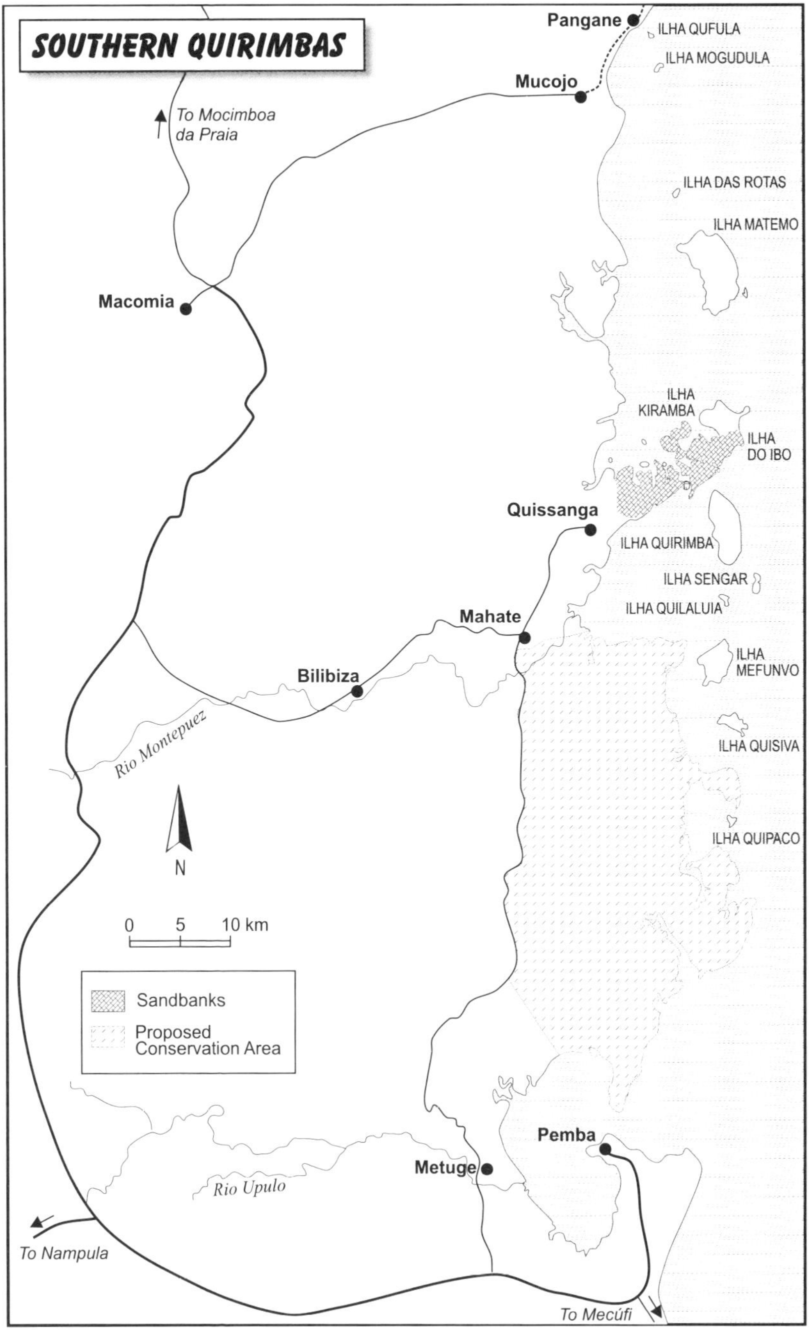
SOUTHERN QUIRIMBAS
Pangane
ILHA QUFULA
ILHA MOGUDULA
Mucojo
To Mocimboa da Praia
ILHA DAS ROTAS
ILHA MATEMO
Macomia
ILHA KIRAMBA
ILHA DO IBO
Quissanga
ILHA QUIRIMBA
ILHA SENGAR
ILHA QUILALUIA
Mahate
ILHA MEFUNVO
Bilibiza
Rio Montepuez
ILHA QUISIVA
N
ILHA QUIPACO
0 5 10 km
Sandbanks
Proposed Conservation Area
Pemba
Metuge
Rio Upulo
To Nampula
To Mecúfi

ancient trails. Further along causerina trees have been planted on the coast to prevent erosion, with coconut palms lending a tropical atmosphere.

Wimbe is the top coastal resort in the north of the country and offers several accommodation options. The **Complexo Turistico Nautilus**, an upmarket hotel situated right on the beach, has self-catering chalets, a restaurant and bar overlooking the bay. A few hundred metres further on you will find the **Complexo Turistico Caracol**, a self-catering complex comprised of two-roomed units equipped with a double bed, two single beds and a kitchenette.

Those geared for camping can head for the **Cashew Camp** situated a short way off the beach amid cashew nut trees. It offers shady camp sites with a pit latrine and cold water showers.

A popular outing for Pemba residents over weekends is to Mecúfi, a pretty beach resort to the south. If you want to avoid crowds, go in the week and take a picnic along. From Pemba take the E.N. 106 for 15 km to a village where you turn left onto a gravel road. Heed the signs warning you against causeways and after about 9 km you reach the village of Murrébuè. After another 14 km the road traverses a mangrove estuary with some impressive baobabs forming a scenic backdrop. A short way on the road passes a cross on a hill and then traverses another mangrove estuary. **Mecúfi**, 5 km further, is a small but pleasant coastal hamlet on the banks of an estuary. The lagoon is ideal for swimming and there are extensive stretches of unspoilt beach to explore north of the mouth. The beach to the south is lined by mangroves and therefore not as attractive for swimming.

ROUTE 9

PEMBA TO ARQUIPÉLAGO DAS QUIRIMBAS AND MUEDA

DISTANCE: 575 km **TIME**: 2 days plus **ROAD CONDITIONS**: Pemba to Quissanga 27 km tar, 88 km fair gravel road; Quissanga to Pangane 116 km fair gravel, 34 km potholed tar; Macomia to Mocimboa da Praia 153 km potholed tar (scheduled to be replaced by all-weather gravel); E.N. 243 to Mueda

50 km fair gravel **FUEL**: Pemba, Mocimboa da Praia **LINKING ROUTES**: Route 8

For anyone who has travelled so far north, a visit to the Arquipélago das Quirimbas should be seriously considered. From Pemba, backtrack for 27 km along the E.N. 106 to the signposted turnoff to Metuge. Turn right here and continue for 12 km to Metuge and another 59 km to Mahate. This section of the coast is still inhabited by a variety of game, including elephants which migrate as far south as the Londo Peninsula. They are rather elusive though, as they move about mainly at night. Predators such as leopard and hyaena are spotted occasionally in the early mornings and late afternoons. As a result, most of the area stretching between the Londo Peninsula and the Rio Montepuez has been earmarked as a game reserve, bounded in the west by the road to Quissanga.

From Mahate continue north for 15 km to the police station at Quissanga, from where it is 1,5 km to a fishing village nestling along a small bay fringed with mangroves. **Ilha Quirimba** lies about 10 km offshore, directly opposite the village, and it is possible to arrange dhow trips from here. As an alternative, ask for directions to Tandanhangui (accessible by four-wheel drive vehicle only), from where dhows can be arranged to **Ilha do Ibo** (see p 151). To the south of Quissanga lies **Ilha Mefunvo**, where there is a small population of dugongs (see p 86). The island has been earmarked for inclusion in a planned multi-purpose use marine reserve.

If you plan to visit the Quirimbas, arriving at low tide will cause a long wait until the tide is in, so plan your trip accordingly. Ask for the *senhor de barqas* and bargain with him for the price of the trip, making it clear that you will only pay on your return. Vehicles are best not left unattended and you should make arrangements with someone to look after your vehicle.

To explore the coast further north, backtrack to Mahate where you turn right and continue for 18 km to the settlement of **Bilibiza**. On reaching the E.N. 243 some 26 km beyond Bilibiza, turn right and continue for 35 km along a badly potholed road to **Macomia**, where you turn right onto a gravel road. After travelling for 34 km you will enjoy your first glimpse of the sea and 7 km from there the village of Mucojo is reached.

At the village square, cut diagonally across to your right and then continue with a sandy four-wheel drive track to a large reed and mud fishermen's village. Take the 'main road' through the village and then head north to Pangane along a sandy track, negotiable by four-wheel drive vehicle only. For the next 9 km the track meanders through an extensive coconut plantation with views of the ocean, islands and reefs to your right. It ends at a headland flanked on one side by a small bay and the crystal clear ocean on the seaward side. The beach at **Pangane** is without doubt the most spectacular spot along the Mozambican coast, with excellent possibilities for snorkelling, a dhow trip to the nearby islands, or simply to relax. Unfortunately, though, the beach on the seaward side is used as an open-air ablution at low tide.

Facilities at Pangane are limited to a camp site started a few years ago by a group of young British ravers who planned to hold rave parties here. They subsequently all left (leaving behind their sophisticated disco equipment) and the site has since been taken care of by a local man, Achime Abubacar. The camp site has an undercover dining area, cold water showers and a pit latrine.

Another option is to ask for directions to the pensão run by Suki, a well-known Chinese resident. Here you can usually also buy cold beer, fish and vegetables.

There are plans to set aside the coastline from Pangane to just north of Quiterajo as a game reserve that will combine game-viewing of species such as elephant and buffalo with the attractions of the coastal environment with its swamps and mangroves.

From Pangane backtrack to Macomia where you turn left if you want to return to Pemba (188 km). To continue to Mocimboa da Praia turn right onto the E.N. 243. It was badly potholed in October 1998 and the 153 km journey to Mocimboa will take anything up to five hours. This road is, however, scheduled to be replaced with an all-weather gravel surface road.

About 103 km north of Macomia you reach the junction to Mueda; turn left here and travel for 50 km along a gravel road that ascends steadily to Mueda, the Makonde capital. The Makonde, who also live in southern Tanzania, are renowned for their fighting spirit and came under Portuguese control only after World War I. They can be recognised by the scars cut into their foreheads and cheeks when they are initiated, while some of the older people still have plugs through their noses, discs through their lips and teeth filed into sharp points. They are also renowned for their Makonde art (see p 23) which is much sought after by collectors throughout the world.

The focal point of **Mueda** is the administrator's office where over 600 unarmed people were killed when Portuguese soldiers opened fire on a crowd of peaceful demonstrators on 16 June 1960; the massacre is reminiscent of South Africa's Sharpeville shooting of a mere three months earlier. Mueda became a symbol of colonial oppression and provided the impetus for the liberation struggle launched on 25 September 1964, when Frelimo attacked the northern outpost of Chai.

Not surprisingly, Mueda became the main operational stronghold and air force base of the Portuguese military in Cabo Delgado. The Makonde formed the main support base of Frelimo and in 1966 a policy was implemented to resettle the local population in *aldeamentos*, or fortified villages, to isolate them from Frelimo. Despite this policy, Frelimo controlled large parts of northern Mozambique by the late 1960s.

In May 1970 the commander-in-chief of the Portuguese armed forces, General Kaulza Arrianga, launched Gordian Knot, a major offensive involving 35 000 troops and over 100 aircraft, to regain territory lost to Frelimo in northern Mozambique. Although the offensive achieved its objective, it resulted in a shift of the war to Tete Province.

If you are headed for Mocimboa, continue to the right at the T-junction along a 50 km stretch of badly potholed tar, scheduled to be replaced by a gravel road. **Mocimboa da Praia** lies within a sheltered bay and is the northernmost port along the Mozambican coast and an important maritime link with Tanzania. It was the first port to be privatised, in 1997, in line with Mozambique's policy of privatisation, and because navigation of the bay is difficult it is planned to ship cargo by barge to and from vessels at anchor outside the bay.

The bay is fringed with mangroves and as a result the water is murky and uninviting for swimming. The largest prawns in Mozambique reputedly come from the waters off Mocimboa which also offers good angling opportunities. Commonly caught species include kingfish, wahoo and rock cod.

Mocimboa has two pensãos: **Pensão Padaria Nina** in Rua Comércio and **Pensão Residencial Magig** in Rua Aeroporto.

From Mocimboa da Praia it is a further 126 km to the Rio Rovuma which forms Mozambique's northern boundary with Tanzania. From Mocimboa a gravel road in fair condition continues for 84 km to **Palma**, which lies alongside a palm-lined lagoon. North of Palma the road deteriorates into a sandy track best tackled in a vehicle with high ground clearance, or a four-wheel drive.

At present, travelling beyond Mocimboa da Praia serves little purpose, unless you are determined to see the Rio Rovuma. There is no bridge across the river and the only way of crossing into Tanzania is by dugout canoe. The most likely place for a bridge across the river has been identified at Negomane, about 250 km upstream of the river mouth.

There are plans to set aside a conservation area that will run parallel to the Rovuma in a 20 km-wide strip and about 125 km upstream from its mouth.

ROUTE 10

TETE TO LAGO NIASSA VIA MALAWI

DISTANCE: 980 km plus optional 180 km **TIME**: 2 days plus **ROAD CONDITIONS**: Tete to Mangochi 455 km good tar; Mangochi to Mandimba 5 km tar, 53 km potholed tar and rough gravel; Mandimba to Lichinga 155 km good gravel, but can become corrugated; Lichinga to Meponda 4 km tar, 60 km gravel; Lichinga to Metangula 78 km good tar, 30 km fair gravel; Metangula to Cóbuè 105 km rough track 4x4 only **FUEL**: Tete, Moatize, Blantyre, Zomba, Mangochi, Lichinga **LINKING ROUTES**: Routes 7 and 11

Although Tete (see p 145 and route 7) falls within Central Mozambique, it is a convenient departure point to the northern province of Niassa and Lago Niassa. Take the 800 m-long suspension bridge spanning the Rio Zambeze from Tete and then head along the E.N. 103 for **Moatize**, an important centre for the nearby coal mines.

The road now strikes northeast and 72 km beyond Moatize ascends steadily for 10 km. About 99 km out of Moatize you reach the turnoff to the Planalto de Angónia (Angonia

Highlands), but your route continues along the E.N. 103 for 15 km to the border. At the Malawian border post, Mwanza, you will be required to take out third party insurance (Malawi K50) and pay Malawi K75 for a temporary import permit for your vehicle. Once you have completed the border formalities continue to Blantyre and then on to Zomba which is probably the best overnight stop *en route* to Lichinga.

Situated on the slopes of the Zomba Plateau, the luxurious red brick **Ku Chawe Inn** is reached after a spectacular 8 km drive along a narrow tar road. Nearby is a **forestry camp site** with basic facilities and little shade, while **Chitinji camp site** is about 5 km further along a gravel road. This delightful camp site, shaded by tall pines, has hot and cold water showers.

From Zomba head for Liwonde and Mangochi, where it is advisable to fill up with fuel which is considerably cheaper here than in Lichinga. The road now heads northeast and 2 km out of Mangochi you cross the Shire River and then continue along a badly potholed stretch of tar and gravel for 7 km before ascending steeply for 8 km along a rough gravel pass. As you approach the summit of the mountain, the gravel gives way to a 5 km stretch of potholed tar before returning to gravel. **Namwera** is 40 km beyond Mangochi and the Malawian border post is another 12 km. A further 7 km brings you to the Mozambican border post, **Mandimba**.

At Mandimba you join the gravel surfaced E.N. 249 to Lichinga. The road has been rebuilt and although stretches were corrugated in September 1998 the road was generally in fair condition. From the border, the road initially passes through a densely populated area where much of the vegetation has been cleared. Unlikely to escape your attention are the interesting granite outcrops that punctuate the miombo woodlands.

The turnoff to **Massangulo** is reached 60 km beyond Mandimba. The village is scenically situated about 1,5 km off the main road below a rocky outcrop. Of interest in the settlement, its streets lined by cypress trees, is the long-abandoned **Roman Catholic Church**.

Continuing along the E.N. 249, the road ascends steeply for 3 km and then descends to cross the Rio Luambala. The area is less populated than further south and 107 km from Mandimba you pass through the settlement of Lione. The road then winds high up along a spur with interesting granite outcrops to the west and east. About 37 km beyond Lione, a pine plantation in the distance suggests that you are nearing Lichinga and 3 km on you will pass through a customs post.

About 1 km beyond the customs post you join a tar road; turn left and after travelling a short way along the edge of a pine plantation you will reach **Lichinga**, the capital of Niassa Province.

At an altitude of close to 1 300 m on the Planalto de Lichinga, the city of 40 000 people enjoys a temperate climate. Although the construction of a railway line linking Lago Niassa to the coast was approved as early as 1912, this ideal was only achieved in 1969 when the line reached Lichinga, a sure indication of just how remote it is.

Prior to independence Lichinga was known as Vila Cabral, a name given in honour of José Cabral who served as Mozambique's Governor-General for 12 years from 1926-38. The city's wide double-lane *avenidas* are still lined with flame trees and jacarandas, but years of neglect have reduced it to a drab place, lacking in atmosphere. The availability of fuel can be unreliable over weekends and as there are few shops, supplies must be obtained at the *Mercado Central* (central market). There is a BCM bank and a TDM *cabine pública* in Avenida Samora Machel.

The town has several accommodation establishments, the best option being the **Residencial Rival**, with clean rooms at reasonable prices. Another option is the **Pousada Lichinga**, which is also the best eatery in the city.

Lichinga is served by regular scheduled LAM flights from Nampula and is linked by bus from Cuamba and Mandimba.

In Lichinga you might well bump into one of the Afrikaner farmers who settled in the Majune District, east of Lichinga, following the signing of the Mosagrius Agreement by President Nelson Mandela and his Mozambican counterpart, Joaquim Chissano, in 1996. The first 14 farmers settled in the province the following year on part of a 50-year renewable concession over 220 000 ha of land negotiated by the South African Chamber of the Development of Commerce in Africa (Sadaca). In terms of the concession 100 000 ha was to be used for crop production, 100 000 ha for cattle ranching and 20 000 ha for fruit growing and ecotourism. The main crops under production are maize, tobacco and cotton. The plan has not been without criticism and shortly after the arrival of the first settlers, the local inhabitants complained about being forced off the land. Another grievance was that the Mozambican government did not consult local chiefs.

From Lichinga, head north along the E.N. 249, a good tar road which traverses the grassy highlands of the Planalto de Lichinga. About 4 km north of Lichinga a turnoff to the left leads to **Meponda**, the southernmost settlement on the shores of the lake. From the turnoff a gravel road strikes westwards and then meanders steeply down to reach the lake shore after about 60 km. The old town consists for the most part of derelict military buildings dating back to the second half of the 1960s, when the Portuguese military established a strong presence here after Frelimo began infiltrating Niassa Province in 1966.

Continuing along the E.N. 249, the scenery becomes increasingly dominated by the 1 863 m-high Serra Jessi as you approach Maniamba, a fairly large village shaded by tall eucalyptus trees. The tar road ends here and for the next 10 km a gravel road ascends steadily before meandering steeply downhill through magnificent miombo woodlands. Then suddenly, with about 4 km to go, the lake comes into view; the sight is especially stunning in the late afternoon just before sunset.

Metangula, the largest of the three settlements on the lake shore, consists of an attractive village of densely clustered traditional mud and reed huts and the old Portuguese settlement and military base on the hill overlooking a sheltered bay with pure white sand and translucent water. The bay is a hive of activity, as this is where fishermen put their craft to the water and land their catches.

Once a terminal point of an ancient trade route linking Lago Niassa and Ibo Island, Metangula's former name, Augusto Cardoso, honours the naval officer who participated in an expedition from Ibo Island into the interior in 1885. Cardoso took over the leadership of the expedition after the leader, Major Serpa Pinto, became ill. After reaching the shores of Lago Niassa he continued to the Shire Highlands before calling off the expedition early the following year.

Metangula is situated virtually opposite Nkothkhotha in Malawi, once the major slave terminus along the western shores of the lake. It no doubt marked the start of the long overland march for thousands of slaves to Ilha do Ibo (see p 151), which featured prominently in the slave trade during the mid-18th century.

From Metangula a rough track heads north along the lake shore, where baobabs grow almost to the water's edge. After about 6 km you will reach the small settlement of **Chiwanga**, where the lake shore makes a sweeping bay with white sand and crystal clear water. Facilities are basic and consist of a few rustic reed and thatch structures available for hire from the owner, *Senhor* Catawala. The spot is popular over weekends with residents of Lichinga, so try to avoid such a time.

Cóbuè, the northernmost of the three villages on the shores of the lake, lies some 99 km to the north along a rough track. The journey can only be tackled with a four-wheel drive vehicle and takes at least four hours. To make the effort worthwhile you should plan to spend at least one night at Cóbuè. There is very little traffic between Metangula and Cóbuè and if you are backpacking you must either be an eternal optimist or extremely lucky if you catch a lift on the off chance. During the rainy season it is inadvisable to attempt this journey as you might have problems negotiating some of the rivers and streams. Most of the bridges were blown up during the war years and have been replaced by log bridges. The strength of some of these bridges is suspect and you might want to inspect them before crossing.

Although not signposted, the track to Cóbuè is easily followed once you're on it; ask at Chiwanga for directions to *estrada* Nova Coimbra. Still better, try to negotiate with a local who knows the route to guide you there. About 6,8 km from Chiwanga you will pass through **Nova Coimbra**, a settlement that was optimistically named the new Coimbra after the city in central Portugal that served as the Portuguese capital from 1190-1260. About 16,5 km on you will reach a large river where the bridge has been blown up. Although the river is quite shallow it is difficult to build up enough momentum to negotiate the steep incline up the other side.

About 85 km from Chiwanga the track meanders across a hill, ascending and then descending steeply. Just when you are about to give up hope of ever reaching the lake it comes into view unexpectedly and 2 km on you reach **Cóbuè**, the smallest of the three lake shore settlements.

Cóbuè is today nothing more than a few ruined buildings with a striking church and mission buildings as its focal point. The mission has fallen into total disrepair; the paint on the walls has faded, but the revolutionary slogans of the mid-1970s and 1980s are still there. The mission was one of several established along the eastern shores of the lake by the Universities Mission to Central Africa of the Anglican Church (UMCA) after it extended its work to Likoma Island in 1882. This enabled the British to lay claim to the island when the Nyasaland Protectorate was created in 1891, despite the fact that the islands are in Mozambican territorial waters.

Likoma Island lies a few kilometres off the Mozambican coast and features an impressive cathedral built between 1903 and 1905. The mission also played an important role in controlling the slave trade and a boat was used on the lake to intercept Arab dhows carrying slaves. In recent years Likoma has become a popular offbeat destination with adventure travellers. The easiest way to get there, though, is to catch the steamer, *Ilala,* which makes a trip from Monkey Bay in Malawi up the lake once a week. Adventure travellers wishing to visit Cóbuè from Likoma do not require a Mozambican visa, provided their stay in Mozambique does not exceed two days.

ROUTE 11

LICHINGA TO PEMBA

DISTANCE: 960 km **TIME**: 2 days plus **ROAD CONDITIONS**: Lichinga to Mandimba 155 km fair gravel; Mandimba to Cuamba 50 km gravel under construction, 98 km good gravel surface; Cuamba to Marrupa 233 km good gravel surface; Marrupa to Balama 155 km track requiring vehicle with a high ground clearance; Balama to Montepuez 53 km rough gravel; Montepuez to Metoro 112 km potholed tar; Metoro to Pemba 95 km reasonably good tar surface. **FUEL**: Lichinga, Cuamba, Montepuez, Pemba **LINKING ROUTES**: Routes 8, 9

It has not been possible to use the direct route from Lichinga to Pemba, via Majune and Marrupa, since the bridge over the Rio Luambala was washed away by floods in 1997. The bridge had not been repaired by September 1998 and until it is travellers will have to use the longer route to Maruppa via Cuamba. This route is over a distance of 960 km and you will have to overnight somewhere along the way.

From Lichinga, take the gravel road through Lione and Chinengue to Mandimba on the border with Malawi. From here a gravel road (under construction in September 1998) winds through beautiful miombo woodlands and stretches of countryside that are sparsely inhabited. About 50 km beyond Mandimba you join a good gravel road and after 23 km cross the disused railway line to Lichinga, the first of numerous crossings. This section is more densely populated and 148 km after leaving Mandimba you will reach **Cuamba**.

Formerly known as Nova Freixo, Cuamba became an important railway centre when the railway line from Nacala reached it in 1950. In 1969 the rail link to Lichinga was completed and the following year the 78 km line to Entrelagos on the border with Malawi was taken into use. During the civil war the railway line fell into disuse and Cuamba became a ramshackle town with potholed roads. Following the establishment of the Nacala Development Corridor in 1997, however, the town's fortunes are likely to change for the better. Although the fuel supply can be unreliable, it is advisable to fill up here as the next fuel stop is at Montepuez, 445 km away.

There are a number of accommodation options in Cuamba. The **Hotel Vision 2002** has clean, air-conditioned rooms and a restaurant with a varied menu, while **Pensão Sao Miguel** is a good choice for backpackers. Another option is the **Pensão Namaacha**.

Cuamba is linked by a daily rail service to Nampula in both directions and can also be reached by rail from Liwonde in Malawi via Nayuchi/Entrelagos. For overland travellers there is a daily bus service which runs from the terminus opposite the station in Cuamba to the *Mercado Central* in Lichinga. There is also a bus between Lichinga and Cuamba.

Retrace your tracks to the Marrupa turnoff, about 1,5 km after passing under the railway bridge. Turn right and after 6 km an abandoned tank serves as a reminder of the country's bloody history. The road traverses the Planalto Moçambicano and further along the miombo woodlands are interspersed with imposing granite outcrops. About 65 km beyond the turnoff, a sign welcomes you to **Metarica**, a small village with streets lined by mango and jacaranda trees.

Beyond Metarica the road continues in a northeasterly direction and massive granite outcrops dominate the scenery. **Maua**, a small village with a few old Portuguese buildings, is

69 km beyond Metarica and just over 7 km further on you will pass the turnoff to the Missão do Jesus, a mission station built below a massive outcrop.

The road now winds through granite outcrops and becomes more undulating. About 35 km out of Maua the road passes an outcrop that resembles the profile of a man's head and after another 60 km **Marrupa** is reached. During the mid-1950s several thousand peasant families in the north of the country were resettled in *aldeamentos*, or irrigated settlements. The policy was devised by the Portuguese to promote the production of crops and in Marrupa more than 300 families were settled on cotton-growing *aldeamentos*. Despite its remote location the town showed signs of a revival in October 1998 with a newly painted school and a colourful cultural centre.

Marrupa is the gateway to the Reservo do Niassa (see p 161) and large herds of elephants still roam the area. The reserve is several hours' drive (150 km) further along a rough track and if you are heading there ask for directions to *estrada* Mecula in Marrupa as the road is not signposted.

The road to Montepuez is also not signposted, but if you head in an easterly direction and stick to the most used road you should have little difficulty finding it. Again it will be useful to ask for directions to *estrada* Montepuez to make sure that you are on the right track. As you head east, the scenery is increasingly dominated by a cluster of large granite outcrops and some 20 km from Marrupa the road meanders through them. More outcrops loom up ahead and 39 km beyond Marrupa you reach the village of Nungo.

The landscape east of Nungo is drained by several tributaries of the Rio Messalo and there are numerous pole and plank bridges across streams and rivers. About 59 km out of Marrupa you pass a large outcrop with a sheer east-facing cliff on your left and 13 km on you cross into Cabo Delgado Province. After about 29 km you will reach a large village with traditional round huts with reed walls and some 15 km further the village of Xamia, which serves as a depot for collecting cotton cultivated in the area.

Balama is reached 32 km beyond Xamia and here you join a gravel road. About 20 km beyond Balama you pass through a neat traditional village with coconut palms and 18 km on you reach another traditional village, Mapupulo. The village of Montepuez is just 16 km away.

Montepuez is a pleasant town with streets lined by frangipani trees and a square decorated by a Portuguese Air Force Dakota shot down during the liberation war. In the late 1950s, Montepuez featured prominently in Portugal's *aldeamento* policy, designed, among other reasons, to boost crop growing. More than 1 000 peasant families were resettled in irrigated settlements in and around the town and in the 1970s a large number of white Portuguese were settled on *colonatos* (irrigated settlements of small farms) in Montepuez to counter Frelimo.

Services in Montepuez include a BMC bank, filling station, a number of restaurants and a busy *Mercado Central* (central market), but there are few shops.

At Montepuez you join a potholed tar road which formed part of the network of roads built in the 1970s for military purposes and to develop the north of the country. About 10 km beyond Montepuez you pass the ruins of Bela Vista and further along the road winds past extensive cotton fields. About 108 km out of Montepuez you reach Metoro at the junction of the E.N. 106 south to Nampula and the E.N. 106 east to Pemba. This is also the junction with route 8 (see p 163).

Continue straight at Metoro and after 12 km you will reach the turnoff to Macomia and Mocimboa da Praia. Your route lies straight ahead, however, and 80 km beyond Sunate (also known as Silva Macua) you reach Pemba (see route 8).

10

WHERE TO STAY

Since the mid 1990s, Mozambique's hospitality industry has made considerable progress in rebuilding and refurbishing hotels and pensões that became derelict during the civil war. In addition, several new hotels and accommodation establishments have been opened and a hotel grading system has been introduced. Where possible, star gradings have been indicated. The following system applies:

★★★★★ excellent

★★★★ super

★★★ very good

★★ good

★ standard

In the major cities, hotels, pensões and camp sites are listed under separate headings, but in other cities and towns no such distinction has been made.

Away from the main centres, many of the pensões still offer fairly basic but comfortable accommodation in establishments dating back to the late 1960s and early 1970s. As the economy improves, the standard of service at these establishments is likely to get better.

Most hotels and lodges in the major cities and tourist resorts charge US dollar rates and, given the performance of the South African rand against the dollar, accommodation in Mozambique is rather expensive.

As an alternative to making your own accommodation reservations you can use the services of companies such as Mozambique Connection, tel RSA (011) 803-4185, or the Mozambique National Tourist Company, tel RSA (011) 339-7275, fax 339-7295, e-mail entur@virconn.com.

Accommodation

The list of accommodation establishments is arranged according to the tourist regions used in this guide and placed under the nearest town.

Maputo

Hotels

Cardoso (★★★★), PO Box 35, Maputo, tel (01) 49 10 71, fax 49 18 04

Carlton, 186 Rua Bagamoyo, Maputo, tel (01) 30 03 56

Central, 266 Rua Bagamoyo, Maputo, tel (01) 43 16 52

Escola Andalucia (★★★★), PO Box 1135, Maputo, tel (01) 42 30 51, fax 42 24 62

Moçambicano (★★★), PO Box 2961, Maputo, tel (01) 42 92 52, fax 42 31 24

Polana (★★★★★), Central Reservations, PO Box 87534, Houghton 2041, tel RSA (011) 484-1641, fax 484-6206

Rovuma (★★★★), Pestana Hotels & Resorts, PO Box 1214, Saxonwold 2132, tel RSA (011) 447-3528, fax 788-6499

Santa Cruz, 1417 Avenida 24 de Julho, Maputo, tel (01) 30 30 04, fax 30 30 66

Tamariz, PO Box 112, Maputo, tel (01) 42 25 96, fax 42 86 09

Terminus (★★★), 587 Avenida Francisco Orlando Magumbwe, tel (01) 49 13 05, fax 49 12 84

Tivoli, PO Box 340, Maputo, tel (01) 30 76 00, fax 30 76 09

Turismo, PO Box 1393, Maputo, tel (01) 42 61 53, fax 42 49 37

Universo, PO Box 831, Maputo, tel (01) 42 70 03, fax 42 51 26

Pensões

Pensão Acijol, Avenida Moçambique, tel (01) 47 05 62

Hoyo-Hoyo Residencial, 837 Avenida Francisco Orlando Magumbwe, tel (01) 49 07 01, fax 49 07 24

Pensão Martins, 1098 Avenida 24 de Julho, tel (01) 42 49 30, fax 42 96 45

Pensão Nini, 586 Avenida Julius Nyerere, tel (01) 49 18 46

Residencial Kaya Kwanga, 321 Rua D João de Castro, tel (01) 49 22 15, fax 49 27 04

Sommerschield House, Sommerschield suburb near Hotel Polana, tel RSA (083) 726 0577

The Burger Inn, Bairro do Triunfo, tel (01) 45 52 11

Triunfo Guest House, Bairro do Triunfo, tel RSA (083) 726 0577

Outside Maputo

Casa Lisa, tel RSA (013) 744-9412 ask for 433

Inhaca Resort Hotel (★★★★), Pestana Hotels & Resorts, PO Box 1214, Saxonwold 2132, South Africa, tel RSA (011) 447-3528, fax 788-6499

Msala Bush Camp (Reserva Especial do Maputo), Polana Tours, tel (01) 49 35 33

Southern Mozambique

Bilene

Centro de Férias dos CFM, tel (022) 13

Complexo Turístico Lagoa Azul, Mozambique National Tourist Co, PO Box 31991, Braamfontein 2017, South Africa, tel RSA (011) 339-7275, fax 339-7295

Complexo Palmeiras, Mozambique National Tourist Co, PO Box 31991, Braamfontein 2017, South Africa, tel RSA (011) 339-7275, fax 339-7295

Hotel Bilene, Bilene, tel (022) 5 90 14

Humula Complexo Turistico, Avenida Amilcar Cabral, tel (022) 2 24 09

Parque Flores, Mozambique National Tourist Co, PO Box 31991, Braamfontein 2017, South Africa, tel RSA (011) 339-7275, fax 339-7295

Praia do Sol, PO Box 2131, Edenvale 1610, South Africa, tel RSA (011) 392-1381

Chidenguele

Paraiso de Chidenguele, PO Box 3016, Cresta 2118, South Africa, tel RSA (011) 782-1026

Inhambane and surrounds

Albatroz, PO Box 244, Inhambane, tel (023) 2 90 05

Barra Lodge Beach Resort, PO Box 6921, Halfway House 1685, South Africa, tel RSA (011) 314-3355, fax 314-3239

Barra Reef, PO Box 3110, Glenvista 2058, South Africa, tel and fax RSA (011) 867-3982, e-mail execupol@mweb.co.za

Casa Barry, PO Box 188, Amanzimtoti 4125, South Africa, tel (023) 2 90 07 or RSA (031) 904-3524, fax 904-3545

Guinjata Bay, Pro-Advent, PO Box 5338, Nelspruit 1200, South Africa, tel RSA (083) 283-6918, fax (013) 741-3149

Hotel Inhambane, Avenida Independência, tel (023) 2 08 55

Nordin's Lodge, tel (023) 2 90 09

Paindane, PO Box 651, Wapadrand 0050, South Africa, tel RSA (012) 807 1464, fax 807 1461

Turtle Cove, Mozambique Connection, PO Box 2861, Rivonia 2128, South Africa, tel RSA (011) 803-4185, fax 803-3861

Limpopo River mouth

Zongoene Lodge, PO Box 35555, Menlo Park 0102, South Africa, tel RSA (012) 346-1286, fax 346-1269

Marracuene/Macaneta

Incomati River Camp, tel Mozambique (cell 082) 30 53 68

Jay's Beach Lodge, PO Box 1753, Maputo, tel Mozambique (cell 082) 30 01 43, fax (cell 082) 33 01 43

Macaneta Lodge, tel (01) 49 94 55, fax 49 94 66, e-mail mlodge@ m-global.com

Marracuene Camping Park and Chalets (Parque de Campismo de Marracuene), tel RSA (011) 609-7806, fax 452-9576, e-mail: thalia@mweb.co.za

Ponta do Ouro

Motel do Mar, PO Box 36112, Menlo Park 0102, South Africa, tel RSA (012) 362-1355, fax 362-1321, e-mail ponta@icon.co.za

Ponta do Ouro Holiday Resort, Mozambique National Tourist Co, PO Box 31991, Braamfontein 2017, South Africa, tel RSA (011) 339-7275, fax 339-7295

Ponta Malongane

Ponta Malongane Holiday Resort, Intercontinental Explorers, PO Box

73089, Lynnwood Ridge, Pretoria 0004, South Africa, tel RSA (012) 348-4262, fax 348-1252

Praia do Xai-Xai

Complexo Turístico Halley, PO Box 180, Xai-Xai, tel (022) 2 29 43

Parque de Campismo da Praia do Xai-Xai, Praia do Xai-Xai, tel (022) 2 29 42

Závora

Závora Lodge, Mozambique National Tourist Co, PO Box 31991, Braamfontein 2017, South Africa, tel RSA (011) 339-7275, fax 339-7295

Central Mozambique

Bazaruto Archipelago – Bazaruto

Bazaruto Lodge, Pestana Hotels & Resorts, PO Box 1214, Saxonwold 2132, South Africa, tel RSA (011) 447-3528, fax 788-6499

Bazaruto Archipelago – Benguerra

Benguerra Lodge, PO Box 87416, Houghton 2041, South Africa, tel RSA (011) 483-2734, fax 728-3767, e-mail benguela@icon.co.za

Marlin Lodge, PO Box 15013, Sinoville, Pretoria 0129, South Africa, tel RSA (012) 543-2134, fax 543-2135, e-mail marlinlodge@mweb.co.za

Magaruque Lodge, The Brokerage, PO Box 2603, Rivonia 2128, South Africa, tel RSA (011) 706-7624, fax 706-7627

Beira

Hotels

Embaixador (★★★★), PO Box 1249, Beira, tel (03) 32 31 21, fax 32 37 88

Moçambique, (★★★★) PO Box 147, Beira, tel (03) 32 50 11, fax 32 50 60

Tivoli Beira (★★★), 363 Avenida de Bagamoio 3, Beira, tel (03) 32 85 70

Miramar (★★★), PO Box 377, Beira, tel (03) 32 22 83, fax 32 95 58

Pensões

Residencial Infante (★★★), PO Box 18, Beira, tel (03) 32 30 42, fax 32 30 41

Camp sites

Biques Camping, Avenida das FPLM, Beira, tel (03) 31 30 51, fax 31 26 22

Clube Náutico (camping), Avenida das FPLM, Beira, tel (03) 31 30 93

Chimoio

Complexo Nhamite, Estrada Nacional N? 6, Chimoio, tel (051) 2 24 48

Estalagem Flor Vouga, Rua Dr Araújo Lacerda, Chimoio, tel (051) 2 20 27

Executive Manica Hotel, PO Box 402, Chimoio, tel (051) 2 31 35, fax 2 31 29

Hotel Moinho, B? Muzingazi, Chimoio, tel (051) 2 31 30

Inhassoro

Hotel Seta, PO Box BW 297, Borrowdale, Harare, Zimbabwe, tel and fax Zimbabwe (04) 87-0930, e-mail welch@icon.co.zw

Maxise

Campiso de Maxise, PO Box 149, Maxise, tel and fax (023) 3 03 51

Morrungulo

Morrungulo, Dive the World, tel RSA (011) 791-2634, fax 791-0337

Quelimane

Complexo Turístico Kass-Kass, tel (04) 21 23 02, fax 21 21 32

Hotel Chuabo, Avenida Samora Machel, Quelimane, tel (04) 21 31 81

Hotel 1 de Julho, PO Box 3067, Quelimane, tel (04) 21 30 67

Pensão Quelimane, Avenida Eduardo Mondlane, Quelimane, tel (04) 21 23 59, 21 21 32

Pensão 24 de Julho, Avenida Filipe Samuel Magaia, Quelimane, tel (04) 21 27 31

Tete

Complexo a Piscina, Avenida Liberdade, tel (052) 2 40 21

Hotel Kassuende, PO Box 80, Tete, tel (052) 2 25 31

Hotel Zambeze, PO Box 230, Tete, tel (052) 2 30 03, fax 2 30 02

Pensão Alves, PO Box 190, Tete, tel (052) 2 25 23

Vilankulo

Aguia Negra, 125 Beach Road, Strand 7140, South Africa, tel RSA (021) 853-7050, fax 853-7195, e-mail http://www.vilanculos.com

Baia do Paraiso, tel RSA (01553) 40591

Hotel Dona Ana, PO Box 2, Vilankulo (no telephone number)

Vilanculos Beach Lodge, PO Box 23821, Claremont 7735, South Africa, tel RSA (021) 683-5337, fax 683-5336, e-mail info@vilanculos.co.za

Northern Mozambique

Cuamba

Hotel Vision 2000, PO Box 65, Cuamba, tel (071) 6 26 32

Pensão San Miguel, PO Box 63, Cuamba, tel (071) 6 26 00

Lichinga

Hotel Chiwindi, Avenida Julius Nyerere, tel (071) 23 45

Pousada Lichinga, Avenida FPLM, tel (071) 28 41

Mocímboa da Praia

Pensão Padaria Nina, Rua Comércio, Mocímboa da Praia, tel (072) 140

Pensão Residencial Magig, Rua Aeroporto, Mocímboa da Praia, tel (072) 159

Mocuba

Pensão Cruzeiro, PO Box 25, Mocuba, tel (04) 184

Pensão São Cristóvão, Avenida Eduardo Mondlane, Mocuba, tel (04) 156

Nampula

Hotels

Lúrio, PO Box 742, Nampula, tel (06) 21 25 20

Nampula, PO Box 96, Nampula, tel (06) 21 21 47

Tropical, Rua Macombre, Nampula, tel (06) 21 22 32, fax 21 32 20

Pensões

Avenida, PO Box 444, Nampula, tel (06) 21 38 93

Central, 17 Avenida Paulo S Kankhomba, Nampula, tel (06) 21 25 19

Estrela, Avenida Paulo S Kankhomba, Nampula, tel (06) 21 49 02

Marques, Avenida Paulo S Kankhomba, Nampula, tel (06) 21 25 27

Nampula, 10 Rua 3 de Fevereiro, Nampula, tel (06) 21 24 56

Residencial Brasilia, 26 Rua Continuadores, Nampula, tel (06) 21 21 26

Residencial Monte Carlo, Rua Cidade Moçambique, Nampula, tel (06) 21 27 89

Pemba

Hotels

Complexo Turístico Nautilus, PO Box 219, Pemba, tel (072) 35 20, fax 37 17

Hotel Cabo Delgado, PO Box 65, Pemba, tel (072) 25 58, fax 35 52

Hotel Pemba, Rua Ten Romeu, Pemba, tel (072) 25 48

Pensões

Baia, Avenida 1 Maio, Pemba, tel (072) 28 48

Residencial Lys, 444 Rua Forças Populares, Pemba, tel (072) 34 32

11

Miscellaneous Information

Mozambican Diplomatic Missions Abroad

Mozambique has diplomatic missions in the following countries: Belgium (Brussels), Ethiopia (Addis Ababa), France (Paris), Germany (Bonn), Great Britain (London), Italy (Rome), Malawi (Lilongwe), Portugal (Lisbon), Spain (Barcelona), Swaziland (Mbabane), Sweden (Stockholm), Switzerland (Geneva), Tanzania (Dar es Salaam), United States of America (New York and Washington DC), Zambia (Lusaka) and Zimbabwe (Harare).

In South Africa, there are Mozambican consulates at the following addresses:

Johannesburg: 252 Jeppe Street, 7th Floor, Cape York House, tel (011) 336-1819, fax 336-9921
Cape Town: 45 Castle Street, 7th Floor, tel (021) 26-2944, fax 26-2946
Durban: 320 West Street, 5th Floor, tel (031) 304-0200, fax 304-0774
Nelspruit: 43 Brown Street, tel (013) 752-7396, fax 753-2088

Diplomatic Representatives Accredited to Mozambique

All based in Maputo – dialling code (01)

Africa

Algeria
121 Rua Mukumbura
Tel 49 20 70

Angola
783 Avenida Kenneth Kaunda
PO Box 2954
Maputo
Tel 49 36 91, fax 49 39 30

Egypt
623 3rd Floor, Avenida Mao Tsé Tung
PO Box 4662
Maputo
Tel 49 23 55, fax 49 14 89

Malawi (High Commission)
75 Avenida Kenneth Kaunda
PO Box 4148
Maputo
Tel 49 31 89, fax 49 02 24

Nigeria
812 Avenida Kenneth Kaunda
Tel 49 29 92

South Africa (High Commission)
41 Avenida Eduardo Mondlane
PO Box 1120
Maputo
Tel 49 00 59, fax 49 30 29

Swaziland (High Commission)
608 Avenida Zimbabwe
PO Box 4711
Maputo
Tel 49 24 51, fax 49 21 17

Tanzania (High Commission)
852 Avenida Mártires Machava
PO Box 4515
Maputo
Tel 49 01 10, fax 49 12 28

Zambia (High Commission)
1286 Avenida Kenneth Kaunda
Tel 49 21 20, fax 49 18 93

Zimbabwe
820 Avenida Kenneth Kaunda
Tel 49 00 25, fax 49 00 56

Europe

Bulgaria
118 1st Floor, Rua Dr Egas Moniz
Tel 49 33 05, fax 49 17 55

Denmark
1500 Avenida 24 de Julho
PO Box 4588
Maputo
Tel 42 90 52, fax 42 05 57

Finland
1128 Avenida Julius Nyerere
PO Box 1663
Maputo
Tel 49 05 78, fax 49 16 62

France
2361 Avenida Julius Nyerere
Tel 49 04 44, fax 49 30 64

Germany
506 Avenida Damião Góis
Tel 49 27 14, fax 49 28 88

Great Britain
310 Avenida Vladimir Lenine
Tel 42 16 95, fax 42 16 66

Ireland
213 Rua D. João IV
Tel 49 63 12, fax 49 30 23

Italy
387 Avenida Kenneth Kaunda
PO Box 976, Maputo
Tel 49 17 99, fax 49 20 46

Netherlands
285 Rua Mukumbura
PO Box 1163
Maputo
Tel 49 00 31, fax 49 04 29

Norway
620 Avenida Agostinho Neto
PO Box 828
Maputo
Tel 42 94 11, fax 42 94 10

Portugal
720 Avenida Julius Nyerere
Tel 49 03 16, fax 49 11 72

Romania
59 Rua Gorongosa
Tel and fax 49 29 99

Russian Federation
1027 Avenida Agostinho Neto
Tel 44 00 91

Spain
347 Rua Damiãos Góis
Tel 49 20 25

Sweden
1128 Avenida Julius Nyerere
PO Box 338, Maputo
Tel 49 00 91, fax 49 00 56

Switzerland
1213 Avenida Julius Nyerere
Tel 49 27 44, fax 49 24 74

North America, South America and the Caribbean

Brazil
296 Avenida Kenneth Kaunda
Tel 49 27 51, fax 49 09 86

Canada
1128 Avenida Julius Nyerere
Tel 49 26 23

Cuba
492 Avenida Kenneth Kaunda
Tel 49 36 73

United States of America
193 Avenida Kenneth Kaunda
PO Box 783, Maputo
Tel 49 27 97, fax 49 36 95

Australasia and the Middle East

Australia
749 9th Floor, Avenida Julius Nyerere
Tel 49 30 72, fax 49 28 88

China (People's Republic)
1309 Avenida Mártires Machava
Tel 49 11 96

India (High Commission)
167 Avenida Kenneth Kaunda
PO Box 4751
Maputo
Tel 49 24 37, fax 49 23 64

Iran
1600 Avenida Mártires Machava
PO Box 1470
Maputo
Tel 49 07 03, fax 49 20 05

Emergency Numbers

Air Ambulance

Medical Rescue International, tel RSA (011) 403-7080

Ambulance

Maputo, tel (01) 42 20 02

Beira, tel (03) 197

Chimoio, tel (051) 2 24 15

Tete, tel (052) 2 21 52

Breakdowns

Maputo, tel (01) 197

Police

Maputo, tel (01) 42 50 31 and 42 20 02

Beira, tel (03) 199

Chimoio, tel (051) 2 22 13

Cuamba, tel (071) 6 26 62

Inhambane, tel (023) 2 08 28

Lichinga, tel (071) 28 28

Nampula, tel (06) 199

Pemba, tel (072) 28 30

Quelimane, tel (04) 21 31 31

Tete, tel (052) 2 30 88

Xai-Xai, tel (022) 2 20 79.

Private hospitals and clinics

Maputo

Centro Medico Phoenix, 671 Avenida Orlando Magumbwe, tel (01) 49 16 39

Clinica Especial, Hospital Central de Maputo, Avenida Eduardo Mondlane, tel (01) 42 46 33

Clinica de Sommerschield Clinic, 52 Rua Pereira Lago, tel (01) 49 39 24

Cruz Azul, 414 Avenida Karl Marx, tel (01) 30 51 46

Urgências Médicas Domiciliárias, 823 Avenida 24 de Junho, tel (01) 42 46 33

State or provincial hospitals

Beira, tel (03) 31 20 71

Chimoio, tel (051) 2 24 15

Cuamba, tel (071) 6 25 33

Inhambane, tel (023) 2 02 11

Lichinga, tel (071) 22 11

Nampula, tel (06) 21 30 01

Pemba, tel (072) 23 48

Quelimane, tel (04) 21 30 00

Tete, (052) 2 21 54

Useful Information Lines

Tourist information

Maputo, tel (01) 42 79 56

Beira, tel (03) 32 36

BIP (Bureau de Informaçao Pública), corner of Avenida Eduardo Mondlane and Avenida Francisco O Magumbwe, tel (01) 49 12 26

Airports

Maputo International Airport, tel (01) 46 58 29

Beira, tel (03) 30 19 08

Chimoio, tel (051) 2 22 42

Inhambane, tel (023) 2 03 12

Airlines

LAM, 1747 Avenida 25 de Setembro, Maputo, tel (01) 42 60 01; Maputo International Airport, tel (01) 46 50 74

SAA, 17 Praça 25 de Junho, Avenida Samora Machel, Maputo, tel (01) 42 07 40

Weather forecasts

Maputo, tel (01) 46 51 38

Beira, tel (06) 30 20 36

Government offices (Maputo)

Direção Nacional de Florestas e Fauna Bravia (Directorate of Forestry and Nature Conservation), Praça Heróis Moçambicanos, tel (01) 46 00 36 Praça Heróis Moçambicanos

Direção Nacional de Geografia E Cadastro (DINAGECA), 537 Avenida Josina Machel, tel (01) 30 25 55

Direção Nacional do Turismo (Directorate of Tourism), 1203 Avenida 25 Setembro, tel (01) 42 50 12

Direção Nacional Migração (Directorate of Immigration), tel (01) 42 04 72

Useful Portuguese Phrases

A fair standard of English is generally spoken at upmarket hotels, lodges resorts and popular seaside towns frequented by tourists and the language is now spoken and understood by far more people than a few years ago. In the rural areas, however, little English is spoken and you will find people very willing to help if you can speak even a few phrases in Portuguese. It is, therefore, highly recommended to gain a basic knowledge of Portuguese before visiting Mozambique. Following are some useful phrases and words.

Basic words and phrases

Good morning	Bom dia
Good afternoon	Boa tarde
Good evening/night	Boa noite
Goodbye	Até logo, Adeus, Ciao
Excuse me (calling waiter)	Faz favor
Excuse me	Com licença
How are you?	Como está?
I am well	Estou bem/bom obrigado
No problem	Não faz mal
Thank you	Obrigado
Thank you very much	Muito obrigado
Too much	Demais

Do you speak English?	Fala Inglês?
I don't speak Portuguese	Não falo Português
I don't understand	Não compreendo, or Não percebo
What is your name?	Como é que se chama?
My name is ...	(Eu) sou ...

child	criança
father	pai (papa)
friend	amigo
man	homen
mother	mãe (mamá)
woman	mulher

good	bem
here	aqui
never (no way)	nada
no	não
nothing	nada
now	agora
please	se faz favor
when	quando
where	onde
who	quem
yes	sim

Accommodation

camp site	campismo
guest house	pensão
hotel	hotel
lodging	pousada

bed	cama
bathroom	casa de banho
room; single/double	quarto; simples/duplo
shower	chuveiro
toilet, ladies'	senhoras
toilet, men's	senhors
water, cold/hot	água fria/quente

Do you have a room?	Tem um quarto?
May I camp here?	É permitido acampar aqui?
Where is the bathroom?	Onde é o quarto de banho?

Banking

bank	banco
bank notes	bilhete (notas)
money	dinheiro
rate of exchange?	qual é o cambio?
travellers cheques	cheques de viagem

Dining/Eating Out

to eat	comer
breakfast	matabicho, pequeno-almoço
lunch	almoço
dinner	jantar
menu, handwritten	ementa
menu, printed	cardápio
desserts	doces, sobremesa
poultry	aves
sauces	molhos
starters	entradas
Please bring the bill	a conta, se faz favor
the receipt	recibo

Beverages (Bebidas) and Wine (Vinho)

beer	cerveja
coffee	café
juice	sumo
soft drink (fizzy)	refresco
tea	chá
water	água
wine	vinho
wine list	carta de vinhos
wine, semi-sweet	vinho meio-doce
wine, dry white	vinho branco seco
wine, dry red	vinho tinto seco
wine, sparkling	champanhe

Breakfast

bacon and eggs	ovos com bacon
eggs, boiled	ovos cozido

eggs, fried	ovos estrelados
eggs, scrambled	ovos mexidos
omlette, plain	omlete simples
omlette with ham	omlete com fiambre
omlette with cheese and tomato	omlete com queijo e tomate

Meat (Carne)

beef	carne de vaca
chicken	frango
chicken, fried with peri-peri	galhina frita com peri-peri
pork	porco
pork, grilled chops	febras de porco na brasa
steak, fillet	filete
steak, ladies fillet	filete pequeno
steak, rump	bife
steak, rare/medium/ well done	filé bife mal passado/médio/ bem passado

Seafood (Frutos do mar)

calamari	lulas
calamari, fried	lulas fritas
catch of the day	peixe do dia
crab	caranguejo
crab, boiled	caranguejo cozido
fish	peixe
fish, boiled with vegetables	peixe cozido com vegetal
prawns	camarão
prawns, boiled	camarão cozido
prawns, fried	camarão frito
prawns, grilled	camarão grelhado
seafood platter	pratos de frutos do mar

Miscellaneous

cake	bolo
cheese	queijo
fried onion	cebola frita
ice cream	gelado
potato, baked	batatas cozidas
potato chips	batatas fritas
salad	salada
salad, mixed green	salada mista

sweet potato	batata doce
vegetables	vegetais
vegetables, mixed	vegetais misturados

Medical

ache	doer
casualty department	banco de sorcorros
diarrhoea	diarréia
doctor	médico
fever	febre
headache	dor de cabeça
hospital	hospital
ill	doente
malaria	malária, paludismo
stomach ache	dor de estômago
I feel sick	Estou enjoado
Take me to the hospital please	Levar-me para hospital, faz favor
Where is a doctor?	Onde está um médico?

Officials

police	policia
traffic police	policia de trânsito

Places

city	cidade
small town	vila
village	aldeia
avenue	avenida
lane	travessa
plaza	praça
road	estrada
square	largo do
street	rua
bank	banco
beach	praia
church	igreja
museum	museu

nightclub	boite
pharmacy	farmácia
police station	policia
post office	correio
restaurant	restaurante
school	escola
swimming pool	piscina
bridge	ponte
lake	lago
mountain	montanha
ocean	oceano
river	rio
sea	mar

Shopping (Compras)

bakery	pastelaria/padaria
bottle store	lojas de bebidas
butchery	talho
curios	artesanato
market	mercado
market, fish	bazar do peixe
shop	loja
supermarket	supermercardo
book	livro
film (photographic)	película
magazine	revista
newspaper	jornal
post card	postal
stamps	selos
bread	pão
butter	manteiga
cashew nuts	castanha de caju
cheese	queijo
eggs	ovos
fish	peixe
fruit	fruta
lobster	lagosta
meat	carne
milk	leite

mineral water	água mineral
onions	cebola
pepper	pimento
potato	batata
rice	arroz
salt	sal
sugar	açúcar
tomatoes	tomate
vegetables	vegetais
closed	fechado (m), fechada (f)
Do you have ...?	O senhor têm ...?
Give me ...	Dê me ...
How much?	Quanto custa
I'll buy it	Vou comprar
I would like to buy ...	Eu queria comprar ...
I would like this ...	Quero isto ...
more	mais
open	aberto (m), aberta (f)
What is this?	Que é isto?
Too expensive!	Muito caro!

Travel

customs	alfandega
passport	passaporte
visa	um visto
aeroplane	avião
airport	aeroporto
bus	machimbombo
car	carro
car rental agency	agência de aluguer de carros
journey	viagem
mechanic	mecânicos
minibus taxi	chapacem
taxi	taxi
train	comboio
train station	estação de caminho de ferro
corner	esquina
far	longe
left	à esquerda

long	longo
map	mapa
near	perto
right	à ireita
short	curto
straight	à direito
How much is the fare?	Quanto é que custa o bilhete?
How far to ...?	Quanto kilometros até ...?
I am lost	(Eu) estou perdido
I have lost my passport	Perdi o meu passaporte
I want to go to ...	Quero viajar parñ ...
My car is broken down	Meu carro está quebrado
Name of this village?	Nome desta vila?
Name of the next village?	Nome da proxima aldeia?
When does the bus arrive?	Quando chega este machimbombo?
When does the bus leave?	Quando sai este machimbombo?
Where is ...?	Onde é ...?
Where is the nearest village?	Onde é próxima vila?

Time

day	dia
month	mês
week	semana
year	ano
morning	manhã
night	noite
today	hoje
tomorrow	amanhã
yesterday	ontem
Sunday	Domingo
Monday	Segunda-feira
Tuesday	Terça-feira
Wednesday	Quatra-feira
Thursday	Quinta-feira
Friday	Sexta-feira
Saturday	Sábado
January	Janeiro
February	Fevereiro

March	Março
April	Abril
May	Maio
June	Junho
July	Julho
August	Agosto
September	Setembro
October	Outubro
November	Novembro
December	Dezembro

Numbers

one	um, uma
two	dois
three	três
four	quatro
five	cinco
six	seis
seven	sete
eight	oito
nine	nove
ten	dez
eleven	onze
twelve	doze
thirteen	treze
fourteen	catorze
fifteen	quinze
sixteen	dezasseis
seventeen	dezassete
eighteen	dezoito
nineteen	dezanove
twenty	vinte
twenty-one	vinte e um
thirty	trinta
forty	quarenta
fifty	cinquenta
sixty	sessenta
seventy	setenta
eighty	oitenta
ninety	noventa
one hundred	cem
two hundred	duzentos/as

three hundred	trezentos/as
four hundred	quatrocentos/as
five hundred	quinhentos/as
six hundred	seiscentos/as
seven hundred	setecentos/as
eight hundred	oitocentos/as
nine hundred	novecentos/as
one thousand	mil
two thousand	dois mil
one million	milhão

Bibliography

The following sources were consulted and are useful if you wish to obtain more detailed information.

Apps, P (ed). 1996. *Smithers' Mammals of Southern Africa: A Field Guide.* Southern Book Publishers.

Ash, P. 1999. "Natural High". *Out There* 41, 48-51.

Birmingham, D. 1992. *Frontline Nationalism in Angola & Mozambique.* James Currey.

Branch, G M; Griffiths, C L; Branch, M L and Beckley, L E. 1994. *Two Oceans — A Guide to the Marine Life of Southern Africa.* David Philip.

Briggs, P. 1997. *Guide to Mozambique.* Bradt Publications.

Clancey, P A. 1996. *The Birds of Southern Mozambique.* African Bird Book Publishing.

Da Silva, C. 1995. *Olhar Moçambique: Tete, Zambezia, Manica, Sofala.* Centro De Formação Fotográfica.

Da Silva, C. 1996. *Olhar Moçambique: Inhambane, Gaza, Maputo.* Centro De Formação Fotográfica.

Dutton, P. 1990. "The Bazaruto Archipelago Mozambique's juvenile Galapagos". *Endangered Wildlife (Journal of the Endangered Wildlife Trust)* 4, 3-6.

Dutton, P. 1994. "A Dream Becomes A Nightmare". *African Wildlife* 48 (6), 6-14.

Korrûbel, J and Cockcroft, V. 1997. "Dire Days for Dugongs". *Africa Environment & Wildlife* 5 (1), 28-33.

Maclean, G L. 1985. *Roberts' Birds of Southern Africa.* John Voelcker Bird Book Fund.

Michler, I. 1998. "Mozambique's Niassa Reserve". *Africa Environment & Wildlife* 6 (5), 28-33.

Newitt, M. 1995. *A History of Mozambique.* Witwatersrand University Press.

Palgrave, K C. 1992. *Trees of Southern Africa.* Struik Publishers.

Raw, H (ed). 1995. *Railways of Moçambique 100 Years.* Manica Moçambique and CFM-Moçambique Railways.

Ryan, P. 1996. "Birding in Mozambique Orioles and Akalats". *Africa Environment & Wildlife* 4 (1), 34-36.

Skelton, P H. 1993. *A Complete Guide to the Freshwater Fishes of*

Southern Africa. Southern Book Publishers.

Skinner, J D and Smithers, R H N. 1990. *The Mammals of the Southern African Subregion.* University of Pretoria.

Sinclair, P J J. 1987. *Space, Time and Social Formation - A territorial approach to the archaeology and anthropology of Zimbabwe and Moçambique c 0-1700 AD.* Societas Archaeologica Upsaliensis.

Slater, M. 1997. *Guide to Mozambique.* Struik Publishers.

Slater, M. 1997. *Globetrotter Travel Guide: Mozambique.* New Holland Publishers.

Steele, D. 1996. "Daring the Deep in Southern Mozambique". *Getaway* 8 (3) 28-38, 128-131.

Swift, K. 1974. *Mozambique and the Future.* Don Nelson.

Tinley, K. 1979. "Gorongosa Kaleidoscope". *African Wildlife* 33 (5), 10-15.

Van der Elst, R. 1993. *A Guide to the Common Sea Fishes of Southern Africa.* Struik Publishers.

Von Etzdorf, B. 1996. "Mighty Mouth Whale Sharks — the world's largest fish". *Africa Environment & Wildlife* 4 (1), 59-65.

Wagner, P. 1997. "Dances with fishes". *Getaway* 9 (6), 74-82, 162-3, 165

Waterhouse, R. 1996. *Mozambique Rising from the Ashes.* Oxfam.

INDEX

A

B

C

N

P

Q

R

Ondeh

0826307788

TREAT YOUR OWN NECK PAIN

A step-by-step guide to
self-treating neck pain and injury

By Christopher David Handbury

Cover design and illustration by Christopher David Handbury.

Author's Disclaimer

The information in this book has been gathered by the Author though continued academic study, personal experience and through many years of active treatment and conversations with other practitioners, patients and students.

This publication has been designed to provide information regarding the subject matter covered. The author will not in any way be held responsible for any injury caused by the incorrect use or practice of the methods within this book. The techniques and methods detailed in this book are to be used at the reader's own risk.

The practice of Qigong and self-applied massage techniques is very safe when performed according to the advice given in this book. Cautions and advice have been provided where needed. The author recommends the guidance of a trained practitioner to provide the best possible experience of the information provided.

Readers are advised to seek professional advice or treatment for any medical conditions prior to undertaking a new form of health exercise or therapy.

The author does not recommend unsupervised practice of Qigong or the practice of the massage points in this book for those who are experiencing symptoms associated with terminal illness, severe psychiatric conditions (e.g., severe depression, active suicidal ideation, schizophrenia), current severe medical conditions for which exercise is contraindicated, chronic addiction to alcohol or drug abuse, or for pregnant women.

About the Author

Christopher David Handbury has been a qualified practitioner of Traditional Chinese Medicine (TCM) since 2006 gaining recognised training in Traditional Acupuncture, Microsystem Acupuncture, Tui Na Medical Massage, Traditional Indonesian Massage and Heaven and Earth Qigong.

He continues to pursue training with some of the most respected teachers in their line of practice and passes this knowledge onto patients and students at his clinic situated in the heart of Gloucestershire, south-west England.

Christopher has successfully treated thousands of patients using the methods of TCM and helped many of them to discover the practice of Qigong health exercise and self-massage methods. This allows each person to actively take part in their own recovery and maintain personal health, ultimately to reduce the need for prescription medications.

Traditional Medicine often states that the best doctor is you, yourself and Christopher continues to promote this powerful belief.

In 2018 Christopher released his first publication titled 'What is Qigong? – A step-by-step guide to growing a successful practice of Qigong' which has gained him worldwide acknowledgement by readers and practitioners.

His mission is to provide simple and effective education to those who seek to improve their health through the positive methods of traditional eastern medicine.

Contents

Author's Introduction

Let me start by saying thank you for opening this book. I hope the information within these pages will help you to live a happier life, with less stress and less pain.

Each section in this book will help you learn how to relieve the discomforts that come with daily neck pain and the associated symptoms of injuries in this area.

I feel it's true to say that neck pain and discomfort are by far some of the most exhausting and debilitating conditions that we may suffer. For the majority of us we can still manage to get along with back pain, shoulder aches or joint pains, but when it comes to the neck it can feel like an uphill struggle, especially if our daily duties are adding to our pain.

Throughout the day we can spend around 70% of our time balancing this heavy bowling ball of a head on top of our spine, with constant support by the neck muscles to make sure it doesn't fall off!

You may be surprised to know there are around 26 individual muscles that support this heavy weight and another 24 that have a secondary support action! That's around 50 muscles used to help support and protect the spine through the neck. No other junction or joint in the human body has as many amazing structures and connections as the neck, so there's no wonder it can cause so many problems.

To add some perspective, the head can weigh around 5 kg (11 lbs), equivalent to five or six bags of flour or sugar. For the lucky ones among us we can get through the day with the odd ache and pain, but what about those who must endure everyday pains, stiffness, headaches, muzzy heads and various signs of fatigue often associated with neck problems.

Neck pain is rarely a life-threatening condition so it's often passed off as a temporary disorder that will correct itself. Sometimes this is true, and sometimes the pain can become an unwanted burden of daily life.

For this reason, there is a huge lack of support and the drug medications that are prescribed rarely have a lasting effect. If anything, they upset our digestive system and disturb sleep patterns, giving us even more stress to deal with.

There are numerous causes of neck pain, such as whiplash injuries, car accidents, falls and degeneration of the physical body. Stress, emotions, trauma and most commonly, poor structure or posture all play their role in causing daily discomfort.

If you are a chronic sufferer you may have gone out at some point and spent your hard-earned money on 'magic' pillows that claim to improve your posture or even worse invested huge sums of money in a mattress that boasts it can relieve neck and back pain.

You may have tried the latest ointments and gels, the electronic massage contraptions or committed to a lengthy course of physical therapy with no lasting results.

I myself have a long-standing neck injury and my journey of pain and emotions led me right here, to write this book! I understand the pain, the sleepless nights, the lack of solutions and I also understand how far the ripples of injury can travel though our personal lives.

Like many sufferers I've tried the whole bag of tricks and gimmicky products, or at least the ones that had a degree of theory behind them. The results never lasted very long. I do however remember the amazing effect it had on making the money disappear from my wallet!

Through my own suffering, I eventually reached a point of pure frustration, exhaustion from sleepless nights and the ever-increasing hours of pain. I knew that something had to change, and it did!

I discovered some remarkable and effective methods that allowed me to eventually treat and manage my own neck pain. They were simple, easy to learn and provided me with a great sense of relief, on a daily basis. These methods quite literally changed my life forever!

In fact, these methods also changed my career, my family life and allowed me to go on to help hundreds of other sufferers regain their happiness and enjoy daily life with less pain, less stress and more energy!

One of the main reasons why I believe they are so effective is because they address the symptoms holistically. It's not just the physical effects of neck pain that cause problems, it's the emotional trauma and constant daily pain that gradually wears us down too.

In order to have any kind of lasting results you need to treat both aspects of any illness or injury.

So, with this book and the methods I am going to share with you, we are going to hit this from both physical and emotional angles. You are going to learn some miraculous things here.

Will it work for you too? Hell yeah! But it also depends on how much time you are willing to invest in getter better.

All you need is to spare just a few minutes every day to run through the techniques in this book and before you know it, you'll be able to treat your own pains and discomforts and become master of your own health! And that's a powerful skill to have, so, let's get started.

Chapter 1

Getting Started

Building the Foundations

Cautions and Safe Care

As we are dealing with pain and in some cases chronic medical conditions, we need to develop the right mindset from the beginning.

With any condition or injury where there is pain, it is very important to get a professional opinion from a trained practitioner or medical doctor before beginning any new health practice.

Try not use search engines or attempt self-diagnosis. A professional practitioner may find something that requires a specific treatment model.

That being said, once you have the all-clear, the methods in this book will work very well alongside any recommended treatment and in most cases, provide a stand-alone practice of pain relief.

Getting to Know Pain

Firstly, it's very important to become aware of the pain and discomfort you are experiencing. There are good pains and bad pains, manageable pains and more serious pains.

Pain that is tight, restrictive or feels like a dull ache is usually caused by muscular tension and restrictions in the tissues. Pain that is sharp or stabbing could mean deterioration of the joints or inflammation of the tendons. It's worth getting it checked out just to be sure.

Most of us will suffer from the former: aches, tightness and a dull pain. In this case it's usually okay to move forward and start with the methods in these pages.

If in doubt, get checked out. The last thing I would want is for you to be in more pain or discomfort.

So, what causes the pain? Why does it come and go? Let's have a quick look at some basic reasons why you may be suffering.

A Brief Look at Causes

There are numerous causes of neck pain, some of which I have already mentioned. We can have pain from muscle fatigue, where the muscles have been overused or had little time to recover from repetitive activities.

There are also those dull aches we get after a long day at work when we feel like we just need to rest our bones. Days when usually, a good rub and soak in the bath can be a great remedy.

At some point we will all get those 'tension pains' from the result of emotional stress, where tension in our shoulders pulls and tightens, making us feel tired and wound up like a spring.

Deviations in posture or poor structure can cause pains where the muscles pull in all directions to keep our bones in alignment. The modern tasks we perform on a daily basis can sometimes reduce the natural flow of the body and cause problems with our structure. This is often seen in jobs where you are seated all day like office work or driving.

We can also get into bad habits with our posture and over time the structure changes and the muscles begin to fatigue and ache. If this is continued, muscles can become short or locked, pulling the bones out of position and compromising our natural balance and equilibrium.

Inevitably, this can affect the nearby nerves and we get localised or referred pain in different areas of the body. It only takes a slight change in muscle tone or bone movement to place pressure on a nerve, causing even more pain and discomfort.

Deterioration of the joints, slipped discs, bulges or herniated discs are quite serious injuries and can cause a lot of pain. In many cases they require manipulation to correct the alignment of the structure, sometimes surgery.

If this is the case, then the methods in this book will serve as a great rehabilitation and recovery programme following any hospital treatment.

Arthritic symptoms are one of the most common conditions we experience as we get older. The joints of the bones become inflamed or deteriorate; the structure becomes weakened, and the muscles around the area become fixed and stiff in order to protect the body. This protective nature is a great process, but it doesn't always feel like it when you're in pain.

Arthritis also has a knack of showing up many years after an injury has taken place. I have treated horse riders who have had a fall as a young rider and not had any problems until their 50s or 60s!

The same goes for minor car accidents where your recovery has been relatively positive but in later years you develop a chronic pain condition. I'm sure a few readers can relate to that.

Other traumatic conditions can result from car accidents, falls and sports injuries. These injuries always affect the neck to some extent because the spine has often taken the shock of the trauma. Injuries literally ripple through our entire being, physically and emotionally.

In my own experience, and through many years treating patients, these injuries are never simple, they are multi-layered. Not only do they affect the neck area, but also the supporting systems of the shoulder, chest and upper back.

Eventually, with the additional pains, we can easily forget what the original injury actually was and go around in circles trying to discover the best solution and remedy.

It's not just the physical impact of the injury that causes pain, it's also the emotional impact that makes recovery even harder. The stress from not being able to enjoy the activities you once loved only adds tension to the body and mind.

Lack of sleep due to pain reduces our recovery and lengthens our suffering. Not being able to carry out simple, daily tasks at home or work becomes a burden and we feel useless, tired and drained. It's just no fun at all!

Throughout these pages we will look at the effect of neck pain and possible causes you might not be aware of and we will seek to use specific techniques to remedy each ailment.

As many of the methods in this book are from traditional eastern systems, it's worth giving you a brief explanation of how this medicine works.

Traditional Chinese Medicine (TCM)

TCM is one of the most tried-and-tested medical systems available today. Its roots go back over 5,000 years. The science of TCM was developed through the observation of how the body reacted to the seasons, what patterns presented during illness and injuries and how the mind was affected by change, especially the emotions.

It's a very deep and powerful system that is beyond the pages of this book, but I will try to give you an idea of how it will help.

In TCM, the energy of the body called 'Qi' (pronounced: Chee) moves in specific pathways to nourish the physical body and our mental self so that we may complete the functions of daily life. When these pathways become restricted or do not function correctly, we can experience illness and pain.

The application of TCM restores and aims to correct any imbalances in the pathways so that we can return to good health.

So, what exactly is 'Qi'?

Qi is not exactly 'a thing' and then again, it is many 'things'! There is always a lot of confusion regarding the idea of 'Qi' and its explanation depends entirely on the context in which it is being used at any given time. For the purpose and simplicity of this book let's look at the character for a basic understanding.

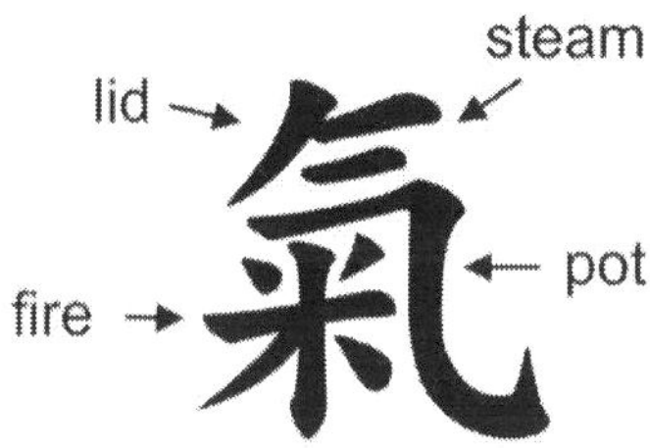

Fig 1.1

In the Chinese language 'Qi' is a common character used to describe the quality or relationship between two 'things'. Let me try to explain.

The character symbolises a pot of water being heated over a fire and the result of this heating process creates an additional form of energy, the steam. *(Fig 1.1)*

This represents the 'Qi', or the result of fire, water and heat combined. You can feel and see the pot and the water, but the steam is more elusive. You know it's there because you can see it, yet it cannot be grasped like the pot of water. It's a different form of energy with a different quality and substance to it.

Another example is the air we breathe which is a form of 'Qi' because it has been produced by the world around us. We do not see it being made, but we know it is there because we are alive and we never give it any more thought.

This air nourishes our physical body, circulates in our blood, converts our food into energy and provides our 'Qi' for the body to exist.

I have also included a picture of my own that separates the components of the Chinese character. *(Fig 1.2)*

Fig 1.2

The idea of 'Qi' can seem quite alien or confusing if you are not familiar with its use or meaning. In Western publications it is often described as energy, life force or even breath or gas, but for me it's simply a word to describe an activity or quality.

In an attempt to simplify the matter, think of it like this. A tennis ball has little Qi (life, activity) when you hold it in your hand, but if you bounce it, it has lots of Qi!

In terms of our health, if we are weak and frail, we can lack vibrant Qi or at least any that has a lively quality, we are empty or deficient. When we are happy and healthy, we are abundant in Qi, active and energetic, we are full of good Qi, we are flowing and have vitality.

It's a big subject that has commanded many volumes of writing on the subject. I hope that this brief explanation has helped.

Although modern Western scientists are still contemplating the understanding of Qi, they are, however, now beginning to understand the pathways of TCM as they are very much like those with which we may already be familiar.

Many of you will have received some biology education in school or read books about the human body so you will already have some idea of the various pathways we have inside us.

The vessels of TCM are closely related to the blood vessels, nerve pathways, fascia, tissue connections and fluid pathways that we know from the Western health system. I am fascinated by it! And I hope you will be too.

So, what does 'Qi' have to do with neck pain?

My own injury came before I was exposed to the brilliance of TCM and it wasn't until I started to train in Chinese Medicine that I began to see how my own suffering could be reduced. The theory and the outcomes fitted perfectly and the jigsaw began to come together.

The development of our pain is much more than something we feel in our bones, muscles and joints. The body is not just a machine, there is a process to the symptoms which present in a very specific way. Once I had this knowledge, I started to get great results and some much-needed relief from pain.

After you have read the information here you will see for yourself that TCM has a lot to offer to improve your health. It can seem very different to traditional forms of treatment; those with which we are more familiar and the ideas or beliefs with which we've grown up. But the more you learn, you'll discover that it is, in fact, the most natural system for healing and maintaining personal health.

As we move though the book, I will do my best to help you understand each section so you can develop a very valuable and personal system to treat your own neck pain. You will also notice that in each section I will mention the word 'Qigong' a lot so, it's worth providing you with a brief explanation of this health practice.

Qigong – The Mind-Body Medicine

Qigong forms one of the four pillars of Chinese Medicine; Acupuncture, Tui Na Massage and Herbal Medicine being the others. Its history is rich in health care. Qigong has begun to grow in popularity since it came to Western shores in the 1950s and 1960s.

Most of us are aware of the Eastern practice of yoga, but many are not aware that it was originally a medical system of health and not just the system of stretching and physical development that it has become today.

Qigong on the other hand, seems to have retained its medical heritage, perhaps because of its lack of exposure here in the West or possibly its requirements for long study and practice. Either way, both systems, in their traditional forms, are great for health and healing.

Qigong at its basis can look like any other exercise system and it's often confused with Tai Chi because of its slow movements and flowing nature.

The difference with Qigong is that the movements have been developed and created by medical practitioners to have a very specific goal and outcome. Some movements help with the physical body, some help to restore organ health. Other practices aim to cultivate the mind and spirit through meditation and static postures, as in Zhan Zhuang (standing post) Qigong.

All of the four TCM methods are based on the same medical theory. Acupuncture is the application of needles, Tui Na is the application by hand, herbs by ingestion or trans-dermal (applied to skin) application and Qigong uses the physical body and the intention of the mind.

Together they form a complete and very profound system of health care. Qigong is an amazing system that ticks a lot of boxes for many people. For me, Qigong is the mother of the four pillars and the 'original' health system.

I have not included much detail of the Qigong practices in this book as they require a deeper explanation. However, if you would like to know more about Qigong and get a feel for Chinese Medicine, please see my book *What is Qigong? – A step-by-step guide to growing a successful daily practice of Qigong.* It has proven to be very effective for new and existing students of Qigong.

Another method that I have found invaluable when beginning a specific health practice is to start by making a note of how you are feeling, right here and right now.

Ask yourself these questions and then write them down so you can come back at a later date and check your progress.

This is a very important part of the healing process as often we forget exactly how much our pain and symptoms have affected our lives.

On a scale of 1-10 make a note of the levels of pain or emotions you feel.

1= Low – Not so much, 10 = High – A lot!

- How do your symptoms make you feel every day?
  Tired ______
  Angry ______
  Low /Sad ______
  Exhausted ______

- How much do you feel pain and discomfort?
  Neck area ______
  Shoulders ______
  Head ______
  Arms ______
  Upper back ______
  Lower back ______

Once you have this information written down you can come back to it at a later date and see if there have been any positive changes.

After a few weeks of applying the methods in this book, come back and enter your details below. Hopefully you will see a notable change, but this will always depend on whether you have been committing to a daily practice or just a few times a week.

Just do your best and be patient. Time is a great healer.

- How do your symptoms make you feel every day?
  Tired ______
  Angry ______
  Low/Sad ______
  Exhausted ______

- How much do you feel pain and discomfort?
  Neck area ______
  Shoulders ______
  Head ______
  Arms ______
  Upper back ______
  Lower back ______

Now that we have a brief idea of what we're working with, let me show you what you can do right now to start feeling better and reduce those aches and pains: our first practice.

Swinging the Arms.

I'm a great believer in getting started straight away! We can get to all the details and understanding as you progress through the book.

To begin with, I'm going to teach you a very simple and effective technique that will help to release the tensions and stress.

This method gently improves blood circulation through the body to activate and nourish the muscles.

It's great for overall health and anyone can do it. If you find it difficult to stand, a stool can be used.

Along with increasing blood circulation around the body. It helps to relax the shoulders and neck by gradually promoting blood flow into the area with each swing.

The trick with this practice is to keep the hands relaxed, but not loose, I call that 'noodle hands'. They should be alive! Try to maintain softness in the shoulders and go with the natural rhythm of the swing.

The natural pendulum-like movement has an additional relaxing effect on the mind. Remember to keep the knees soft so that you can begin connecting to the earth. *(Fig 1.3)*

Practice.

1. Stand the feet at shoulder-width apart. Soften the knees and relax into the feet.

2. Gently swing your arms back and forth, forward and back in a relaxed motion.

3. Repeat 150-300 times or set a timer for 3-5 minutes.

You can practise this movement any time you like, if you have the kettle boiling, toast in the toaster, food in the oven or you have the TV on, for example. Just take a step to the side, relax the legs and swing your arms.

Eventually, through regular practice, this simple movement will become very therapeutic and the results will be instantaneous!

Fig 1.3

And we're off!

So, it's official! You have now begun your recovery and have your first, positive practice to learn. Why not spend a few days getting used to 'Swinging the Arms' and once you have the hang of it, come back to the book and we'll move on and look at the physical nature of the neck to get an idea of what we're working with when we're self-treating pain.

If you ever find yourself standing still … just swing your arms.

Chapter 2

What is Causing Your Pain?

Exploring the Body and Mind

The Balancing Ball

In all its essence, the neck is primarily a support system for the powerhouse that is our brain. Basically, it's a ball that sits on top of a spike supported by many ropes working in harmony to maintain the structure and safety of the skull.

If you can imagine a huge ball resting on just the smallest of spikes with numerous support ropes all working together to maintain the balance, you will not be far off what we have on top of our bodies.

This ball-like mass must be constantly balanced from all sides so that it does not fall. When one rope becomes slack the opposite rope must pull or restrain itself to restore the balance.

If the rope is pulled too hard, when there is a traumatic injury for example, it may stretch too far or at worst, tear or break! If this happens, it is up to all the other ropes to take the strain and eventually that could mean pain. It's a never-ending juggle to maintain the balance.

Each rope has a job to do and they must all work together to be able to turn the ball, tilt the ball, rotate the ball, move with the eyes and ears, be supportive when we talk or eat and move it to whichever position we choose. How exhausting is that?!

Not only do we have to balance the ball on top of the spine, but we also have the added pressure of gravity pressing down on us too. Luckily, the spine is designed to cushion and minimise the effects of this through correct posture, but how many of us feel we have correct posture?

How often do you feel like your head is a ball balanced on a spike? I can tell you this: 8 out of 10 patients I see in clinic do not have a healthy posture!

If we don't balance the head properly then any deviation from the centre will travel through the spine and hips. The body will adjust itself to maintain whatever position is least uncomfortable.

This is not always the right position, but as it 'feels' better you might see it as the right way. If this happens, and because you have adjusted the structure, you may begin to feel other pains too. The shoulders will ache, the back will have pain, the hips will hurt and the feet will become painful, all because the head is not supported in the correct position by the neck.

It all starts at the top, so taking care of the neck can also have many subsequent benefits for the whole body and mind.

In general, there are three main types of neck conditions that cause pain and discomfort: degeneration, trauma or injury. These symptoms are the most common I see in clinic, top of the list are repetitive strains from overuse.

Degeneration

Degeneration is when the structures and tissues of the cervical area begin to age from wear and tear. The pads in between the discs can wear and cause pain when the bones meet, or they can compromise any nerves that are situated close to the injury. These discs can also become dehydrated and more prone to cracks and tears.

Most of us will have some level of degeneration in the cervical neck bones, and most of us will never know until the area has been scanned. Some level of degeneration is normal as it's a very well-used part of the body.

Excessive or early degeneration can be problematic and there doesn't seem to be many solutions on offer from doctors here in the West. I feel that educating people as to how the body works, how to use the body more efficiently and the possible effects its poor use can have is one of my goals in life.

Education of this type is less favoured in schools in the UK, but it should be the number one subject. Just think how much money could be saved on medical bills if everyone had a better knowledge of how to look after themselves better! Money that could be used to help those more in need or with fewer advantages than the average.

I also find that degeneration is considered by Western medicine to be an irreparable condition. I'm a great believer in the healing power of the body and mind and I have seen some quite remarkable outcomes of cases that doctors had decided could not be treated.

Even if your condition is thought to be on the excessive side of degeneration, DO NOT give up! You can still have a positive effect on your own health if you actively take steps to improve the symptoms.

In 2014, after my own MRI scan, the doctors and surgeons all looked very bleakly at my results. Excessive degeneration, herniated disc and the bones closing around nerves were just a few of the noted problems. The surgeon felt that the risk of operation could leave me with a loss of use in my right arm.

But five years on, I am, in most part, pain-free and I can't recommend Qigong and self-massage enough. Both methods really tick a lot of boxes for many health conditions if you are willing to invest the time and reap the benefits.

Emotional Causes

When we feel pain, the physical reaction of the body makes us think that the cause is physical too, but that's not always the case. In all cases of physical pain there is always an element of emotions, because that is how we judge the severity of pain, our reaction to pain is emotional.

After I had been training in TCM for a while I began to learn how the emotions presented when I suffered with physical pain. The experience also gave me a great insight into the years I had been suffering myself and I noticed how the patterns of pain and emotions intertwined.

The emotional mind is very powerful. I will talk more about the emotions later.

Overuse/Repetitive Strains

The majority of neck complaints fall into this category. They are caused by extended periods of driving, long hours at the computer (I feel mine tightening right now as I type this) without a break, staying up too late and literally spending too much time balancing this heavy ball of a head all day!

Other factors causing complaints can be occupations necessitating repetitive movement of the neck or, conversely, where the neck is generally in a fixed position for too long on a regular basis.

Similarly, occupations where bending forward a lot is required, like massage, computer work, healthcare work, production line operation, plastering, tiling, building, carpet laying – and this list is not exhaustive – are all likely to impact the neck in the long term. All it takes is a regular break to straighten your spine, have a gentle stretch and BINGO you could save yourself a lot of pain.

If you do have an occupation that is aggravating your neck, it might be worth seriously considering a change of job.

This can be a huge step for sufferers and for many it is not the best option or even possible. I myself had to make this hard decision, twice!

Before I entered medicine, I worked in the construction industry. When my shoulder was damaged through overuse and the constant labour of plastering, I decided to change to wall and floor tiling because the physical demands were easier to manage.

Over time my knees began to suffer, they became painful and sore no matter what precautions I took. I knew then that it was time to change my career completely, my body felt like it needed a break and that compounded my decision to take the leap into full-time medical practice.

It wasn't easy, nor was it achieved overnight, but it was the best solution for my health and it was worth it.

Each transition was a struggle financially as was the emotional impact of having to start all over again, but I knew it was the best solution at the time. For many I understand this can be a hard decision to make.

Perhaps my journey will help inform your own decisions as well as help relieve your pain. There will always be other jobs, but you only get one body.

My main aim of sharing the information in this book is to help you feel better by encouraging your body and mind to heal so you can maintain comfort in daily life. Being able to continue doing what you do without too much change and upheaval is the best solution.

I think you'll be pleasantly surprised at the relief you'll experience in just days of applying these simple yet incredibly effective techniques.

Injury and Trauma

Our next major neck pain complaint is caused by direct trauma and injury from sporting activities, car or road traffic accidents, falls, etc.

As previously mentioned, when the body is forced beyond its range by outside forces, it will do its very best to fix the structure of the body and keep us safe from serious injury, but the way it does this means it takes the strain and there's nevertheless a price to pay for that.

It's a great process but one that we must ultimately suffer for afterwards. Injuries take time to repair so be patient and keep moving forward.

A good way to reduce injury and restrictions in the physical body is to develop a regular practice of 'opening' the body though postures that help to release the tightness in the muscles and nearby tissues.

Later I will explain why 'stretching' the body might not be the most suitable remedy. Having the mindset of opening the body can work wonders for health.

Stagnation

I thought I would include this condition here as it's a main cause of pain and suffering. In TCM, all pain is thought to be caused by stagnation, a less recognised term in Western Medicine.

Stagnation refers to a lack of movement in the body such as movement of blood, fluids or even thoughts. The body and mind are naturally designed to move continuously like the gentle flow of a stream and when this process is altered or even blocked, we can suffer with pain.

When water cannot flow correctly it becomes stagnant like a pond without fresh water. The water becomes cloudy, dirty and the activity of life begins to disappear.

Stagnation is more than just a lack of movement; it is also the accumulation of energy that needs to move. When a flowing stream is hindered by rocks and debris, the movement of the water changes its natural flow, and it can become turbulent.

Objects in the water get stuck and build up like a dam causing congestion on one side and lack of flow on the other. You can also think of it like the flow of traffic. If everything is moving correctly, the traffic lights are all working, and everyone is driving with care and consideration, then there will be very few problems along the way.

But what if there is an accident and a car blocks the road? What if there are roadworks?

The traffic will begin to slow down at the site causing congestion and eventually, there will be a bottleneck with some very angry drivers all trying to reach their destination.

On one side you will have a build-up of energy (stagnation) that has nowhere to move, on the other side, the road will be clear and lifeless as there is no activity from the normal 'flow' of people and traffic. Once the obstruction has been cleared, everything returns to normal and eventually, we have balance.

Much like our hot-headed drivers when they get stuck in traffic, the body also gets hot when blood, fluids and energy can't flow as freely as they should. The effect of this blockage or accumulation of energy is that heat is created. We can experience this heat as inflammation. Bruises and swelling are good examples of stagnation.

A common reaction to inflammation is to immediately apply ice. In some cases, on certain parts of the body, this may be helpful in the initial stage of injury. My advice to patients is NEVER put ice on your neck or shoulders! It's like adding a freak snowstorm to our already chaotic traffic jam. No one will be moving for a long, long time!

This inflammation not only causes more pain at the site of the injury, it also creates excess heat in the body in general which rises, expands, and can exacerbate existing conditions.

Rising heat, such as when you feel the emotion of increasing anger, can cause the emotions to become erratic, overbearing and seem much worse than they actually are.

If there are existing or underlying emotions that have not been resolved, these can create more emotional turbulence, a condition in TCM likened to wind, which can add more energy or increase the severity of symptoms where pain is present. The effect of this 'internal wind' is that pain moves around the body resulting in inflammation in other joints as well as in your neck or shoulders.

In TCM the vessel or meridian system is a great transporter of heat. Heat is naturally deflected away from the organs to reduce further suffering, but this does have some undesirable effects. As heat rises, it often gets 'trapped' in the head often becoming a cause of headaches and muzzy thinking.

Remember our pot of water over the fire? If the lid cannot be lifted to release the steam the pressure will build inside the pot. This can be felt as heat, pain and emotional stress.

If not treated, the build-up begins to cause tension in the neck and shoulders too, making us feel tired, exhausted and low. This book will help to relieve this build-up of pressure and lift the lid of stress and frustration. If left too long there is a good chance the lid will blow and that may be experienced as anger or emotional breakdown.

Being able to self-treat symptoms of pain and stress can greatly reduce many other ailments associated with injury.

Speak Up!

When I first started to study other authors' work on neck injuries and their emotional effects, it was interesting to find many of the books talked about the physical reactions of emotional stress. A common entry in these books was that the neck was related to the way we express ourselves through voice.

The feeling of not being able to express your emotions through voice, or the fact that when you speak, you feel that those around you are not listening, can result in the neck literally choking with emotions. We become silent.

Perhaps when you were young you were told to be quiet, to stop being loud or to stop saying silly things. Is there a fear that what you want to say may not be accepted? Do you get a lump in the throat when you try to share your feelings?

There are many ways that our inner voice can cause tension in the body if it's not allowed to become vocalised. If you feel any of these emotions, it may be worthwhile addressing them and see if your neck pain improves.

We all know how good it feels to let out a loud scream when we are frustrated or angry, imagine keeping it inside for years, not being able to feel free from your own thoughts! No wonder you're feeling tense!

A helpful remedy for this is to have a good sing, hum or whistle. Put a classic pop radio station on, you can bet there's always something catchy to sing along to. Don't worry about what others think of your tone, just do it! It's a great thing to do.

It's also worth mentioning that singing and whistling are something we all do naturally when we are happy and free of tension, especially tension in the neck.

If you do this often enough perhaps the brain will believe you are, in fact, not in pain and relax those tense muscles just a little bit more for you. Give it a go, its free!

Watching TV

You don't need me to tell you that sitting in front of the TV for extended periods is going to mess with your posture! And even if you don't watch much TV, it's worth being aware of your body position for any length of time.

When a patient comes to me with neck pain, especially one-sided pain, the first thing I ask is: imagine you are sitting on the sofa in your lounge, where is the TV? In most cases the patient will turn their head in the direction of the pain!

It's fair to say that since the creation of digital TV it has become much easier to spend hours watching programme after programme. So, if you must do it, try to have the TV in front of you or change to a different seating area to watch the TV. It could save you a lot of discomfort in the future.

Who is at Risk?

Anyone who has a sedentary position in their daily work is ultimately more at risk than those who are more physically active.

As I sit here now, typing these words, I can feel myself constantly correcting my posture because I have spent too long seated, looking at the computer screen, back and forth to the keyboard and getting fidgety in my seat.

These are signs my body is not in a healthy position and it needs to change.

I have my station set up as ergonomically friendly as it can be, but, put simply, we ARE NOT designed to be seated for long periods!

When seated, we can become lazy and fidget in our chairs, rest an elbow on the table, extend an arm out to write or use a mouse. You may be looking up at your screen or down at your keyboard and all this time the neck is constantly adjusting, becoming tired and fatigued. If this is you, I hope this book is a welcome remedy.

Driving occupations are very similar. The head is never really supported. It's in constant motion, reading the road, following other traffic and navigating directions to reach your destination. Driving is immensely stressful at times which only adds to the tension in the neck.

If you were to video someone driving a car or seated in an office chair for an hour then play it back at a faster speed, I think you'd be surprised to see the amount of limited movement and repetitive use of the neck and spine.

Other occupations like hairdressing, massage or beauty salon work, where you are leaning forward all the time can eventually be problematic. My wife and her mother are hairdressers and I have seen for myself the trouble it can cause. Firstly, with the neck and then the back, due to the deviation and balancing act of the spine.

Plasterers, painters, builders, etc., can suffer, especially from working with ceilings or above-the-head tasks. Occupations that use the voice a lot like teachers, speakers and singers can suffer from overuse of the voice and the neck muscles. They too can benefit greatly from the methods in this book.

I could go on, but you yourself will know if your daily duties are causing your pain. In the past I have recommended patients change their job so they can recover properly.

For many this is not an option and that's one of the main reasons for writing this book, to help you manage your health on a daily basis.

We should all be able to continue our daily duties and not have to suffer chronic pain. Regular use of this book will definitely help.

I myself get 'job pains' from leaning over a treatment couch every day. Without regular practice I would be in a lot more discomfort. It really helps keep the pain under control so I can continue my duties and enjoy life.

Throughout the next section I will be teaching you various methods and applications that I myself have successfully used over the years.

They will allow you to build a sense of freedom away from your aches and pains. If you apply the methods daily, they will help. It's like having a toolbox of carefully crafted implements you can use to treat your own symptoms – always there when you need it most.

Now we have looked at those of you who might best benefit from this book. Let's add another method into your box of tools to start easing your neck pain right away.

Rotating the Waist

This movement is great for unwinding the whole spine and forms part of the simple but highly effective warm-up system I share in my book *What is Qigong?* It's a great read if you want to delve into energy health and self-healing.

As you become more relaxed at doing this, it helps to release the muscles in the upper neck, providing great relief for tension in the spine that builds up with seated and sedentary positions.

1. Stand in a shoulder-width stance. Soften the knees and relax the body weight into the feet.

2. Rest the backs of the hands in the small of the back or on the sides of the hips.

3. Gently circle the waist clockwise 10-20 times. Return to centre. *(Fig 2.1)*

4. Gently circle the waist anti-clockwise 10-20 times. Return to centre.

If you find you are seated for long periods during the day, getting up every hour and doing this practice will provide instant relief and reduce the negative effects of being static. That means fewer aches at the end of the day and you'll also help to stimulate the kidneys and digestive system.

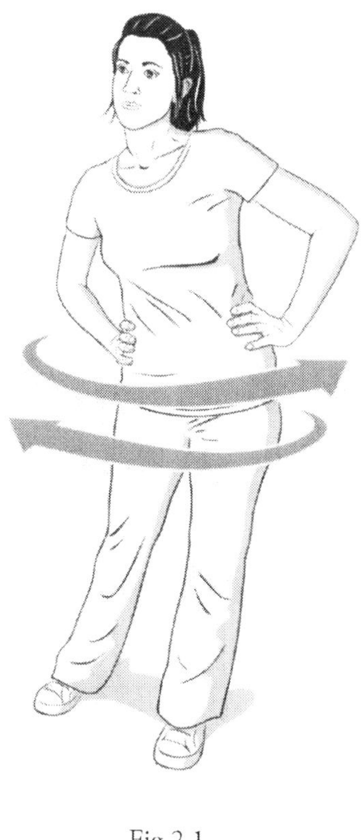

Fig 2.1

And Breathe...

This is great place to take a break and spend a little time getting used to 'Swinging the Arms' and 'Rotating the Waist'. There's no need to jump ahead, enjoy the process and you'll feel much better.

Once you are comfortable with the movements come back to the book and we'll look at how to prepare the neck and create that lovely, cosy warmth that will make everything so much better.

While you are here, why not make a note of any thoughts you have had since beginning this book.

Have you noticed anything you may have forgotten over time, like events that make you feel tension in the neck, or are you doing something physically every day that might be adding to your pain?

Even the slightest bit of information can make a big difference to your recovery and help you get to know how your own individual symptoms are affecting your happiness.

Chapter 3

Preparing for Treatment

Connecting the Mind and Body

Preparing for Treatment

Getting used to spending some time preparing the body and mind for treatment can really help increase the benefits and bring positive results.

The main aim of preparation is to set the mind to the task at hand, connecting your mind to your body and most importantly, when it comes to massage, creating warmth.

Maintaining warmth in the body is crucial to overall health and recovery. The body is designed to work at its most efficient temperature of 37 degrees Celsius (99 degrees Fahrenheit) so let's do our best to keep it that way.

The feelings of tension, pain and discomfort can often be quickly remedied with heat. A warming hand, heated wheat bag or soak in a warm bath can bring instant relief to tired, achy muscles so we must get used to applying warmth when things get cold and stiff.

By warming the muscles, we improve blood flow and can instantly relax any tightness and reduce pain. It's such a simple and effective method and yet something we forget in times of need. Well, not anymore!

Find yourself a comfy seat where you can keep your posture upright and I'll show you how to prepare the neck for treatment. Then we can look at ways the world around you might be adding to your pain.

Warming the Neck

This method can be practised seated or standing at any time of the day when you feel any aches or pains. A good massage really helps with relaxation.

Massage, for me, is by far the most effective form of therapy available. It is the most natural thing we can do to ourselves and others.

When we are injured, we rub the aches away, when we are emotionally hurt the contact through a hug or stroke of the head can bring instant relief and a sense of feeling connected to those around us.

The majority of my patients who have regular massage treatment report fewer feelings of stress and present with fewer painful injuries. It's better to prevent pain than to wait for it to come.

Massage is extremely effective and often needed by the body and mind. If you can get to a Tui Na practitioner the massage will also treat your illnesses too.

Application

Gently rub both hands together until they are warm. If they don't get warm enough quickly you can give them a few claps to divert some blood into the area (always quite funny in a public place, but I'll let you be the judge of that).

Once you have a nice pair of warm palms, place the right hand behind the neck, reaching over to the left side and gently wrap the fingers around the neck. *(Fig 3.1)*

Now wipe the hand back and forth, from left to right across the neck, gently pulling the skin with the palm. *(Fig 3.2)*

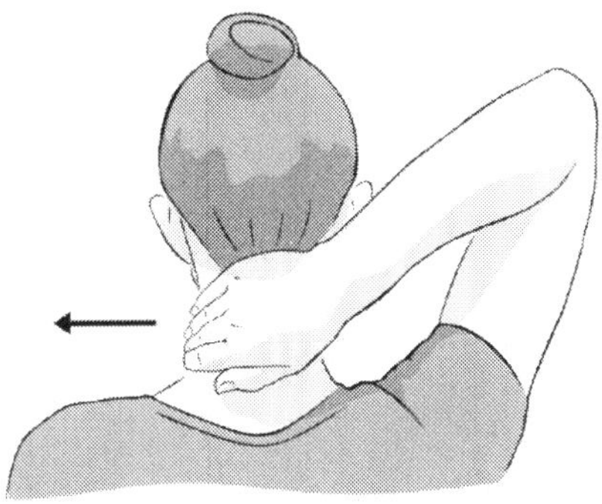

Fig 3.1

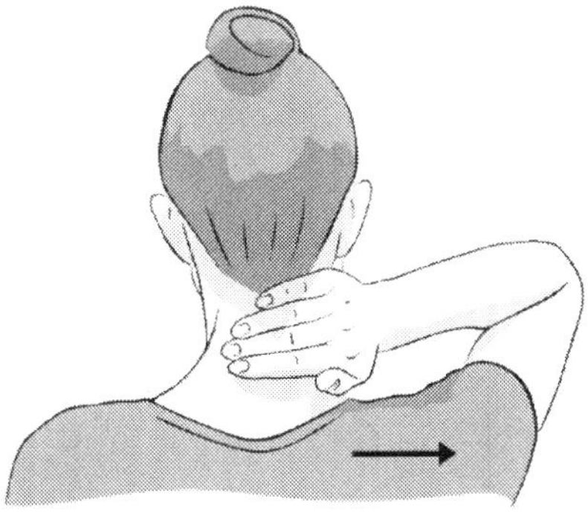

Fig 3.2

Do this movement ten times, then warm the palms again and repeat the same with the left hand, reaching behind and across to the right side of the neck.

Repeat this process on each side a few times to warm the area. Next, do it again but this time slower, adding a little more pressure to the hands to move the skin gently, pulling the palms around the neck towards the side.

It should feel quite comforting as the tissues begin to warm and relax. A simple warming massage like this has a great effect on the neck area.

Using a Towel

This is another very simple exercise to bring warmth and relaxation to the neck area. Grab yourself a large towel. Beach towels work great for this. Roll it up lengthways and place it around the neck holding it at each end.

Now gently move it back and forth to warm the neck, altering the angle of your hand positions to get to the side muscles too. *(Fig 3.3)*

Fig 3.3

When you are nice and warmed up, hold the towel around your neck with both hands at each end and gently move the head back to look up. *(Fig 3.4)*

Then move the head slowly to each side, using the towel as support, like a tube wrapped around the neck.

This will provide a slight amount of traction to the neck area and can bring instant relief to a tight neck. Just make sure you are mindful of the movement and your own neck condition.

Fig 3.4

Be gentle and don't overdo it. A newer towel is best but if you only have an older, stiffer one, then make sure you don't rub too hard on the skin, we are only trying to bring a mild warmth to the area.

It's also a great warm-up before any of the exercises and massage practices listed here in this book. Enjoy!

These two simple techniques can help relieve neck pain and discomfort instantly which feels great after a few hours of driving or working at the computer.

Most importantly it adds warmth and moves blood to the area to relax the muscles and surrounding structures. Cold is the last thing you need near the neck when you are in pain! We ultimately need to warm the body and circulate our blood.

So, how does the blood fit into our self-treatment? Let's take a look.

Blood

Blood is the transporter of life throughout the body, reaching every cell, tissue and structure to keep us alive and healthy. Our physical body helps to move the blood through daily movements so we can restore the functions of the organs and generally feel well each day.

Blood is also our natural heating system and needs constant activity to reduce and expel the ill effects that cold can bring.

The body and mind love warmth and the warmth of blood helps to relax muscles. We all feel much better sat in front of a cosy fire than being outside in the snow and rain.

When things are cold, they become slow and stagnant. Muscles that have become fixed by continued small, repetitive movements, or in most cases, lack of movement, will have a reduced blood supply and therefore feel more tense than usual.

Think of it like this, if you have a bath sponge that has been left on the side of the bath for a while it will become brittle and hard with not much movement at all when you squeeze it in your hand.

Now, add some water and it's a completely different tool altogether, but this doesn't happen immediately either. At first it takes a while for the water to move through the sponge until it is entirely saturated with water, then the water can pass through the sponge so it becomes softer and more pliable to use.

Muscles are very similar. A stiff muscle needs a little bit of encouragement to get moving and once the blood is there it becomes softer and more relaxed. Blood also removes the damaged cells that come with injuries and pain.

This is why periods of being seated, or as Brits we say 'vegging out' in front of the TV, are always followed by a stiff back, neck or hip when you finally decide to get up and move.

This is another reason why the health authorities recommend moving your body for ten minutes every hour. A long plane ride can feel like the worst and people are often a bit self-conscious of taking to the aisles for some much-needed star jumps or yoga stretches so the simple warm-up methods in this book are ideal remedies to use at any time.

In Chinese medicine almost all painful conditions are said to be caused by stagnation, as discussed earlier, or lack of movement in the blood, joints, tissues and fluids. 'Move it or lose it' is always the case for painful conditions, even if it doesn't feel like it at the time.

Quick Tip - If you suffer with a condition that causes you extreme pain when moving, you can improve the functions and flow of your body by just breathing correctly. A few rounds of relaxed and mindful breathing can be a refreshing change to the whole body and mind.

Now that we have discussed blood and the importance of how warmth and flow can reduce pain, let's discuss some of the other ways that the elements around us can affect our pains. You may discover something that could be making your pain and suffering worse.

The External Influences

In TCM there are six external factors that can affect our health. These are wind, cold, heat, summer heat, dryness and damp. In brief, wind can be sudden and changing, cold can be slow, solid and restrictive. Heat and summer heat can expand and energise. Dryness can be brittle and lack movement. Damp can be heavy, sticky and congestive.

In my experience the most prevalent influences are wind, cold and heat during neck injuries. Let's take a look.

Cold

Aside from the hands, the neck area, and the face, are the most exposed areas of the body at any time during the day or night. Our hands go into pockets or gloves when we are cold, and our feet are mostly covered in footwear throughout the day (unless you are one of the 'flip-flop brigade' who can wear your feet proudly all year round).

Yes, we can put a hat on our head, but we also have hair to warm us. And yes, we can wear a scarf around our necks when it's windy, but how many people with constant, nagging neck pain do this religiously? Not many at all.

Remember this: if you have neck pain, cover your neck when it's cold or windy outside!

In order to understand why this is so important we need to look at each of the elements concerned to discover the process of how this can affect your symptoms and ailments.

Cold in nature causes a lack of movement and we become tense to retain heat in the body. When water is in its fluid form, it can move, when it is cooled to extreme, as ice, it is solid with no movement at all. When we are cold, the arms come in towards the body, the shoulders reach up to our ears and we huddle up to stay warm.

If you regularly experience prolonged periods of cold, then eventually it's only going to add to your pain and suffering. Wearing a scarf, neckerchief or light throw will help keep this from happening and your muscles will remain relaxed.

Personally, I carry 'morphs' in all my bags just in case the weather changes or the wind picks up. Cyclists, walkers, sports enthusiasts or runners tend to use them a lot. A morph or 'buff', as my runner friend calls them, is just a simple stretchy band of material that goes around your neck. They fit in a pocket and can make a big difference.

Wind

The next, and probably the most volatile element inflicted upon us is wind. In nature wind is unpredictable, changing course and speed, bringing with it cold and blustery chills.

When wind attacks, it causes muscle spasms and pain to move around the body, especially if cold comes along for the ride too. One of the most common neck complaints I see in clinic is caused by cold and wind. I will give you an example that many of you may have experienced.

It's late, the bed is calling so you make your way to the bedroom and you settle down for a night of sleep. Everything is normal. The next morning you wake, open your eyes, take a great yawn and stretch to the heavens. THEN, suddenly, a pain shoots through your neck, the muscles have gone into spasm and the pain hits your senses like a hammer. OUCH!

So, why does this happen? Nine times out of ten the culprit is an open window or door. Your neck may have been exposed overnight and a cold draught has hit the neck making the muscles stiff and less pliable first thing when you wake.

You then give that 'dried out sponge' of a muscle a quick stretch and BINGO, the muscle recoils like an elastic band, just to stop you from tearing the tissues, and you end up with a stiff neck.

The other causes of a stiff neck can range from poor posture while sleeping when a nerve has been pinched, incorrect pillow-sizing affecting the alignment of the spine, being overly hot at night if you are experiencing menopause or have had too much alcohol or spicy food.

Hold on a minute! Alcohol and spicy foods? Menopause? How on earth can that affect the neck? To understand this better let me tell you some more about heat.

Heat

Excess stress, alcohol and spicy/hot foods all cause heat in the body to rise, especially if this is late at night. To balance out the excess heat in the body, the skin pores open to release heat and sweat forms to cool the skin.

You go to bed all snuggled up but then as you sleep you become hot and you throw off the covers to cool yourself, leaving the neck, upper back and shoulders exposed to any cold or draughts that might be around. A sure recipe for a stiff neck in the morning.

Environmental influences also play their part in our quality of health. For those that work in hot surroundings like a bakery, product manufacturing or a hot climate, heat can take its toll if you are sensitive or have a weak energy system.

Cold environments such as working in cold-produce areas or a winter environment can increase symptoms of cold. Living or working near water can have a damaging effect on your health because of the constant damp and moist environment.

We all know someone who complains their aches and pains have worsened when the dampness of autumn comes. All of these environmental conditions can have a negative impact on your health over a long period of time, especially if you are run down and feel low.

The time of year can also have a bearing on your health. It's cold and windy through autumn to winter so these are seasons to be mindful to wrap up warm. But there is another more cunning time of year that can reap havoc for neck pain – the end of summer.

Quite quickly towards the end of the summer season, the nights begin to lose their heat and become much cooler even if the days remain hot. We go to bed all nice and warm in our summer night attire such as our vests, t-shirts or even our 'forever birthday suits' and think nothing of the changes in temperature overnight.

As the nights become cooler, perhaps we still leave our doors and windows open if we are still feeling hot from the daytime. Doing this can increase the risk of a cricked neck in the morning or even more stiffness added to our already existing pains.

Obviously as I am in the UK writing this, I cannot account for the different climates around the world, but it's definitely worth paying attention to your weather changes if you have bad or chronic neck pain. I've become quite good at watching and reading the seasons now, a bit geeky I know, but it's really interesting ... honest!

Menopause

The menopause is also a culprit, especially if you suffer from night-time sweats and overheating. As you sleep, the heat builds, the skin starts to melt, not literally of course (!) and a swift kick of the duvet sends it to the floor, leaving you exposed to the cold and draughts and the possibility of more pain. It can be a constant balancing act!

I really sympathise with women who suffer menopausal symptoms and I have heard many stories from patients how this can become very problematic.

If you do suffer with menopausal symptoms, I highly recommend going to see an acupuncturist who is trained in traditional acupuncture. I have had great results treating these symptoms and it can make a huge difference to getting a restful and calmer night's sleep. Don't suffer, give it a go.

Some of the following techniques and methods will help calm your reactions to heat, build protection for those overly sensitive to wind and restore a certain resistance to the cold. Keep your eye out for the details of each of the techniques and see which ones best suit your needs.

I must add that not everyone is susceptible to cold, wind and heat but in my experience those with neck injuries often are. If this is not you but you ever hear a friend mention their dislike of the wind or cold, why not suggest a few of these solutions to them. You could be the help they've been looking for.

Better Breathing

There is another cause of neck pain and it is one that is often missed. Breathing. Yes, this simple and automatic process we go through thousands of times a day can also contribute to neck pain.

Every time we inhale, the diaphragm is pulled downwards, drawing air into the lungs ready to be expelled. This continuous cycle helps to bring oxygen to the blood and helps to nourish the muscles. This is the correct way to breathe.

So, what is the incorrect way to breathe? With your neck! Over time, most of us will lose the natural pattern of abdominal breathing like we used to do as children. We'll get into very bad habits and employ the upper chest and neck muscles to breathe superficially.

This constant use of the neck muscles will fatigue them and they will become tight and tense. This is also a natural reaction during stressful periods of life and something that we can all change for the better.

When we experience stress and especially fear and anxiety, we naturally breathe higher in the body to get more air into the lungs quicker. It's okay when we are frightened or in danger because it rarely lasts long.

Repeating this pattern throughout our daily life can have many negative effects on the relaxation of the neck muscles.

Here is a quick test you can do right now to see where you are breathing in your body.

Sit down in a chair and pull up the crown (top of the head) as if being suspended by a string from above (more about lifting the crown later), tuck the chin in slightly and make sure your spine has good upright posture, but don't use force.

Close your eyes and take a slow deep breath inward. Try to notice what parts of your body are moving and expanding to help you bring this new air into your lungs.

Do you feel it in your belly? Are your ribs and chest expanding sideways? Are you lifting your shoulders towards the head? Or do you feel something different?

If you feel you are raising the shoulders, then you will need to retrain your breathing so that you are not causing any undue stress to the neck muscles.

Another test you can perform that will give you an idea of how this can add to neck pain and discomfort is to sit in a chair as before, with good posture.

Now, raise your shoulders to your ears about 3-5 cms (1-2 inches). Continue lifting and relaxing and see how far you can count before it starts to ache. How many? 20? 40? 100?! If you think that during a period of 24 hours, we inhale around 17,000 to 28,000 times per day, you can begin to see how incorrect breathing can be a problematic cause of neck pain and may add undue stress to an existing condition.

There are huge benefits to correct breathing practices so get practising today, your whole body and mind will love you for it ... not just your neck!

The next section will introduce you to the energy points and teach you how to prepare the body and mind to be able to treat your own symptoms. There is no rush so please take your time and enjoy each phase of the learning.

That way you will build a great practice and be able to improve your health. Don't forget! Swing, rotate, warm and breathe. Simple.

This is also a great time to take a breath, relax and recap what we have learnt already.

Swinging the arms is a simple way to reduce stress and relax tension in the neck, arms and shoulders.

Rotating the waist helps to free up tension in the whole spine for better nerve function and overall health.

Warming the neck can bring great relief to stiff, tired muscles that often cause headaches, fatigue and symptoms of pain.

If you can form a daily practice of 'Swinging the Arms', 'Rotating the Waist' and 'Warming the Neck', you will be well on your way to feeling much better with less pain on a daily basis. It really does make a big difference to the day.

Being aware of your own symptoms and condition really helps to build a personal picture of how your health is being affected by your pain.

Also take some time to look and listen to your daily life and the duties you perform to see if there are any external influences that might be affecting your symptoms.

Are there any changes you can make today that will help improve your pain?

Write them down for future reference.

Chapter 4

The Energy Pools

Activating your own medicine

Self-Treatment for Health

Each of the treatment points I share with you are specific points that have a particular effect on the body and mind.

They help to release the connective tissues around the site of treatment. These tissues are like a web that connects and binds our body parts together so each point can also influence areas further away by the way the body is connected like a system of roadways or trainlines.

I have generalised the pathway regions, often known as meridians or vessels, to give you a basic idea of the areas that can be affected. I intend to publish another book dedicated to the vessel systems later, which will delve deeper into the energy functions, so please keep following my work.

These pathways help to transport blood, fluids and the nerve messages through the tissues that help us to perform our daily duties. They also connect all the body parts together and allow the structure of our bodies to move and remain strong.

When there is an injury, lack of movement or blockage along the vessels, we can suffer with pain and discomfort. This can be caused by physical and emotional injuries.

Via the practice of Qigong and deep meditation by past sages, medical practitioners and scholars of Eastern arts, it was discovered that activity and Qi energy would gather or 'pool' at specific areas or points along these pathways.

Through continued investigation it was discovered that these points would have a certain effect on the body and mind when manipulated by touch, some being more reactive than others. Over time, this formed the foundation of what we now know as TCM.

Manipulation of these energy pools can affect the superficial layers, muscles, skin, tendons, etc., and also the deeper levels of the organs, bones and our emotional/mental self.

They provide the map that connects the body and mind as one whole being. These are also common points that are used in acupuncture treatment.

In modern medicine, especially sports therapy, some of these points are now used to release restrictions in the physical body, to relieve tightness and many problems that affect our free movement of the bones and muscles.

When you add the knowledge of TCM and its original method they become very powerful points by which to restore health and well-being.

The application of using the points correctly is very important to be able to achieve the results we desire. It's not just the muscles, tissue and bones we are affecting with our treatment, it is also the balance of the emotional system and the way the mind and body function too.

It may be okay to use points on the neck to release tension, but what if, at the same time, you are increasing heat in the area and later you experience headaches? What if the treatment or incorrect application aggravates the pain or causes disturbed sleep?!

In many cases there may be chronic tension or at worst repressed emotions in the tissues that require a specific model of treatment.

The untrained may just apply the wrong treatment to release the tissues and at the same time, unknowingly, increase the feelings of emotions which can cause further stress and suffering.

As a practitioner of TCM we take any manipulation of the energy system very seriously. It's not just the acute, or immediate symptoms that need treatment. It is the very root of the symptoms that requires attention too.

When you start to manipulate the energy and functions of the body, there is the right way and then there is a better way. The points here are put together in a very specific way so you get the best results for both physical and emotional conditions.

As you can see from the following image, the pathways that run through the neck can affect many areas of the head so when these are clear and the energy is functioning efficiently, we can relieve many common ailments, especially those that affect the emotions. *(Fig 4.1)*

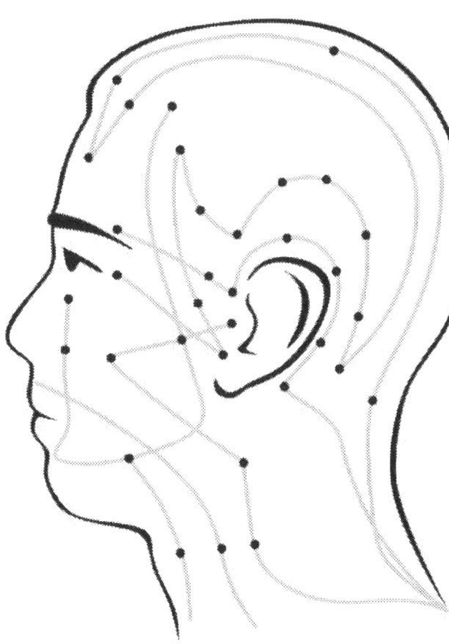

Fig 4.1

I must add that when I talk of the 'energy' of the body, I am not referring to a magic or invisible form of esoteric power, I am referring to the way that the body functions and the movement of activity to keep us in good health.

The generic word for the result or quality of these processes is 'Qi' as we discussed earlier.

Where needed, I will list both the physical and emotional applications of each massage point as we go along. That way you can see which points resonate most with you at that time. You may even start to see a pattern to your symptoms and how they relate to each other.

I hope this book will also serve as a valuable reference for any future injuries and pain you may have, it's a great toolkit.

The following image *(Fig 4.2)* is a chart showing the vast network of energy channels within the body. As you can see, they reach every aspect of the physical body, travelling through the muscles, joints, and bones providing a map that enables those who practise Chinese Medicine to restore health to the body and mind.

When the channels are functioning in harmony, we have less stress, less pain and our vital energy is abundant. This results in our sense of well-being, strength and happiness.

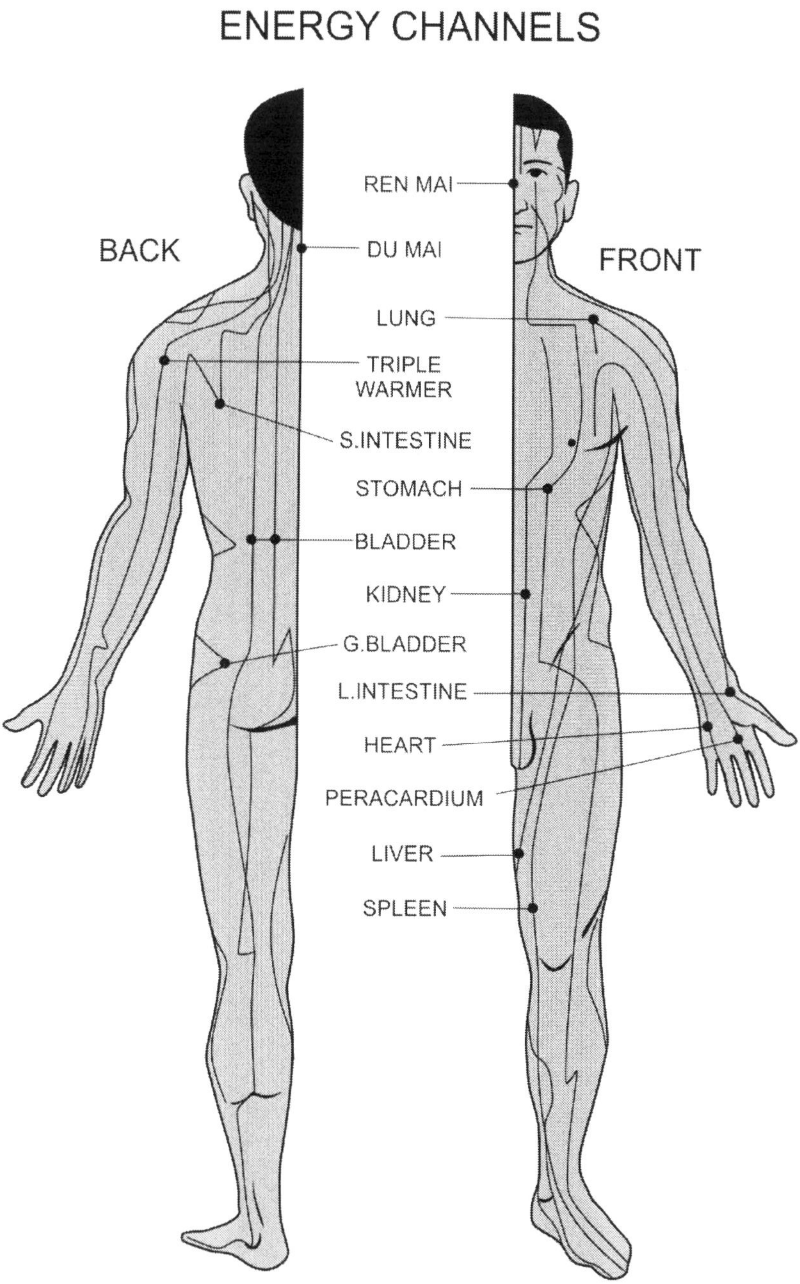
ENERGY CHANNELS
BACK
FRONT
REN MAI
DU MAI
LUNG
TRIPLE
WARMER
S.INTESTINE
STOMACH
BLADDER
KIDNEY
G.BLADDER
L.INTESTINE
HEART
PERACARDIUM
LIVER
SPLEEN

Fig 4.2

Be Mindful of Your Practice

Some of the points we will use have additional benefits and some will have cautions to adhere to when using them. Please familiarise yourself with the information at each section to get the best from your practice.

I will try to add as much detail and description as needed, as sometimes illustrations do not provide the whole picture. So, if you are ready now, let's get started with learning our energy points for treatment and how to apply the techniques.

Application and Pressure

When applying pressure to the massage points, the amount of pressure applied depends totally on your own individual preference. Everyone will have different levels of discomfort and equally different levels of how much pressure is tolerable.

Saying that, there needs to be a certain amount of pressure so that you are affecting the localised area of tissues and structure.

In the beginning take some time to get used to each point and the area you are massaging. You will find that as you progress, the points will become less reactive and feel more therapeutic. You can start by just gently pressing the points for a few breaths, then relax and repeat. After that, you can apply a circling motion with the pads of the thumbs or fingers, gradually increasing the pressure over time.

Duration

The duration for applying the techniques can range from just a few seconds to a few minutes. You may find that applying the techniques will cause your fingers or hands to ache initially. This will pass as you become stronger and more used to the methods.

A really easy way to time yourself is to count your breaths. Start with applying the techniques for five breaths gradually building up to twenty breaths for those stubborn places.

Less is definitely more with these techniques, so don't go pressing and prodding too hard, take your time and as discussed earlier, allow the tissues and body to relax and open. There's no rush, enjoy it.

Cautions and Safety

If you experience any sharp pains or dizziness during any of the methods here, I highly recommend arranging a few treatments with a trained practitioner just to check everything over before continuing.

They will be able to move you through the initial stages much quicker and you'll get even more benefit from your home practice.

A practitioner trained in Tui Na Massage, Shiatsu or Thai Massage would be my best advice as they will work with many of the same points here. That will also give you a great, first-hand experience of what it feels like when you apply the massage yourself.

The Master Pain Point! - Large Intestine 4

Everyone has experienced pain at some time, it's the number one complaint we could all do without, so let's start there with our first massage practice.

Our first massage point is called 'HEGU' which means 'joining valley' in Chinese Medicine, but we'll call it 'The Master Pain Point'.

This point is situated on the web of the thumb and first finger so it's easy to treat this point at any time, whenever you feel like you need some relief. *(Fig 4.3)*

In TCM this is the Master Pain Point that is added to any prescription of treatment that involves pain. It is also an ENT point (ears, nose and throat) so it can treat many problems associated with this area such as painful ears, sinus problems and sore throat.

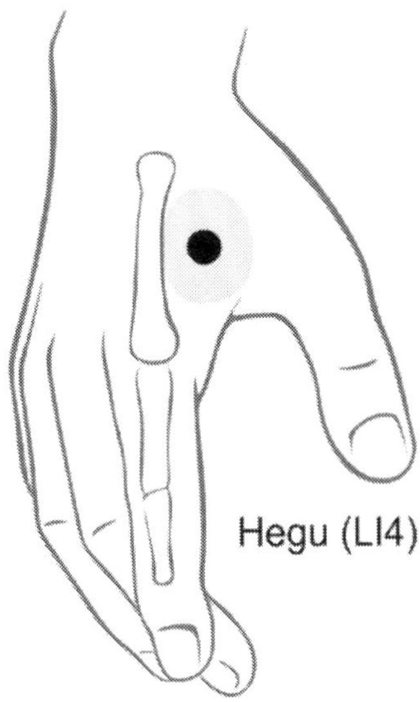

Fig 4.3

For our purposes, its manipulation can also relax the shoulders and face as well as the neck. It helps to release the whole vessel area as shown in *Figure 4.4*.

This Master Pain Point is also a major point for releasing wind conditions, a TCM term for symptoms that move around the body, and for strengthening our resistance to external influences like cold, heat, damp and perhaps the emotions of those around us. Wind symptoms can be neck pain, headaches, dizziness and general aches, all of which come with our neck aches and discomfort.

This point is situated on the webbing between the thumb and first finger, halfway between the ends of the index metacarpal bone. At first, it helps to mark the point with a pen until you get used to where it is.

Once you've found the point, gently place the thumb on top and press towards the bone. Have a search around the area by applying pressure. You will find a noticeable area that is more tender than other places around the point.

After you've found the tender area, apply pressure to the point or a circular motion with the pad or the tip of the thumb.

Rather than count how many times you are circling with pressure, it's much easier to count your breaths. Start with five complete breaths and work up to twenty. Do this gradually and keep in mind that doing more circles or applying more pressure may not necessarily provide better results.

As this is a new health practice you must allow your body time to get used to it gradually. The body and mind must be nurtured and tended, not forced or manipulated. Keep it soft, slow and steady.

The Master Pain Point has many health benefits. As this is a major point for pain, whenever you have any kind of pain, go for this point immediately. It can affect the whole body so just because your pain is not in the area of the point, do not think it won't help. In many cases it can provide faster relief than the time it takes painkillers to work.

This point is good for treating:

- Headaches and migraines
- Pain of the hand and wrist
- Shoulder pain
- Sinus and eye problems
- Dizziness
- General aches and pains
- Tooth and jaw pains
- Abdominal pain
- Constipation and diarrhoea

CAUTION – this point is contraindicated during pregnancy.

While you spend some time getting used to the Master Pain Point, let's take a look at some other methods that we all naturally use when we're in discomfort.

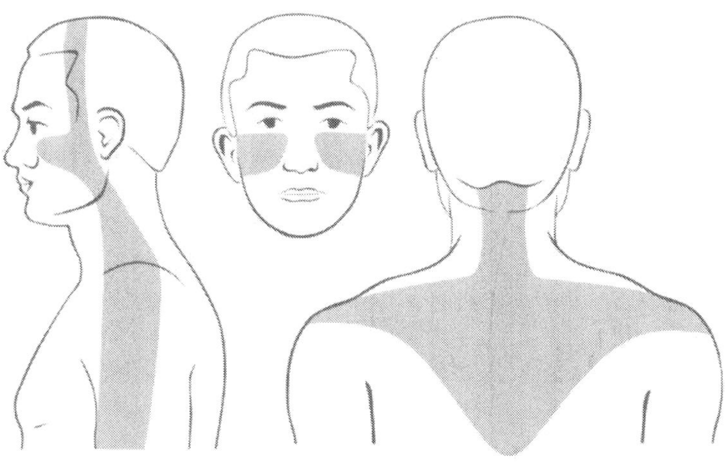

Fig 4.4

Regions affected by The Master Pain Point

Everyday Methods

There are many other useful methods that we are all aware of or may have used naturally during times of pain. They are very basic movements that are often practised incorrectly or in a less efficient manner.

I feel it's going to be of great benefit for you to go over them, just so you know you are getting the best out of each movement and not adding more stress and pain to existing symptoms.

As a musculo-skeletal therapist I often see these simple movements performed incorrectly, especially if you have current pain, so let's get them right from the start.

Rolling the Shoulders

The biggest mistake when people roll their shoulders forwards and back is that they often crane the neck creating pressure in the joints and possibly increasing tension.

Rolling the shoulders correctly allows you to use the muscles at the side of the neck to gently massage the cervical area, exercise the shoulder joint and release the muscles around the collar bone.

To get it right, all it takes is a bit of awareness of what you are doing. This can be performed seated or standing.

Rolling the right way

Take your awareness to the centre of the shoulder joint and imagine a mark on the outermost part of the shoulder muscles. Now, imagine that your head is suspended by a piece of string like the head of a puppet gently lifting the crown upward (see crown point section).

Take a deep breath in and then relax the shoulders as you breathe out gently. You can repeat this process until you feel the shoulders and neck have relaxed.

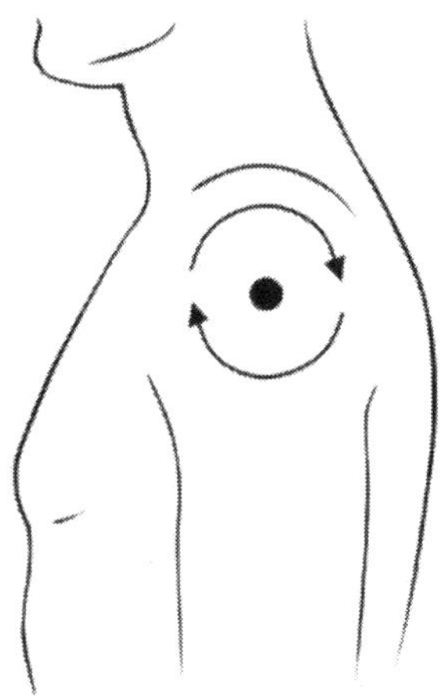

Fig 4.5

Next, begin to make small forward circles from the outer shoulder point. Gradually increase the size of the circles, but not too much. *(Fig 4.5)*

You will notice the muscle of the shoulders rise to gently massage the neck muscles. Then relax.

Take another few relaxed breaths in and out to relax the shoulders again.

Now, slowly circle the shoulders backward, starting with small rotations, then slightly larger ones. You should notice how the movement starts to massage and exercise the muscles at the back of the neck, the upper back and space between the shoulder blades.

Repeat this process ten times forwards and back, working up, over time, to thirty circles. Depending on how you feel on the day, you can adjust the amount to suit your own comfort.

Rolling the wrong way

Raising the shoulder and lifting the chin; tilting the head back or pulling the shoulders too high and too far back; overstretching or forcing this movement – all these actions can easily cause a series of spasms if there is any impingement of the nerves. Take it slow and be mindful of the tissues and structure you're working with.

Do not think of it as something you DO to the body, think of it as something you do WITH the body.

Lifting the Crown Point

I can't stress enough how important the crown point is! It's very clear that the increasing use of computers and mobile devices, as well as more and more seated occupations, will likely contribute to an epidemic of postural problems.

Not only do these cause great pain and discomfort, they also have a chronic effect on the emotions and our ability to function mentally. Lifting the crown point is an important practice in Qigong and Taijiquan and one that everyone should practise, every day.

Through continued flexing of the neck, the muscles are constantly overused and pulled into positions that could eventually become fixed. When this happens, they lose their soft and pliable nature, leading to a rigid structure and pain.

This unnatural position puts pressure on the cervical vertebrae, compromises the surrounding nerve paths and if stiffness in the tissues is chronic, may reduce the flow of blood to the brain.

This means that the brain will not receive an efficient flow of oxygen and blood which in many cases can lead to diminished functions, anxiety and less efficient decision-making. You may also experience headaches, high blood pressure, anxiety, mild depression, fatigue and tiredness. These are all common symptoms I see in patients with this condition. *(Fig 4.6)*

It is thought that the pressure added to the neck when the alignment is chronically deviated can be similar to carrying a large bag of potatoes on your shoulders! For all those hardcore mobile device users, that means you too.

You only have to look around to see how these modern devices are negatively affecting our health. No wonder there is an increase in teenage emotional problems.

It's not just the emotional effects of using digital media that we are beginning to see now, it's also the physical changes in the body and the way this affects the functions of the body and mind.

You can discover this for yourself if you put your device away for a few days. It can literally change everything! Those I've helped to restore correct posture and reduce the pressure in this area have likened it to a river dam being unblocked!

The relief can be profound.

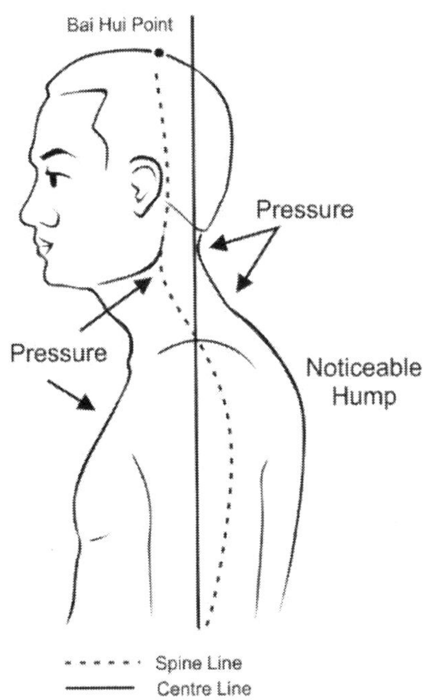

Deviated Position

Fig 4.6

As the posture begins to deviate from its natural shape, the spine begins to curve and some people will develop a noticeable hump on the upper back. The chest cavity will also be pulled inwards creating pressure on the lungs and reducing your ability to breathe in the correct manner.

Ultimately that means less energy for the body to function and over time, fatigue can set in due to the restrictions in efficient breathing patterns. Many cases of anxiety and low mood can be cured by correct breathing patterns, so correct posture is imperative for good health.

This process of deviation can also be caused by emotions. For those of you that are fearful, shy, anxious or experience feelings of trauma, you will naturally move into an overly protective state. The body literally begins to curl up into a ball.

We all know someone who has suffered with emotional turmoil, they talk looking down at the ground, avoid eye contact or place themselves in a position below us so as not to seem threatening or confrontational.

Practising lifting the crown can literally lift a person out of this emotional suffering so they can be part of the world around them, have a voice and hold their heads up high.

During this method, we are consciously correcting any deviations of the posture and helping to restore a healthy body and mind. Practise this every chance you get during the day.

As previously mentioned, the spine is designed to reduce the effects of gravity and keep the spinal nerves safe, uncompromised and functioning so that we can live our daily lives. Continued deviation of this position will always have a negative effect on our overall health – so start today.

Nobody wants to be bent over or in a wheelchair when they are older and for those of you who may need mobile aids, lifting the crown will work wonders for your health too.

How to Lift the Crown Point

Sit in a chair or on a stool being sure that your spine is not touching any surface and you are as upright as you can be. Take a few relaxed breaths and relax the shoulders, neck and arms.

Now imagine a cord attached to the top of your head that gently pulls you upwards towards the sky. You will notice the back of the neck become longer and the chin should tuck in slightly. *(Fig 4.7)*

Remember that the head is a ball on top of a spike that gently balances above the top of the spine.

Now take a few more deep breaths and again, relax the neck, shoulders and arms.

Once you have practised this method a few times, try it standing up. Stand with the feet shoulder-width apart, relax the knees and practise lifting up the crown.

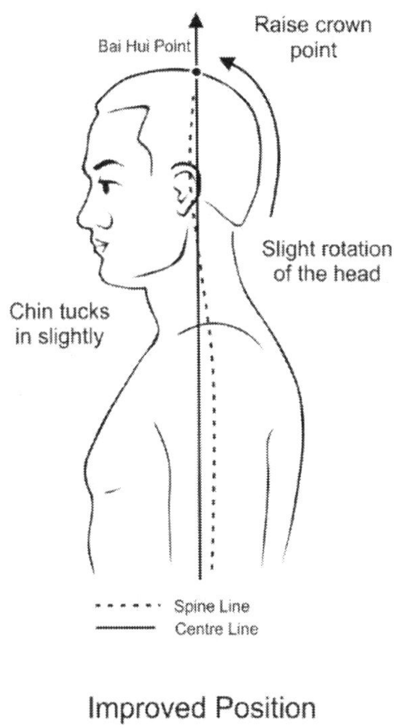

Fig 4.7

Practise this as often as you can. When you are driving, be more aware of your posture.

When you are seated, practise lifting the crown. In fact, at any time at all during the day, just spend a few minutes gently becoming aware of your body and posture.

It has great results for the whole body and mind. A healthy spine that has correct structure is paramount for overall health and well-being. Be mindful in every task and you will begin to feel a great shift in health.

To Stretch, or NOT to Stretch!

Every week I see injuries in clinic caused by incorrect stretching or exercises that have been recommended for various conditions. Poor care and lack of individual attention in yoga or pilates classes, minimal preparation for sports activities, lack of correct knowledge and most of all, taking advice from online videos, are all contributory factors to longer-term pain.

Each injury is unique to each specific person so having hands-on care or being coached in person will always provide the best results.

Most stretches are fine to do, it's just the mindset accompanying them that is often wrong. When it comes to stretching, the common idea is that the muscles are like elastic bands that become tight, so a good stretch is all that is needed to get more range and mobility.

For me this is the wrong mindset and goes against the nature of the body. The tissues in the body should not be stretched during injury, they should be allowed to open!

Each of the muscles are made up of individual strings of fibres that have a certain degree of movement. When this range is exceeded, the strain is passed to the tendons that connect the muscles to the bones.

You cannot go beyond what is not there. The muscle fibres can become damaged, stiff or bind together during an injury. Overstretching is a disaster just waiting to happen!

Think of it like rolling dough or pastry. If you just bundle it up and pull it apart the structure will tear. Now, if you tend it, knead it and nurture it, it will change shape and lengthen. It will stretch and become a more usable material.

If you want to change the shape of your body, it must be nurtured (plus, a good bit of kneading now and then is good for the body and mind).

Through regular warming and opening of the muscles, the fibres can become lengthened thus increasing our range of mobility. Your body will adjust to its needs NOT what is forced upon it.

This incorrect mindset may still be residual from previous generations when we had to be much more physical to survive, but there was a real lack of scientific knowledge at that time.

The thing that I feel is still missing is a basic understanding of what happens to the muscles during injury. Let me explain.

When there is a danger to the spine, nerve paths or joints, the muscles do their very best to stabilise the injury. If there is a danger of a spinal disc being pulled out of place, the muscles will gather and pull with all their might to fix the joint and reduce any serious injury.

If a shoulder is in danger of being pulled from the socket, the shoulder, neck and chest will pull everything together and fix it to reduce injury. This is the pain you feel after an injury. It's the muscles doing their best to save your body from damage.

Other injuries occur when the muscles have been pulled beyond their range and the tissue tears or when the muscles have been used so much that they begin to rub against other tissues and structures.

This can cause the tissues to bind and the nerve fibres to bundle up like an unwound roll of string. Nerve messages become compromised and the result is pain, stiffness and spasms. If you treat the body like a machine, it will break like a machine!

If this is the case it really pays to take a little more care and let the body know that there is no danger when you are stretching. All you need to do is allow the body to open.

So, this is how I do it.

When I apply an increased range of movement I only need to go as far as feeling a slight change in the tissues or muscles. This could be a slight tightening or a feeling of light pressure.

Then I take a few seconds to breathe. When the brain has registered that I am relaxed and in control, it will gently allow the tissue fibres to open, which means increased range of movement.

The reason why, during an injury, you have to be actively mindful of your recovery is that in many cases there is trauma attached to injuries.

If you have been in a car accident and you stretch your neck with the pain, the brain will think it is in danger and recall the imprint of the accident. It will pull the muscles to fix the structure and you experience what is called a spasm. The muscles literally lock up.

If you can let your mind know you are not going to hurt it while performing your rehabilitation exercises, it will be more likely to help you. That way you will always be moving forward with your health and not taking steps backwards because you went just that little bit too far. Slow and steady is best.

I am not saying that this is the best way – it's a very soft and natural approach to the body and mind and one that is based on over a decade of treating in clinic. Being hard rarely has a positive effect.

Turning the Head

For me personally and in my own clinical experience, less is definitely more when it comes to turning the head. I have seen numerous patients with neck injuries who force their neck to turn or tilt, hoping that they are making a difference. They are not!

If you can remember our discussion of the head being a ball on top of a spike which is supported by many guide ropes to maintain the balance, it will help you get the right movement when turning the head.

The guide ropes that I mention are just the superficial muscles, the outer layer we all see in the mirror. Inside the neck, at a deeper level, there are many more, like a series of supportive bands providing opposing forces.

When one side is pulled, the opposite must be lengthened, and the tissues are relaxed. This complementary movement in the muscles is what keeps our spinal nerves and blood systems safe and intact.

Lack of mobility and range of movement in the neck can have some unwanted side effects that you may not relate to your neck problem. This is notably evident when driving a car. Being able to see other road users around you is paramount for your safety and the safety of other road users and passengers.

Not being able to see over your shoulder at turns and junctions can leave you feeling very vulnerable and this adds to your stress.

Feelings of apprehension can quickly turn to feelings of fear and anxiety. It may not be on a large enough scale for you to feel overwhelmed, but it is there, nonetheless.

Over time this can affect the balance of the body and mind, weakening the system and causing undue symptoms of stress like irritable bowel syndrome (IBS), headaches and anxiety. Practising turning the head can relieve these symptoms and restore a sense of confidence and security.

Correct Practice

Take a breath in and out, relax the shoulders. Suspend the crown as discussed earlier. Be aware that the head is a heavy ball, gently balanced on top of the spine. Now, take your awareness to just behind the left ear and imagine that there is a stretchy band attached to the ear that runs around behind the head to the spine.

Very slowly, imagine the band pulling the ear towards the spine until you feel a slight change or lengthening of the muscles in the right side of the neck and shoulder, then slowly release the tension, back to centre.

One thing I have found helpful is to also be mindful of the tip of the nose. As you turn the head, try to keep the nose moving in a smooth horizontal plane. Applying warm hands to massage the neck in between turning the head adds even more therapeutic value.

Repeat this process up to ten times each way. Warm the palms and gently move them across the neck from both sides as previously practised.

Incorrect Practice

Forcing the neck and head to turn can have the opposite effect of relaxing the muscles and can be painful too. The neck is very protective of any undue movements and does not like being forced beyond its range.

When the muscles are relaxed and there is blood in the area, the range of movement naturally increases. It takes time to change this protective process, especially if you have had an accident where the memory of the injury has become embedded in the neck tissues. It will come in time.

At this point, why not take a mental picture of the range of movement and the level of discomfort in the neck? Then see how you feel and what positive changes have taken place when you have reached the end of the book. In fact, let's jot this down so we have a physical record for future reference.

Grab a pencil and mark on the graph what direction your nose is facing when you turn your head left and right. You can use this as a before-and-after record or even come back after a few weeks of practice and see how you have progressed. *(Fig 4.8)*

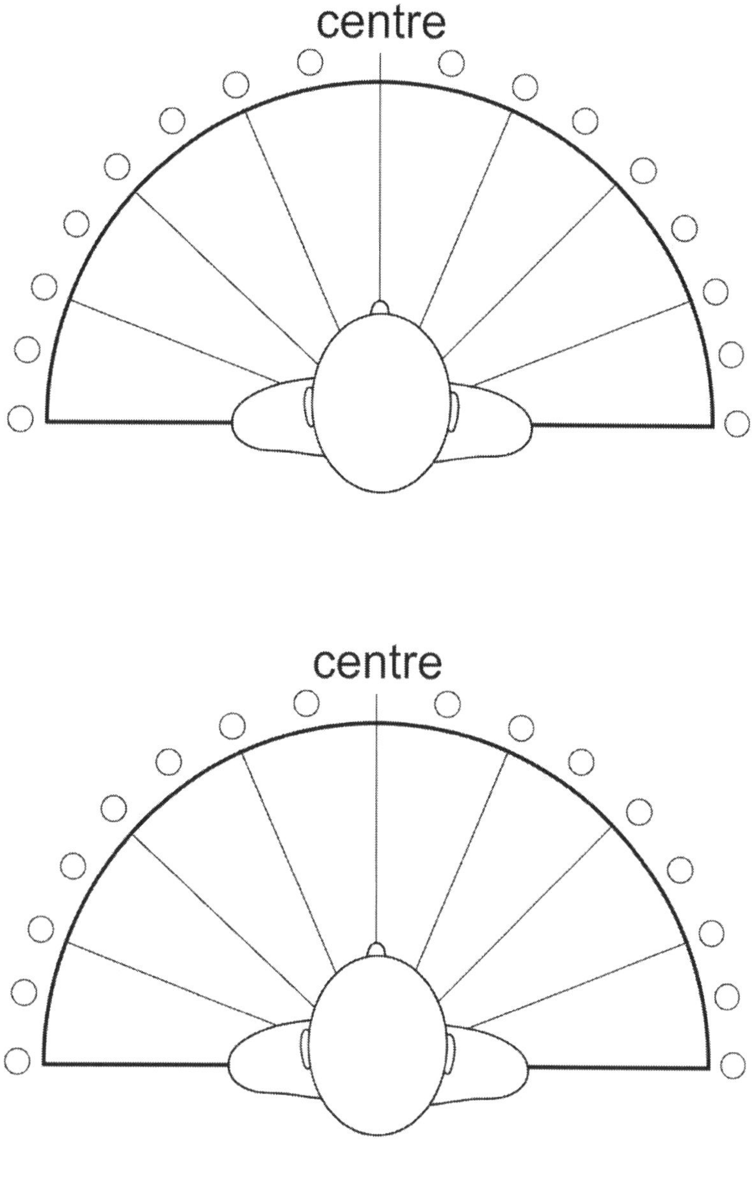

Fig 4.8

Putting it Together

At this stage, let's look at what we have learnt so far and how we can fit this into a daily practice routine. Firstly, we have 'Swinging the Arms' to gently increase our blood and relax the neck.

Then we have 'Rotating the Waist' to release the spine and relax the neck. Our two preparation methods of 'Warming the Neck' and 'Using the Towel' help to connect the mind to the body and set ourselves for treatment.

Developing efficient breathing helps to nourish the whole body and reduces the effects that poor breathing patterns can create for existing neck pain.

Next, we have our 'Master Pain Point' to relieve acute pains throughout the body followed by 'Rolling the Shoulders' to release the neck and 'Lifting the Crown Point' to correct and improve our spinal posture.

We then finish off with gently 'Turning the Head' to engage and relax the area, releasing tensions and stress from the pains. What a great little system!

To put this into a routine, here is everything so far listed for you. Take some time getting used to this routine as it has great value prior to using the energy points for massage which we will look at afterwards.

- Swinging the Arms
- Rotating the Waist
- Warming the Neck
- Breathing Gently
- Massaging the Pain Point
- Rolling the Shoulders
- Lifting the Crown Point
- Turning the Head

How simple is that!

Get to know the routine and enjoy every step as you progress, then when you are ready, come back to the book and we can move forward into our applications of energy point massage.

Take all the time you need. These are skills for life.

Chapter 5

Energy Points of the Neck

The Magic is Inside of You

Now that we have some great skills to help with our symptoms of neck pain, we can move forwards onto our physical application of massaging the energy points of the neck.

These simple, yet very effective points can treat a whole host of symptoms related to neck pain. They also treat many other symptoms you may have, so keep your eyes open for the details in each practice.

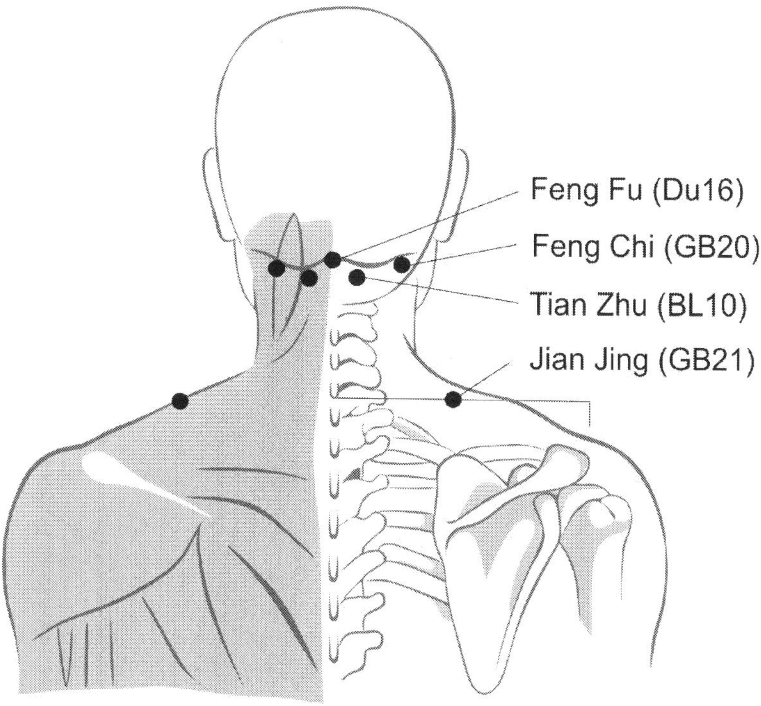

Fig 5.1

Energy points at a glance

Feng Chi – 'Wind Pool' – Gallbladder 20

Hopefully by now you are already enjoying the benefits of Swinging the Arms, Rotating the Waist, Turning the Head and treating yourself with our Master Pain Point.

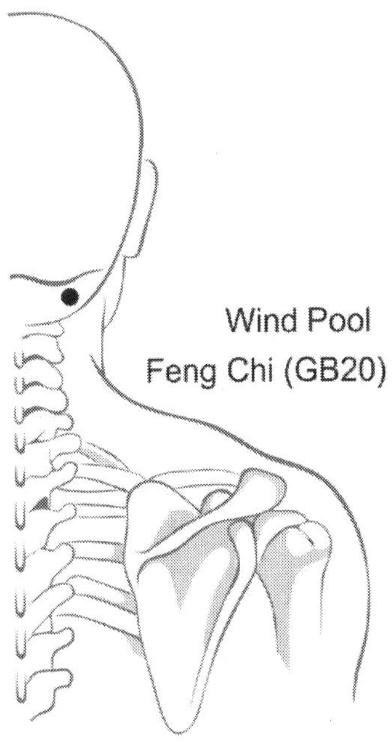

Fig 5.2

The next point we are going to use is called 'Feng Chi' which translates as Wind Pool. *(Fig 5.2)*

We have already discussed the impact that wind can have when it affects the body, so let's now use one of the most important points to relieve those effects.

Most sufferers with neck pain and headaches will experience a tightness in this area and around the point we are treating.

This is likely to be those of you who suffer from thick, muzzy headaches that emanate from the base of the skull causing you to feel tense and tired.

Regular treatment of this point can have an immediate release from discomfort and clear the mind of that stuffy, muzzy feeling we often get.

It's good practice to warm the hands and neck prior to any massage, just to make sure we are not adding any undue cold. Wiping the hands across the neck and using the towel method is a great start.

Firstly, let's familiarise ourselves with the location of the point. Place your index or middle fingers behind the ear lobes. You will feel a bony protrusion at the base of the skull.

Now apply a little pressure and run your fingers slowly up and in towards the spine following the line of the base of the skull. It will feel like the fingers climb a slight mound and then fall into a space between the muscles. You may need to repeat this a few times to get it right.

When you feel you have found the point, use the fingertips to search around the area until you find the point that is most tender. Then you can begin applying slight pressure or a circling motion to the point.

Remember to breathe. Once you have finished, take a few relaxed breaths before moving on to the next point for treatment.

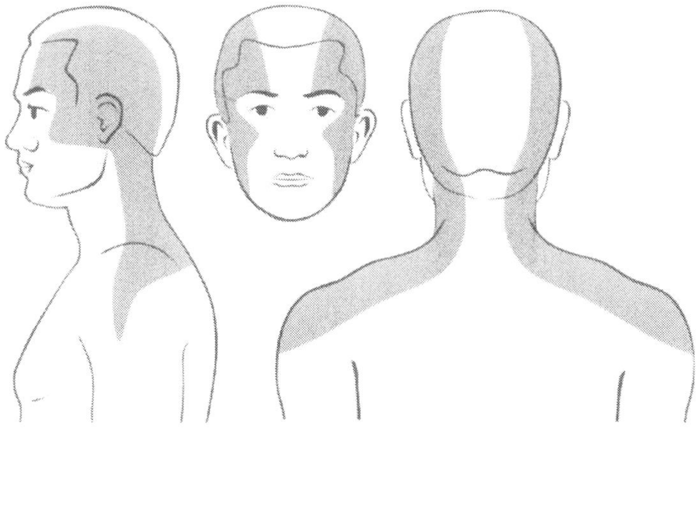

Fig 5.3

Regions affected by Feng Chi – GB20

Tian Zhu – 'Celestial Pillar' – Bladder 10

The next point we are going to treat is called Tian Zhu, the Celestial Pillar. It's great for headaches, stiff neck, stiff back and expelling wind that often causes spasms.

The point is located further along the occipital ridge from our previous point Feng Chi.

If you continue to run the finger along the ridge towards the spine, *(Fig 5.4)* the tips of the fingers will run over another muscle structure, like a small hump. The point is situated on the highest point of this small hump, approximately 2 cms (approximately 1 inch) from the spine.

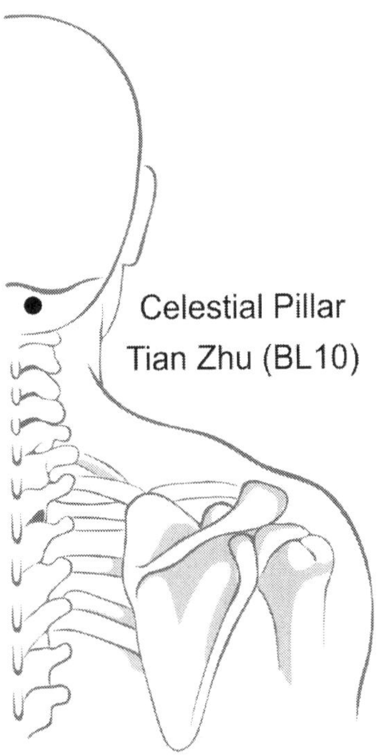

Fig 5.4

Search this area to find the spot that may feel most sensitive and apply the same techniques as before.

Celestial Pillar is also a 'Sea of Qi' point in TCM which means it has a great energetic effect on the flow of energy in the body.

Tense and tight muscles can restrict this energetic flow and reduce or block activity which can cause pain and discomfort.

As this point is situated in the neck area it also has a clearing effect for the mind and we'd all like a clear head.

Have a look at the regions image to see what areas can benefit from treating this point. *(Fig 5.6)*

Benefits of Tian Zhu:

- Regulates energy
- Benefits the head and senses
- Strengthens the lower back
- Expels wind to calm emotions

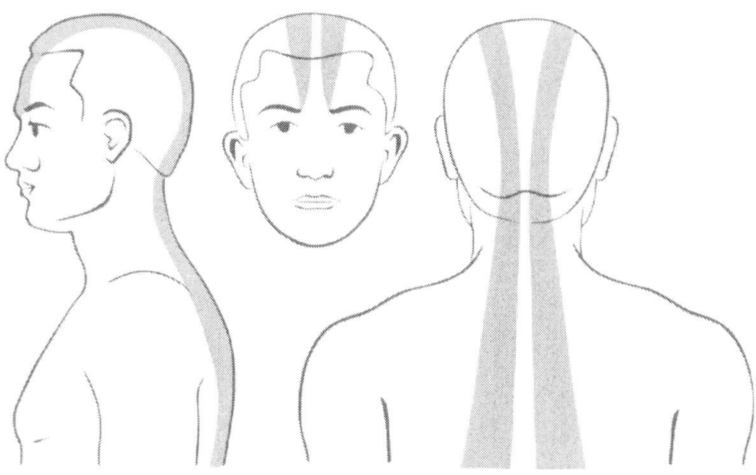

Fig 5.6

Regions affected by Tian Zhu

Feng Fu – 'Wind Palace' – Du 16

Following on from the last point, we come to Feng Fu or 'Wind Palace'.

For local treatment, it has a similar effect to Tian Zhu, helping to release a rigid neck and relax the tissues. It has a slightly more calming effect on the emotions than the two previous points, and that means releasing those tensions and stress.

It's a great addition to help with neck tension caused by emotional stress.

Location

For this point we move into the centre of the spine. You can treat this point with just one finger or alternate with other fingers or the thumb if you like. When you find the centre of the spine there will be a noticeable depression.

Now, move upwards slightly and you will feel a small bony protrusion at the base of the skull. Our point is situated just below this protrusion. Gently apply the same techniques as before.

When you have finished, take a few relaxed breaths and enjoy the relaxing effect of energy moving through the area we have worked on so far.

It's a great feeling when the aches and pains are leaving the body and mind.

Benefits of Feng Fu:

- Clears the mind
- Helps to expel wind conditions
- Relaxes the neck and shoulders
- Clears excess heat
- Calms the emotions

This point can really calm the emotional reactions we get when we are in pain. That could also mean better sleep patterns and ultimately better rest and recovery.

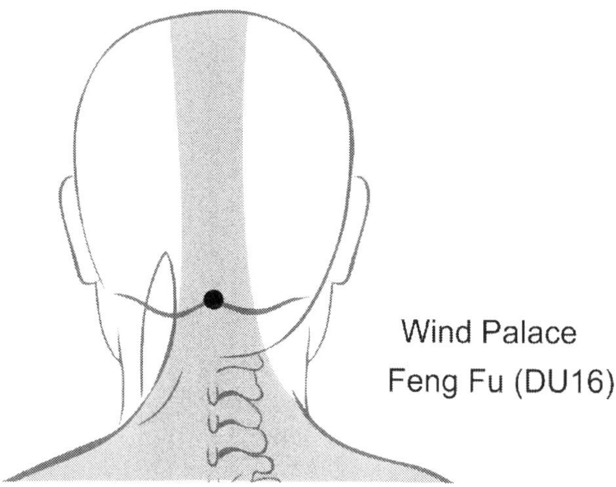

Fig 5.7

Regions affected by Feng Fu

Jian Jing – 'Shoulder Well' – Gallbladder 21

Jian Jing translates as 'shoulder well'. It helps to release the upper shoulders and neck. This point is always a little tender and those with recurring stress, that is not addressed, will often feel a build-up like a small knot or ball under this point. A sure sign that you really need to address your existing emotions and lifestyle decisions.

The build-up can also occur through continued raising of the shoulders, a typical movement during long periods of emotional problems and incorrect breathing patterns.

Jian Jing has a grounding effect on the body and helps to bring us back to our body when we feel overwhelmed by emotions that can make us feel detached and disconnected mentally.

CAUTION

This point is contraindicated during pregnancy.

Location

To find this point, place your right hand onto the left shoulder and feel around at the back of the shoulder for a noticeable bony protrusion at the end of the top of the shoulder blade. *(Fig 5.8)*

Now, run the fingers across the top of the shoulder muscles towards the spine. The point is midway between the end of the shoulder and the spine.

Search with your fingertips and apply pressure to find the point. You know when you have found Jian Jing!

Application

Make circling movements with your fingertips, gradually increasing the pressure. Then, press the point downwards and turn the head to look right.

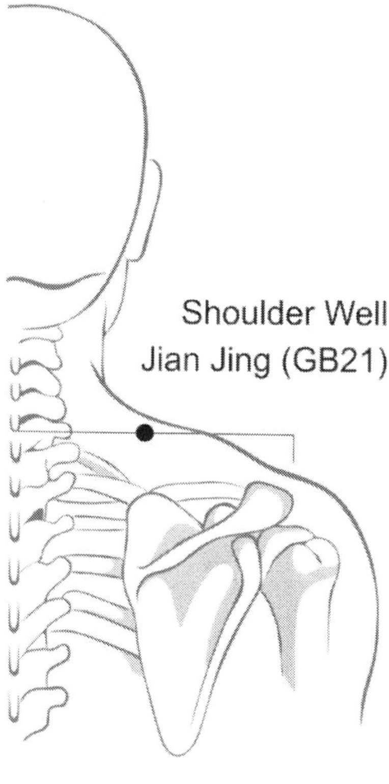

Fig 5.8

Do this three times. After a few breaths on this side, repeat the process on the right shoulder by reaching across the front of the body with the left hand.

Finish by warming the area by gently moving the hands across the tissues and roll the shoulder forwards and back ten times.

It may take a while to break down the knotted tissues and relax this area but stick with it! You'll really appreciate it in the end.

Additional tips

Sometimes applying these techniques with the fingertips can cause slight aches if you are not accustomed to using your hands in this manner or if you have arthritic symptoms.

You can also use a small ball such as a squash ball or a soft ball such as those we use for dogs. Another great tip is to lay down on the floor and place your hands under the head to apply massage to some of the previous points used.

This way you can utilise the weight of the head and apply less pressure with the fingertips. Not so easy at work, but hey, workplace health will catch up eventually.

Benefits of Jian Jing:

- Helps with vertigo and tinnitus
- Alleviates pain in the neck, head and shoulders
- Treats headaches and migraines

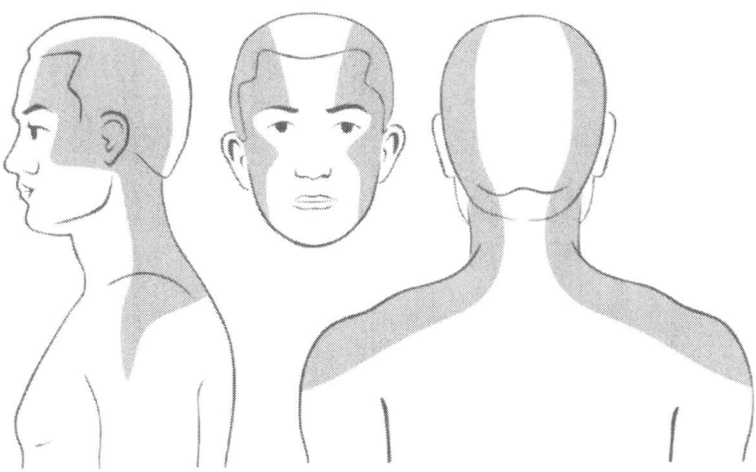

Fig 5.9

Regions affected by Jian Jing

Zhong Zhu – 'Central Islet' – Sanjiao 3

Our next point for treatment is Zhong Zhu. This point helps to clear heat from the head and relax the neck muscles. (Fig 1.1)

Location

To locate this point, run the tip of your little finger from the webbing between the opposite little finger and fourth finger over the knuckles and you should notice a slight depression in the tissues. *(Fig 5.10)*

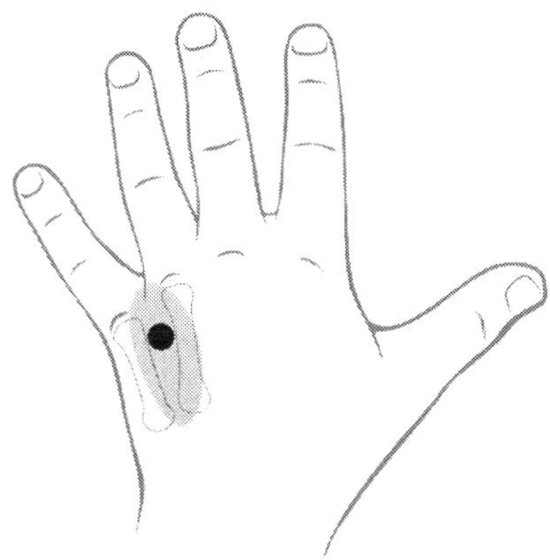

(Fig 5.10)

This can be easier if you make a loose fist. You may feel a noticeable gap in the structure beneath the tip of your finger. Once you have found the point you can apply a static press and hold for a few breaths or use the tip of your index finger to massage the point while you breathe.

This point can feel quite sensitive at times so gradually work up the pressure when you treat it. Remember to do both sides so that you feel balanced and harmonised.

Benefits of Zong Zhu:

- Reduces heat and helps relieve a sore throat
- Benefits the eyes and ears
- Alleviates shoulder and arm pain

Chapter 6

Closing Your Treatment

Protecting Your Vital Energy

Washing Away the Excess

This method is the perfect way to finish any kind of massage work in the upper body, especially when there are emotions and pain involved. It's very relaxing and helps to calm the mind too.

Lay the fingers over the cheeks and gently circle the hands up the sides of the nose, around the forehead and down the side of the face and jaw. Do this several times as if you are washing with your hands.

Now, do the same again but place the hands to the sides of the face. Move the palms upwards and circle the fleshy part of the thumb over the ears, around the sides of the head and gently down the neck with the fingers. Repeat this several times.

To finish, using both hands, one after the other, gently caress the front of the neck in downward strokes. Do this several times to cool and calm the body. Now, with the right hand, reach over the left shoulder towards the spine and gently move the hand over the shoulder and down the arm to the fingertips, as if dusting yourself off or trying to remove static energy. Repeat several times.

Warm both the palms together and sit quietly for a few breaths. Notice what changes have taken place. Are there any areas that feel in need of more attention? If so, you can address these the next time you apply your treatment.

Try to remember these things or make notes ready for your next practice. Some techniques will work better for certain people and their symptoms. They may also work differently at different times so try to explore your symptoms and get used to what your body is telling you.

If you are currently seeing a practitioner for additional help with your recovery then providing this information will help them to do a better job for you, and that means quicker recovery and reduced onward pain.

Yong Quan – 'Bubbling Well' – Kidney 1

An additional point I like to finish with, especially if the head feels hot or your mind is still slightly overactive, is 'Bubbling Well' – one of the most important points of the energy system and especially for those practising Qigong.

This point is our connection to the earth and stimulates both yin (nourishing) and yang (active) aspects of our health. Everybody loves a good foot massage!

This point has a great grounding effect on the body and mind, it's also a major water point, being the first point on the kidney channel, and helps to reduce the internal fire that comes with stress and pain.

Regular daily massage can provide remarkable results for health improvement.

Location

To locate this point, slide the thumb up the centre of the sole of the foot until its stops at the fleshy part. Press down and circle the thumb until you find the tender spot, it's very noticeable. *(Fig 6.1)*

Application

Gently massage this point as you breathe softly and enjoy the calmness and cooling effect of Bubbling Well.

Author's Tip

Get yourself a good quality tennis ball and gently roll it back and forth along the length of the sole of the foot, it feels very soothing and comforting!

When you have had a hard day on your feet, this can be a very welcome form of treatment for tired feet and fatigue. Try it for plantar fascia pain too!

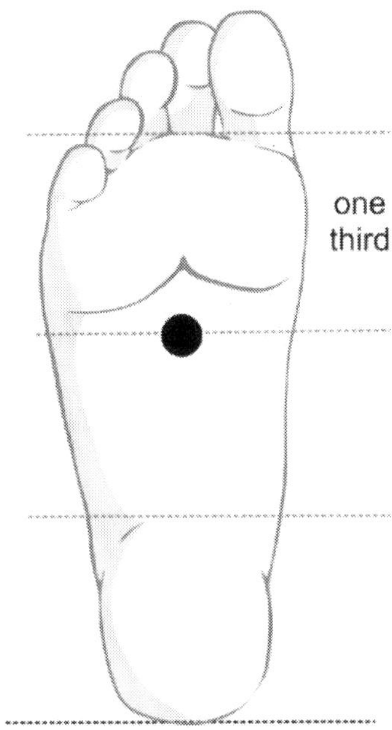

Fig 6.1

Yong Quan – Bubbling Well – Kidney 1 Point

How Simple is That?

And there you have it, a simple, easy to learn and effective solution for neck pain and the associated emotions which can accompany it. Take your time going over the methods here, get to know how YOU feel and how the points feel when you are treating them.

If you have suffered pain for some time, it may take longer to achieve the results you want but stick with it. Every time you apply the methods you will be moving forwards to better health and less pain.

There will be bad days and good days. Life is full of change, injuries and emotions. Just keep practising and soon you will experience how much power you have to maintain your own health when you need it most.

So, before we finish, here is a brief rundown of the methods to recap and remember. Yes, the points are effective on their own but not as effective as when applied in this exact prescription of treatment.

It has been designed this way for maximum results.

Building your Practice

Here is a simple list for you to practice so you can form a specific sequence of the methods in this book. I have added some prompt words to help you remember.

As previously mentioned, the points are very effective on their own, but the magic is in the way they are used together.

Give it a go and see how it feels for you. Enjoy every part and get to know each practice as you move through the methods.

- Swinging the Arms (relax the arms)
- Rotating the Waist (clockwise then anti-clockwise)
- Warming the Neck (with hands or the towel)
- The Master Pain Point (on the web of the thumb)
- Lifting the Crown Point (suspend the head)
- Feng Chi (the outer neck point)
- Tian Zhu (just to the side of the spine)
- Feng Fu (at the centre of the base of the skull)
- Jian Jing (midway on top of the shoulder muscle)
- Zhong Zhu (on the little finger knuckle)
- Turning the Head (looking left and right)
- Washing Away the Excess (dusting off the body)

Closing Thoughts

I do hope you have enjoyed reading this book and that you are well on your way to becoming a master of your own symptoms. Please do keep in touch with a trained practitioner if you have access to one, they can really help minimise the duration of painful conditions.

Although I have done my best to describe the techniques in the book, it always helps to see how they should be practised first hand.

Practise, Practise, Practise is the key here! The more you apply the techniques the more your symptoms will subside, and you will be able to manage any daily pains and discomforts.

Ideas of Interest

Over the years I have gathered many ideas and formulas. I have heard thousands of interesting remedies and methods that patients mention during our time of treatment together.

Some have proved to be very valuable pieces of information and some at least have been very amusing. It just goes to show that what works for one person doesn't necessarily work for another.

I'm a great believer in making health cost effective and getting the best bang for my buck, that is why I teach others, in the end the methods are priceless skills for life!

In this final section I will share some of my own findings for you to think about. Who knows, it may just be the gem of information you need to help relieve your pain.

Enjoy!

Pillows

How is your pillow? How is your sleep? Have you got the latest highly recommended memory foam, cool-layered, organic fibre, chiropractic recommended pillow that straightens your spine and ensures your body is in the optimum position for health? If so, does it work for you?

Believe me I have tried them all and all I can say is, what a waste of money! I do however know people that have said they have found relief from their 'scientific' pillows, but in all cases a pillow is just a pillow, isn't it?

Yes and no. Let me share a few things with you and you can decide for yourself.

When it comes to neck pain and sleep, we need a pillow that will support the neck in a neutral position while sleeping. This must also support the weight of the head.

Now, if we all slept in the same position, had the same bodies and our heads were the same size, I would say YES! These magic pillows are amazing. But we are not all the same.

Here are a few guidelines I have picked up and tested along the way.

A simple and general rule is: one pillow if you are a back sleeper, two pillows if you are a side sleeper. If you are a back sleeper you need to find a pillow that your head sinks into the centre of so that it can support the neck. If you are a side sleeper it's a little trickier.

The distance from our neck and shoulders is different for everyone and even the softness or hardness of your mattress (more on that next) will alter this distance to be able to support your neck. You need to find the right height that will fit from shoulder to neck and support it in a neutral position.

So how do you do that and how do you know the right height? You don't! But you can get as near as possible.

To start with, find a nice new comfortable pillow you are happy to sleep on. Forget the gimmicky pillows, just find one you like. This will be your main pillow. Next, we need to do a bit of detective work.

Take a towel and fold it so it is around 2-3 cms (1 inch) thick. Place it under the pillow and have a few nights' sleep with it. If you find that your hand is sliding under the pillow to support your neck, it's not high enough.

The next thing to do is fold the towel more and repeat the process until you find you are not sliding your hand under the pillow as much. Then you can either place the towel in the pillowcase with the pillow or you can go to the store and buy a piece of foam roughly the same thickness and place it under or in with the pillow.

It's not scientific but at least it will be as near to your own needs as possible, and much cheaper than the 'highly recommended' ones.

Also, if you have continued neck pain (hopefully not so much after reading this book) I feel you should renew your pillow every 18-24 months. They do lose their support and can easily aggravate an injury over time.

I have a simple shredded foam pillow that can be washed, and the insides changed. It was £25 ($30) and I buy a new one every year. A good night's sleep is priceless in my opinion.

Types of Pillows

It is worth discussing other pillow types, particularly the feather and memory foam variety. Previously we discussed hot and cold temperatures and how they can affect the neck.

Certain types of pillows may exacerbate existing problems.

Feather pillows are generally cold and can remain cold if there is cool air in the room. This can be ideal if you are a warm person but if you have cold or wind in the neck, they may make symptoms worse.

Memory foam on the other hand is the opposite. It heats up with body heat and retains the heat. This added heat can sometimes cause extra heat around the neck and you may even sweat a little.

The pores can open to release the excess and you can easily get a cold invasion and stiff neck afterwards. In addition, I do not recommend memory foam for those experiencing menopausal night sweats.

It's just an observation and one that has proved to have a positive result for some sufferers, but it could have a significant impact on your sleep if you change your pillow.

Mattresses

We spend up to 30% of our lives lying on a mattress so it's very important to have the right one. I'm not a big fan of the 'highly recommended for health' mattresses for the reason stated earlier ... we are all different.

Mattresses are a secondary support system for the body when it comes to neck pain. If every night you are putting your body into a position that is bad for your structure, eventually it will have a negative effect.

Generally, you will need something that supports your weight. If you share your bed this becomes a bit tricky so it may be better buying a mattress that minimises the body rolling to the bed's centre. Most modern mattresses will have a model with centre support.

Often shoppers will go with something that feels comfy in the furniture store. Its great fun trying mattresses out in a public store so you are probably more relaxed and at ease, but will the same mattress feel as comfy after a long day in pain?

It's a bit of a minefield really and trying out different mattresses is sometimes not an option. I would suggest getting a model that is cooling and can breathe, memory foam can be overly hot at times, and that goes for mattress toppers too!

Also, I feel that people are not renewing their mattresses often enough. They used to last for a good 10-15 years but now the recommended time is around eight years. How old is yours?

The rule of thumb here is that if you look at your bare mattress and there are any dips, sags or uneven parts, it needs to be renewed as it will have lost its support.

Manufacturers will often give a sliding money-back guarantee if the bed is less than five years old. So, if after just two years, the mattress is showing signs of wear, you can often be reimbursed some money towards a new one.

My wife and I did this after three years and were reimbursed 40% of the original price which we put towards a new one.

Mattresses shouldn't be too expensive either. Around 5-8 years ago I found a reputable model with a 'climate cool' top layer for half price at £300 ($370).

We have since bought another one and intend to renew every 4-5 years. It has made a big difference to our sleep quality and that means more recovery time and less stress with less pain.

It's definitely worth looking into if you have had the same products for a long time, or you are suffering with chronic daily pain. It's a very worthy investment.

Food and Drink

Most of you will never consider food or drink to be a cause of neck pain and suffering. With all pain conditions it is very easy to develop a pattern of eating or drinking the same items every day.

It's worth spending some time just checking your dietary intake for a couple of weeks as we often use some foods to mask emotions and pain. In terms of recovery, poor food choices can add to existing symptoms or hinder natural healing.

Dairy, sugar and fat are the most common 'go to' foods when there is stress and pain. They are all heavy, sticky foods which literally hold or weigh down the emotions we feel when we are in pain.

In TCM the emotions are related to certain foods and body parts (see organ chart below). You may have a sense of loss (grief/sadness) attached to your neck pain, which most of us do, you may find yourself eating more fiery, spicy foods.

If you are worried and anxious you may find sweet foods help to calm you during the stress of pain. You could have feelings of anger attached emotionally to your pain which can lead to what TCM calls 'liver stress' so regular alcohol may have become a remedy. If your confidence has been rocked, salty and savoury foods could be your regular daily intake.

This is not to say that what you are eating is unhealthy, only you know if the foods you supply your body are working for you or not, but it's worth noting down the food you eat regularly, possibly without even noticing so much and changing this habit. You may see an improvement in your health within days.

The main trouble with eating or drinking excessively is that it can cause weight gain, dehydration of the muscles and bones and also trigger sleep problems making an existing condition far worse!

And yet again we have another problem to solve. What we are trying to achieve is the removal of any action or possibility that could be making our pain worse.

Quick Tip: If you experience an injury or you are going through a particularly emotional period, I advise you to eat foods at room temperature or above and avoid cold and iced foods. They drain much needed energy.

When you ingest them, the body has to warm them immediately and that means stoking up the furnace and wasting energy.

Warm is best. Poaching, steaming and stir-frying are great ways to cook during injury and stress. Ditch the coffee and go for green tea, fruit teas, or make your own fruited water with fresh fruit and spring water.

Below is a simple chart that shows the five element organs and associated body parts, tastes and emotions.

RELATED ORGAN	ELEMENT and TASTE	BODY PART	EMOTIONS
LUNGS and LARGE INTESTINE	Metal Pungent	Skin	Sadness Grief
KIDNEYS and BLADDER	Water Salt	Bones	Fear Apprehension
LIVER and GALL BLADDER	Wood Sour	Tendons	Anger Frustration
HEART and SMALL INTESTINES	Fire Bitter	Blood Vessels	Joy Over-Excited
STOMACH and SPLEEN	Earth Sweet	Muscles	Worry Pensiveness

There are many great books available on the subject of 'five element' nutrition. I hope to delve deeper into this subject in a future publication, so please keep following my work.

So, for now, I bid you farewell and wish you great health on your journey through life.

Enjoy the magic!

A special thank you to my family, friends, patients and students. Your help, knowledge and support continue to inspire me to share the traditional healing arts.

Thank you for your time reading these pages. I hope it has provided you with some valuable tools to use on your journey of health and well-being.

Christopher.

For more information, video tutorials and further training options please visit

www.chrishandbury.com

Also available by Christopher David Handbury

What is Qigong? A step-by-step guide to growing a successful daily practice of Qigong

Top 10 Amazon Bestseller

Available in Paperback and E-Book on Amazon

PLUS! access video tutorials online

- Activate the body's own **natural medicine** and feel GREAT!
- **Improve energy flow** to remove harmful blockages
- Harmonise the internal organs to **promote healing** from illness
- Excite the digestive system for **improved energy**
- **Tone the muscles** for strength and vital health
- Strengthen the bones and joints for **less pain**
- **Sleep better** and feel alive with life!

Printed in Great Britain
by Amazon

55225609R00081